LEAVING THE FOLD

CANDID COVERSATIONS

WITH INACTIVE MORMONS

• BY JAMES W. URE •

SIGNATURE BOOKS

SALT LAKE CITY

COVER DESIGN BY RON STUCKI

Preparation of this work was funded in part by a grant from the Utah Arts Council and the National Endowment for the Arts.

Published by Signature Books. Signature Books is a registered trademark of Signature Books, Inc.

Leaving the Fold: Candid Conversations with Inactive Mormons was printed on acid-free paper and was manufactured in the United States of America.

04 03 02 01 00 6 5 4 3 2

LIBRARY OF CONGRESS CATALOGING-IN-PUBLICATION DATA

Leaving the fold : candid conversations with inactive Mormons / by James W. Ure.

P. Cm.

ISBN 1-56085-134-1 (pbk.)

1. Mormons—United States—Religious life. 2. Ex-church members—Church of Jesus Christ of Latter-day Saints Interviews. I. Title.

BGX8656.U74 1999

289.3'092'2—dc21 99-36057

CIP

Contents

Acknowledgements

Graciously supporting this project were a number of men and women whose efforts are reflected on every page.

To my wife, Susan Luxton Ure, goes the grand prize for patience and insightful inquiry. Susan lived this book with me, asking the most probing questions. As a result, I came to see certain elements in a different light—a light which, I believe, resulted in a better book. Her demanding honesty ended any thoughts I had entertained about easing through this project with minimum introspection.

My brother, Joseph McCune Ure, measured the book's progress and provided comments on our own upbringing in Mormonism. Many of our conversations took place on some of the West's finest trout waters, which seem to have a particularly keen effect on clarifying memories.

The book was honed by my longtime friend Jim Woolf, who agreed to interview me so that I might know what my subjects were undergoing, and so that I might also improve the questions I asked. We discussed the style, approach, and progress of this project on many occasions, and his contribution was significant.

William C. Bailey provided important clarification of LDS church doctrine and terms that arose from my interviews. Bill was especially helpful in providing an active Mormon's view of some of the questions posed in the process of preparing this book. Douglas ("Duff") Clawson provided cogent observations and suggested some persons who provided excellent interviews.

Richard Kagel, professor of marketing research at Brigham Young University and president of Kagel and Associates, helped me frame the approach to this book, since originally I was thinking of a statistical work in combination with a study of attitudes. As it turned out, Dan Jones of Dan Jones and Associates had ready numbers due to his vast experience in Utah; I am grateful to him for sharing this knowledge.

Peggy Fletcher Stack, religion writer at *The Salt Lake Tribune*, was instrumental in helping me arrive at the scope and voice of the book. I came away from our conversations with a satisfied sense of knowing what to do next.

Those who helped ferret out information were Steve Purhonen, U.S. Navy (retired), and Larry Smith, professor of social work at the University of Utah. Purhonen also undertook the daunting task of transcribing three of the more difficult interviews from tape to computer disk, and I grew to trust his judgments implicitly. Jeanene Anderson also lent a hand on some research.

At the LDS Church Office Building, Don LeFevre was gracious and helpful, and we both looked back with wonder and laughter on our days together at *The Salt Lake Tribune.*

Suggestions for interviews flowed from many sources, including the interviewees themselves. Brent Cameron was especially helpful in directing me to some interviews.

Many thanks to Sandi Olson, who bore the brunt of transcribing the interviews. Her intelligence and cheerfulness made the editing go smoothly. Susan Coon transcribed many of our interviews with dedication and perseverance, in spite of the burdens of a new baby.

Moving from idea to published book requires resources of many kinds. John Netto and J. Lynn and Diana Lady Dougan provided support that enabled this book to come to fruition, as did the Utah Arts Council and the National Endowment for the Arts. They helped fire the confidence necessary to complete a work revealing such varied opinion.

Overview

Journalism is an extraordinary and terrible privilege.
—*Oriana Fallaci*

If you were raised Mormon in Utah, most likely the church is at your very core, whether you're active or inactive. You are part of the culture, and no matter how you may try to escape its influence, it's always with you—like a kid sister or brother tagging along.

Through family and friends, Mormonism shaped your life, insisted you make choices, brought you joy and conflict, estrangements and communion. If you are devout, you know the church has all the answers. If you aren't, you must find your place in our unique cultural landscape by following another path. Sometimes that path presents uncomfortable footing and struggle, as you'll recognize when you read the personal stories that follow.

Living in Utah almost demands that you choose sides on religion, and it's difficult to convince some believers that there is no harm in a thoughtful examination of the Church of Jesus Christ of Latter-day Saints (Mormon).

This work is an exploration of the LDS church as seen by well-known Mormons, most of them Utahns, all of them inactive (non-practicing or infrequently practicing) in the church after being active at one time in their lives. This is not an anti-Mormon work; its purpose from the beginning is to create and foster understanding.

You may find criticism in these interviews: no institution with the worldwide profile of the Mormon church is immune to it. But it is also interesting to note that many interviewees articulate honor and respect for the church and individuals in its leadership and its membership. Their views most often reflect thoughtful consideration. And in almost every one, there's a hint of disappointment and longing, as if they're searching for a promised ideal not yet achieved, perhaps ironically the result of the idealization and perfection taught them by the church.

It is fair to ask, "Do some of these interviews misunderstand the LDS church?" In some instances years have passed since an interviewee was last active. Changes in the church during intervening years may have removed or altered certain factors that escorted an individual from involvement. However, reading will indicate that an individual's reasons for leaving active participation are usually layered and complex.

SELECTING INTERVIEW SUBJECTS

There's no reference available to the public that indicates a person's level of activity in the LDS church, so I established three criteria interview subjects had to meet.

1. They had to be members of the church (not excommunicated or disfellowshipped and not having asked to have their names removed from the official roles).

2. They once actively attended church functions.

3. They don't regularly attend church at the present time and don't pay tithing.

Avoided were those whom Peggy Fletcher Stack calls "Evangelical Jack Mormons," those who regularly and vigorously foment against the church. I also avoided those transitioning out of the church. This isn't the place for their stories.

Sought were men and women of intelligence who offer thoughtful commentaries as a result of life experience within the LDS community.

This sampling is not a representative reflection of the attitudes of inactives, but you'll find recurring themes: repulsed by the zeal of an individual; intellectualized rejection of doctrine; an inactive parent; the politics of gender; and politics in general.

ARRANGING AND CONDUCTING THE INTERVIEWS

At the outset, I sketched a list of about seventy-five individuals who were thought to meet the above criteria. If you've lived in Utah all your life, and if you've been part of the Mormon milieu, it isn't difficult to identify the activity status of a fellow Mormon.

The next step required a certain delicacy, since I was encroaching on the most personal of psychic space. The individual would receive a call which offered an overview of the project, including my criteria for interview subjects; they were then asked if they felt they fit my criteria.

If the answer was no, I thanked them for hearing me out. If they answered yes, an appointment for an interview was made in the setting of their choice, usually in their home or office. If they agreed to consider an interview, they were sent a printed overview of the project. A few I called were not Mormon. Three calls turned out to be to active Mormons.

There were a number of possible subjects who for various reasons were not interviewed. One woman declined as she was in the process of being called in by her local church authorities for questioning. One former beauty queen was about to become active again. Two members of the gay community who were still on the rolls agreed to interviews, then backed out due to possible repercussions. Interestingly, a number of inactive women and one man who are involved in the Utah arts community declined after first accepting interviews. Follow-up conversations indicated they feared the economic consequences as a result of revealing their status. Some turn-downs had to do with possibly hurting active family members. One famous athlete simply said, "It would kill my mother."

In two instances, interviews were completed before I learned my subjects had been excommunicated, and I reluctantly decided not to include them. I thank these two women for their courage and stories, but they too belong elsewhere.

One interview went for over an hour before my elderly subject revealed he was currently active in church affairs. This in spite of the materials I'd sent ahead.

In total, I taped forty-two interviews. After transcription, I set aside ten who did not fit the criteria. The initial manuscript ran to more than 800 double-spaced pages, and would have been excessively expensive to publish. A decision had to be made: fewer complete interviews or excerpts from all? In looking at the manuscript, I saw that the interviews fell into two distinct categories: those who'd left active LDS membership when they were older and those who'd left as adolescents or young adults.

With the support of the publisher, I decided to feature in this volume mostly the interviews of those who left activity when they were older. A second volume may follow, which would include the interviews of those whose decision to leave came in their younger years.

All interviews took place during the last half of 1996 and the first half of 1997. Each interview was transferred from tape to computer disk. Printed transcriptions were checked against the recordings. Each interview was edited in draft form and all were returned for a final view for accuracy by the interviewee. This was to make certain of names and spellings, and to avoid mistakes that may have occurred in the transcription process. (I frankly don't trust my own ears sometimes, having recently heard radio commercials offering what sounded like Chili Flavored Rolaids and another product containing a Mickey Mouthwash Ingredient). Most interviewees made few corrections; some made none.

The question of anonymity arose early in the project. Before I began, I was uncertain how many subjects would agree to use their names. Surprisingly few did not want to be identified.

STATISTICS RELATIVE TO INACTIVES

Utah politicians have long operated on the assumption that the state is "one-third active LDS, one-third inactive, one-third gentile." At the turn of the twenty-first century, is this an accurate representation? I asked noted Utah pollster Dan Jones to summarize the statistical status of active and inactive members of the LDS church in Utah, figures which his company, Dan Jones and Associates, has developed as a result of long-term research for politicians, businesses, and institutions:

- 69 percent of all Utahns are Mormon.
- Of that number, 55 percent claim to be "very active."
- 20 percent claim to be "somewhat active."
- 25 percent claim to be "inactive."

Jones's figures differ from those generated by the Mormon church, he says, which claims that 75 percent of Utah is Mormon and that 60 percent of those are "very active." However, "tithing receipts don't match those claims," says Jones, adding that Brigham Young University's Department of Sociology has independently confirmed his 69 percent figure. In addition, 75 percent of all LDS call themselves Republicans. Inactives are "definitely more liberal," Jones adds. Perceptions of the "very active" are that they pay full tithing, attend church regularly, and have current temple recommends. According to these figures, 45 percent of all Mormons in Utah are what the church itself calls "less active."

Let's look at Jones's percentages as numbers: of the state's roughly 2 million population as of 1997, approximately 1.4 million are Mormon—770,000 are active, 280,000 are "somewhat active," and 350,000 are inactive.

The church now counts on its rolls 10 million people; if Utah's figures represented members everywhere, some 2.5 million Mormons world-wide are inactive.

Many of interviewees used "Jack Mormon" to describe their status within the LDS church, while others objected to this name. It is a term that has risen to popular use and is often applied to those less active. It has an interesting history. One of the first references to "Jack Mormon" comes from B. H. Roberts's *Comprehensive History of the Church*, volume 2, page 322, in a footnote. Apparently, Thomas C. Sharpe, editor of the *Warsaw Signal*, an anti-Mormon newspaper of the 1840s, was one of the first to use the expression "Jack Mason" to refer to anyone who refused to take part in the anti-Mason activities of the 1830s. Sharpe later used the term "Jack Mormon" to refer to people who were not members of the Mormon church but sympathized with the Mormons and refused to terrorize and punish them. For many years thereafter, the term referred to anyone who supported or sympathized with the church who was not Mormon.

Today the term has taken on a different meaning, but no one seems to be able to offer a fully satisfactory explanation of how it evolved. Suggested as analogues for current usage are "jack salmon" and "jack pine." For Washington state fishermen, jack salmon are young, undeveloped salmon which attempt to spawn. In northwestern timberman's parlance, jack pines are small pines, not yet big enough to harvest (there is also a separate species of pine called jack pine). This usage would hint that Jack Mormons have yet to fully effloresce, perhaps an intimation that they will mature, see the light, and become full members, an implication many inactives would find objectionable and condescending.

The LDS church's historical department in Salt Lake City says the term now refers to anyone who is "a member of the Mormon Church who may not keep the Word of Wisdom or other Church commandments, who doesn't live his religion, who isn't valiant in promoting the church."

No one term can accurately characterize all of the interviewees, since all are different. "Unorthodox" doesn't really describe them, since many active, tithe-paying members of the LDS church fit that category. Neither does "liberal Mormon," which implies politics. "Backsliders"? Too pejorative. "Mormons off the beaten track"? Depends on one's point of view. Official church language calls inactives "the less active." "Lapsed Mormon" is occasionally used, but it is deficient as well, meaning falling away from a moral standard, or, as the dictionary puts it, "a falling or slipping into a lower condition."

None has the same meaning as "Jack Mormon." The term feels just right, even a little jaunty. Jack Mormon is in popular use and has a meaning that virtually everyone in the mountain states understands.

A PERSONAL NOTE

I undertook this book to help determine my own place in our unique social landscape. Complex feelings of exclusion came early to me, and I didn't feel I could live up to the standards of perfection articulated by church leaders. These feelings were further amplified by acts and comments of active members in both my family and in my local ward (or congregation).

With a head full of Mormonism and a heart empty of faith, I found rebellion replacing a sense of unworthiness, and soon I sought like-minded friends—many of whom were inactive Mormons.

I'd chosen a path that took me away from active Mormonism, and as I looked back years later, I was haunted by a sense of guilt. I felt lonely, disoriented, and without a cultural community wherein once I'd known everyone in every house within a half-mile radius, thanks to my active Mormonism.

My life had become painful. Feeling hostile and bereft of soul, I embarked on an exploration of my feelings. As an outgrowth of this, I developed a new spirituality, deeply personal, firmly rooted, satisfying in its delivery of answers and serenity. But unresolved questions lingered. I wondered about others who'd left the active practice of Mormonism. Had they found their way? Were they carrying baggage from the past? How did they deal with their feelings, their lives?

This book was a journey to find those others. As I located them and encouraged them to talk, I recognized that for many our interviews were acts of courage. In recognition, to my interview subjects I offer small honoraria in the form of the epigraphs at the beginning of their interviews. Some reflect the character of the person, some contain messages. They are my thank-yous, and the process was delightfully like selecting little gifts.

As we talked, each man and woman provided me with another small piece of myself. I came to recognize the conflict created by some individuals during my early immersion in the church. I remembered feelings of disdain, hostility, arrogance, and defiance. But across forty years, I recalled and felt the love of many active Mormon friends and relatives. Oddly, memory recalls fragrances more than words. At times during the writing of this book, I smelled the freshly mowed grass of my childhood ward, the acrid odor of burning box elder branches in an old stove in a cabin at Tracy Wigwam, the mothball scent on the Sunday suit of my bishop, tomatoes hot from the noon sun of August.

On my journey I renewed ancestral links to those who accomplished so much in settling Utah. The process brought me to respect the lofty goals of the LDS church and created an appreciation for the integrity and unconditional acceptance residing within the hearts of those active Mormons with whom I worked during this project. We can all study the concept of acceptance from truly spiritual men and women, and it's this quality more than anything else that attracts me to an individual, philosophy, or theology.

After a dozen or so interviews, I observed a change within myself; I reached a state of comfort with myself and, in a shower of realization, concluded that it was no longer important if I was active or not. No one can force me to choose sides. Belief in doctrine is not a pre-requisite to giving or receiving love and respect. A feeling of contentment came over me as I realized I had in my own way returned to my tribe, my comforting neighborhood, remingled my blood with that of my great-grandparents who first arrived in Utah in 1849. I realized that all of us—active Mormon, inactive Mormon, former Mormon—must pursue our own paths to salvation, and above all we must respect that in each other.

1.

Calvin L. Rampton

It is not enough to have a good mind. The main thing is to use it well.

—*René Descartes*

Utah's only three-term governor, Calvin L. Rampton, was born in Bountiful, Utah, in 1913. He attended George Washington University and the University of Utah, where he took his Juris Doctorate in 1940. He was admitted to the Utah bar in 1940, and the next year was admitted to practice before the U.S. Court of Appeals. In 1946 he was admitted to practice before the U.S. Supreme Court. Cal was county attorney in Davis County, 1939-40, assistant attorney general of Utah, 1941, and again in 1946 and 1948. He was elected governor, took office in 1965, and was reelected twice. He chaired the Education Commission of the States and was president of the Council of State Governments. He also served as chair of the National Governors' Conference in 1975. Cal was active as a reserve officer in the Utah National Guard, including active duty from 1942-45. For readers who would like to know more, I suggest his autobiography, As I Recall *(University of Utah Press, 1989), in which his political career is interlaced with his romance, marriage, and family life.*

Today Cal's hair is grayer, but the abundant head resting squarely on hunched shoulders will be familiar to anyone who lived in Utah through 1976, when he left office. His eyes are alert for nuance, but his face is confident and open, his manner candid and gentle. The man who directed the state's affairs, who cobbled agreements for industrial giants such as Union Pacific Railroad, sits behind a modest desk stacked with papers in a comfortably small office in downtown Salt Lake City. Wood carvings collected from his travels occupy much of one wall—an African rhythm pounder, a bust of Don Quixote, a soaring eagle. There is spoor from his political past, including signed photographs and sculpted busts of U.S. presidents John F. Kennedy, Lyndon Johnson, Gerald Ford, and Jimmy Carter. Photographs of his family, a plant or two, medals from his World War II service in Europe and his National Guard service in Utah occupy shelves along with numerous books and award certificates. Outside the temperature is already 90 degrees on this overcast August morning. He leans back in his chair.

~

My grandfather had been what they call disfellowshipped from the Mormon church, which is something less than an excommunication. As I understand it, if you're disfellowshipped you can apply and get back in the church, but Grandpa would never have applied. So in Dad's family the church was not predominant, and Dad himself didn't go to church very often. He'd go when the children were named and on special occasions.

My father's family was not anti-Mormon. And my grandfather's best friend and brother-in-law was Mormon general authority Brigham H. Roberts and really I think that it was he who got them to reduce the excommunication charge to a charge of disfellowship. I never heard Grandfather say anything derogatory about the church.

Do you know what he might have said that caused this disenfranchisement?

I don't know what it was. It wasn't a quarrel with an individual. It was a disagreement with policy.

But your mother was active?

Oh, yes. Now I don't remember if my Campbell grandparents were active. Grandmother Campbell died when I was quite young, and I don't remember her very well. Grandfather Campbell lived till I was about sixteen or seventeen. But mother belonged to the Relief Society and she insisted I go to church.

Did you want to go?

I enjoyed certain functions of church. I don't remember if I enjoyed children's primary or not when I was little, but I certainly enjoyed the Mutual Improvement Association and the Boy Scouts when I was a teenager, and I didn't mind sacrament meeting. I thought stake conferences were too long.

There was a social element.

Well, I belonged to the Bountiful 1st Ward, and the ward house was a wonderful big white church that still stands in the full block—in the center of Bountiful. And that was the social center of Bountiful. It wasn't only the ward house; it was the stake house, as well.

Were your parents ever in conflict over the children going to church?

My father also encouraged it. Mother did it because she herself was religious and thought I should go, and I think Dad felt that it was good for me.

When did you become less active? Was it an abrupt event?

I don't think it was an abrupt thing. I continued being quite active in Parley's Ward almost up until the time I was elected governor (1964). I don't mean I was a regular attender, but I was a frequent attender. I taught Sunday school and I was scout master. One day my wife, Lucybeth, and I were sitting in church and a couple of scouts from behind us sniffed and said, "I smell a cigar"; another kid said, "That's no cigar, that's Cal's pipe." So I smoked a pipe and the kids knew it. When they asked me if I'd be the scout master, I said, "Well, do you know I smoke a pipe?" They said, "You don't have to smoke it at a scout meeting, do you?" I said, "No."

Your dad smoked a pipe, too, according to your book. When did you start smoking a pipe?

In the army.

So you were in your late twenties or early thirties.

Yes.

What caused you to pick it up?

Well, I don't know. I'm sure a lot of people took up smoking in the army. I did it principally because nearly everyone else was doing it. It was a peer thing, and a release from tension.

Did you feel any guilt over that? Over breaking the church's Word of Wisdom?

No. Although mother was very active in church, she was also an avid coffee drinker. And we had coffee in our home, and I drank coffee as I was growing up. But the army changed a lot of habits, of course. You're living in an entirely different environment—different than a family environment. I'd never smoked before that. I'd drunk some liquor before that and continued to do so in the army on occasion. Not frequently, we couldn't get it frequently. But I had no feeling against the moderate use of alcohol.

Regarding that, is there less stigma toward the drinker than there is toward the smoker?

No, I think, because you can drink and still be with others and they don't necessarily know it. But they can see you smoke. I think it's a matter of the obvious with some.

How old were you when you first tried alcohol?

I was between high school and college. I'd say I was seventeen.

Did you enjoy it?

No. But we had a bunch of guys go up to Como Springs near Morgan, Utah, and we'd made some home brew in the barn of one of the guys by the name of Weldon Parrish from Centerville. His dad was a bishop, but we made this home brew in his barn without his father's knowledge.

What did you make it from?

Hops and, oh, I don't know. It was a drink like beer. And we were trying to smuggle 'em out of the barn, and one of the bottles dropped and broke on the bishop's front yard. It was a little embarrassing.

I thought maybe your first experience with liquor was related to the time you tried to use young Alton Call as a projectile in a slingshot you made from a standing tree and an inner tube. You broke his arm while attempting to launch him to—

Oh, no. That was when I was twelve or thirteen.

Did alcohol and tobacco seem to be elements that delineated whether people where active or inactive?

Almost the litmus test.

You were elected to public office several times before you became governor. You were also defeated a couple times.

I was defeated more than I was elected.

Did you feel that you had to disguise or hide your habits? I mean, it's not a good idea to go around waving your pipe in Utah if you're running for office.

Well, I didn't make a fetish out of it. On the other hand, I think most people who knew me knew I smoked a pipe. Now, the first time I was elected to office was before the war—I was elected county attorney of Davis County—and I'm sure I didn't smoke a pipe at that time. But I never did hide the fact, but I didn't advertise it either.

There's a story I like to recall because it gives me a warm feeling about politics as contrasted to now. Early in my time as governor, I was in the governors' conference in Minneapolis, the National Governors' Conference, and the set up was in a big ballroom with a horseshoe-shaped table. Governors sat all around the outside, and behind each individual governor sat his staff and newspeople from his home state. Well, most of the governors smoked at that time (I'd say that very few of them smoke now. They quit for the same reason I have, you get older and the doctor tells you you'd better stop). Anyway I was smoking my pipe and I didn't pay any particular attention that there was a pipe in my hand. I looked up, and a newsman from one of the national newspapers snapped my picture. I don`t know if you remember Roy Gibson, the Salt Lake television newsman, but Roy got up and followed that guy, the newsman. They stopped and talked a minute. The newsman opened his camera and gave the film to Roy and Roy brought it over and put it on my desk. Roy never said a word, but I appreciated it. I don't think many of the press would do that today.

In your memoirs, As I Recall, *you mention that because Sherman Lloyd*

admitted he was a social drinker you believe that hurt him in the election in 1962. And I think there were rumors about Lawrence Burton, too ...

Edith Ann Lloyd, Sherm's widow, got very angry at me for even mentioning that in my book. For the fact that I confirmed that Sherm occasionally took a drink, she felt was demeaning to him. She was very angry at me.

That shows you the power of that issue in this state, doesn't it?

Yes. Sherm certainly wasn't a heavy drinker, but a very light drinker. I'm sure that alcohol never affected his conduct.

Do you attend church today?

Occasionally.

Do you go to regular Sunday services or funerals?

I don't like funerals. We lost a daughter, Meg, ten years ago, and funerals bring that back, so if I have a friend who dies, I generally go and see the family and then I leave. But I go to church on occasion. I speak in church occasionally when I'm asked to.

Do you consider yourself active?

No, I would not consider myself active.

What about your bedrock belief in the Book of Mormon? Do you have that?

No, I don`t. That's probably my principle problem with the LDS church. I have a hard time accepting the authenticity of the Book of Mormon stories. On the other hand, I feel that the philosophy of the Mormon church is wonderful. I am, as most people, uncertain about the existence of God. I try to believe in it because I want to believe in it—I sort of make myself believe. I have a hard time forcing myself to accept the Book of Mormon story literally. Just as I have trouble accepting the biblical stories literally. If you do believe in an omnipotent God, they're possible. Anything's possible, if you believe in that. I think this is responsible for the fact that I'm not active as I should be.

When did these feelings first come to you?

As a boy.

Even from early childhood?

I wrote a poem in college that was published in the *Pen* magazine on that subject.

You don't have a copy of that, do you?

I remember it.

Can you recite it?

Well, it's a sonnet:

As forth upon life's perilous cruise I sail,
No vision of my goal invites me on.
Though I watch others cross the horizon,
My sight does not extend beyond death's veil.
I pray, but even while praying doubts assail
My mind. Who hears my prayer? Am I upon
My knees worshipping some false image drawn
In my mind by an age old fairy tale?
Yet I fear to think that when at last
Death's finger points at me my soul must face
An awful empty never-ending night.
Oh, God, if by your hand our fates are cast,
If you can really hear me pray, erase
My doubts, in my heart to let there be light.

It won a prize.

What kind?

I don`t remember, it was a cash prize. Five dollars, maybe.

How did you deal with church "activeness" with your own children?

I encouraged them to be active in the church of their choice.

You didn't restrict them in any way about which church? Lucybeth was in agreement with this obviously. You and she, according to your book, often went to church together, when you were in Washington. Does she continue to go to church?

She continued to go to church pretty regularly until about ten years ago. There was a woman's conference here and she got pretty angry at the church about their involvement. She comes from good religious stock. Her grandfather was first counselor in the First Presidency for a number of years until his death in 1932.

Were you married in the temple?

I was not married in the temple.

What about your brother Byron. Has he been active? [Byron died shortly after this interview.]

About like I am.

And your sister, Virginia?

About the same.

Before your mother's death, did she ever have any feelings about your activity or inactivity? Did she ever mention them?

No, she never did. But then I continued to be fairly active in my participation up to the time I was elected governor. I lived in Parley's First Ward. It was a wonderful ward. We had the finest bishop I've ever known. A fellow named Joe Wood. When we moved to the Federal Heights Ward, we moved to a new ward. I had new responsibilities as governor that were very time consuming. And although the church house was right next door to the governor's mansion (I could just jump out of bed some mornings and go through the back lot to church), I went fewer and fewer times.

Why was that?

I don't know. I guess I didn't feel the same warm relationship to that ward that I'd felt to Parley's First Ward. Although I had some very good friends there. You know Bill Smart, former editor of the *Deseret News*? Bill used to teach the early morning priesthood meeting when I lived in the governor's mansion next door to the ward house. I saw him one Monday and he said, "Oh, it was hot in that meeting yesterday." And he continued, "The very hottest time was while I was teaching the lesson. I heard you start up your car and I knew you were going to the golf course, and I said to myself, 'I hope this is all true.'"

You mentioned some conflicts with the church during your period as governor. They don't seem to be major conflicts.

I got along very well with all of them. I served with four church presidents. I got along very well with all of them.

Who was your favorite?

I'd have to say President McKay. He's one of my favorite people of all time.

He was a very gentle and loving man.

He was when he was old. I understand he was kind of a fire-brand as a young man.

Where you ever angered by official church positions during you governorship?

Yes.

For instance?

The Equal Rights Amendment.

Any others?

The Right to Work law. While this wasn't the subject of a church position, I felt church influence. I wanted the Right to Work law repealed. I felt it was sort of a burr under labor's saddle and wasn't doing any particular good. But I know the church wanted to keep the Right to Work law, although I never heard a church pronouncement on it. That irked me a little bit. Those are the ones that I can remember. Ordinarily the church stayed out of political and governmental matters.

We often hear stories about how they have an "underground" system of letting their political views be known. Do you believe that?

No.

Do you think that communication with the church is affected by a person's active or inactive status?

I don't think so. I enjoyed chatting with church leaders and they seemed to enjoy chatting with me. A cute little story. During my first term, when President McKay was in very good health, he was fairly robust then. I used to enjoy very much going down and talking over matters with him. I can remember one day the Peace Corps director wanted to put work camps in Utah and I was to designate where they went. I decided one should go at the mouth of Weber Canyon (there were some facilities held over from the old Civilian Conservation Corps), and I decided the other one should go to Milford, Utah. But Wallace Yardley, the president of the Beaver Stake, was much opposed to it. And I didn't want to bring those boys from out of state into a hostile atmosphere, so I said to hell with them and made the decision the work camp should go down to Price. I thought I was going to have some others to designate, so thought I'd better talk to the church leaders about it. I made an appointment and I went down and President McKay had President Hugh B. Brown and President Nathan Eldon Tanner there.

I explained the Work Corps concept and said, "Is the church opposed to this new policy?"

President McKay said, "Well, no. It sounds like a good idea to me." He said, "You say Brother Yardley was opposed to it?"

I said "Well, I suppose he's afraid of bringing in these young boys of unknown background among the Mormon girls."

President McKay said, "Oh, I don't think that's a problem unless young men have changed since I was a boy. If there are Mormon girls who are trying to get into trouble, there'll probably be a Mormon boy to take care of it."

You never felt any lack of confidence because of your inactivity or status within the church?

What do you mean, lack of confidence?

You seem to be a completely confident man and with a good self-image.

Do you mean, did I feel somewhat inadequate in my dealings with the church? No, they treated me well.

I guess I mean, did you ever feel inadequate in your own spirituality?

Oh, yes. I wish with all my heart right now that I had a testimony. You don't get that. Maybe if you work at it hard enough you do, I don't know. I wish I did. I envy people who do. I'm sure they are happier. The mind is at ease on a matter that it might be troubled about.

Takes quite a leap of faith, does it?

Uh-huh.

Do you think the church hurts itself in a way by asking that we have faith, yet encouraging us to get the kind of education that might challenge that faith?

Well, I suppose the theory is that your faith should be tested. If it's not tested, it's not strong. And if it's not strong, it could fail.

As a child, do you remember having any feelings about being good or evil according to the way church doctrines had been taught to you? Did you ever feel that when you catapulted Alton Call, for instance, you were doing something bad?

I guess everybody's suffered that type of guilty conscience. If they did something they knew they shouldn't or felt they shouldn't. Like the time we catapulted Alton. I felt bad because Alton was hurt. I wasn't particularly concerned about the fact that I flipped him in the river.

I remember stealing cherries as a kid and feeling very guilty and remorseful.

Well, I don't remember stealing cherries, but stealing a watermelon. In Bountiful it was just a way of life. It's just what you did. It just wasn't considered stealing.

Do you think inactives are more likely to be better educated and have better jobs, more income?

I can't see it. You'd have to do a survey. John Huntsman is very active. George Eccles wasn't active at all.

Do you think many of us become inactive because we don't feel we can live up to the rigid demands of active status in the church?

No, I don't think it's that so much. I think we get awfully tired of going to church Sunday after Sunday and hearing a repetition without evidence of something we can't accept. I think that's the problem. We just can't listen to that anymore.

You mentioned you like the way of life that Mormonism teaches. Can you be more specific?

The Mormon work ethic, the Christian work ethic—that you should work and that nobody owes you a living. The golden rule is not exclusive to the Mormon faith, for all great religions—Christian, Jewish, Muslim, Buddhist—teach you to treat your neighbor kindly. But the Mormon church has a good way of life. Now would I have joined the Mormon church if I'd been born in some other religion? I don't know. Maybe not. But I think all religions have excellent ethical underpinnings that guide us in our lives, and as I was born a Mormon and as the Mormon code was perfectly acceptable to me, I tried to follow it.

What might the church do to reactivate those who become inactive?

I'm sure the church is working very hard on that. I can remember clear back right after Lucybeth and I first moved into Parley's Ward, they asked me to teach a quorum of elders, which came to be called the "Smoking Elders." And I did teach for two years. I had a good Sunday school class. They not only came from our ward, but from other wards. Gus Backman [former executive of the Salt Lake Chamber of Commerce] used to come all the way from where he lived at the Ambassador Club. He'd come Sunday morning and there would be a faint smell of alcohol, hardly dissipated from the night before. The church would make an effort then. I taught the Old Testament and the New Testament, and then they asked me to teach the Book of Mormon. I just didn't feel like I could teach that. I didn't know it well enough and I didn't have enough confidence in it. You see other churches doing the same thing. Some of these evangelical preachers go to all extremes to be startling to bring in their people. I haven't seen anything very successful.

What political issues might be alienating active people from the church?

The church hasn't taken positions on very many political issues. They've taken positions on tobacco issues, but I don't know anybody who quarrels with them very much there, even smokers. Almost everyone today agrees we shouldn't smoke. The church takes positions usually only on moral issues. Or when a political issue becomes a moral issue. Now on the Equal Rights Amendment, I guess it was President Spencer Kimball to whom I said, "Not only do I think you're taking a wrong position, but I don't think you should have a position."

Today many people are disillusioned or become inactive because of the issues of censorship. In 1993 and since, we've had active Mormons resign or be excommunicated as a result of their desire to speak out on issues. For some women I think divorce and their status as divorcees have alienated them. What's your view?

Yes, that's true. You know Alvin Gittins, the painter? Here's a wonderful story. Alvin didn't tell me, someone else did, about the church calling him into a bishop's conference. Alvin had criticized some church pronouncement. Anyway, they said they were seriously considering excommunication charges against him, and would that trouble him? Alvin said it would because his parents are very devout and that would hurt them. He said, "But as far as I'm concerned, if I've done something for which I should be excommunicated, the Lord's already done it. If I haven't, it doesn't matter what you fellows do." Which I think is a pretty rational position.

Was there ever a time that being a Mormon was embarrassing.

No. But I remember a funny incident. My daughter Meg came down to Washington and rode in one of the inaugural parades with us. Someone on the sidelines said, "He's the governor of Utah. He has two wives, an old one and a young one."

As for my children? Two of them have been very devout Mormons and two not. Vince is in the bishopric and Meg's husband was bishop and Meg was Relief Society president. Tony has become an Episcopalian, and I don't think Janet goes to church.

What do you think active Mormons think of those who are inactive?

I get along fine with active Mormons and they seem to get along with me. Sometimes they subtly try to get me to be more active, but I don't resent it because I don't respond.

What do you think happens when we die?

I wish I knew.

2.

Loneta M. Murphy

A great flame follows a little spark.

—Dante Alighieri

Loneta M. Murphy has served as a member of the BYU Women's presidency, and also as president, counselor, or teacher in all of the local women's organizations of the LDS church. She was an active member of the League of Women Voters, of the National Women's Party, of the National Organization of Women, of the Algie Ballif Forum, and also a member of Mormons for ERA.

Loneta has given me careful directions to her Provo, Utah, home, but the street coordinates (or my own inattentiveness) between Orem and Provo once again outfox me, and I'm a little late. It's a sunny March day, and small banks of dirty snow shoulder the north sides of the houses as I check for her address.

After I find her tidy home next to a ward chapel on Provo's east side, she greets me. Loneta, mother of five, grandmother of thirteen, has neatly coiffured blonde hair and wears stirrup pants that accentuate the trimness of her figure in spite of her seventy-plus years. She smiles easily as she shows me inside. The living room is done in autumn colors of orange, tan, and gold. She presents a two-tiered tray with chocolates and candy canes. My eyes fall on the top of a coffee table where a copy of the Ensign *rests.*

~

What year were you born?

In 1924.

And you were born in Wyoming?

In Cowley, Wyoming. My parents lived in the Big Horn Basin in Wyoming, and their parents went there to help settle the Big Horn Basin. My father's folks were from West Virginia. They were converts to the Mormon church. My mother's folks were Danish and had been living in Sanford, Colorado. There were others moving to the northern part of Wyoming to Mormon church settlements, and they journeyed thinking the opportunities would be there for land and for building communities. So about 1905 both families somehow gathered there and became a part of the community for a long time, and made a place for Mother and Dad to raise their children. There were eight of us—nine, actually. One child died in infancy. The community that I grew up in was actually Lovell, Wyoming. Lovell was an interesting little city because it had several churches. It not only had the Mormon church, but it had Methodists and Baptists and Catholics and Lutherans. There were a lot of Lutherans there. I think that made a very healthy community life, looking back on it. We were very active in the LDS church. My Danish grandfather was a patriarch in the church, a very solid member in the community.

Were you a regular attendee at church?

I was. My mother was. My father was active as much as he could be. My mother was the strong one of the partnership and very devoted to the church, as her father was.

When you say your father was not, did this ever create friction between them?

No, he could take it or leave it.

But did he attend church regularly?

No. He was away from home a great deal of my childhood. He worked away from home, and Mother kept the family together and kept the home fires burning and food on the table. But when the children in the family—particularly my sisters—grew up and started having children, then my eyes were open to the fact that the Mormon way of life lent itself to having children, to marrying, and to being content with the same process going on and on. My mother was having babies, and my two older sisters were having babies, and that to me was not the ideal life, and I could see it coming to me if I stayed in that community. So I rebelled or turned away from that emphatically. I said, "This is not Loneta's life."

So you left?

As soon as I graduated from high school.

And came to Salt Lake?

Yes.

What did you do then?

I worked in the Remington Arms plant.

Were you still going to church?

No. I didn't see a need for church. I didn't have any reason to be inactive as far as any conflict goes. It just wasn't necessary to my way of life. I think our church provides a lot for children. I really think that's its stronghold. It provides good social life and good training for children, and I also think it's good for older people in the church. On those two ends of the spectrum, it really is an important part of our lives. But I don't believe it meets the needs of the middle.

That's interesting. Why?

For one thing, if we are thinkers in life, there's no room for thinkers in the Mormon church. But it also doesn't allow for our feminist voice in the church at any age.

I'd like to explore that in more detail later. When you were living in Lovell, did it seem important that you were active?

Yes. It was a peer group thing.

Did you as a youngster have a testimony of Joseph Smith and the doctrines?

No. I think that those who say they did are just saying they did. I don't think a testimony comes that early, if ever, because I don't believe it's true.

So it was a social thing more than anything.

Very much so.

I guess your parents, your mother especially, expected you to do these things, to attend church.

Right.

Does growing up in a diverse community like that put a different light on Mormonism? Did it provide a dimension that may have caused you to view your church differently at some point?

It may have contributed a lot. It may have reflected the outside world, that there are other ways of thinking and doing. Now if I'd been in one of the other towns surrounding Lovell, I may have thought otherwise, because Byron and Cowley, Wyoming, were almost all Mormon people. But Lovell was a cross section and that was very good.

So now you're a young woman, you're liberated, you're working at Remington Arms, and you're the essence of Rosie the Riveter in World War II.

That's pretty much the way it was.

You were suddenly experiencing some unusual freedom, weren't you? In terms of the times?

I was. There were so many soldiers to date, for one thing. My social life was very exciting.

And you were also providing for yourself?

Oh, yes, I was very independent. But my sister was going to BYU at the time I was at Remington Arms, so she encouraged me to spend a year with her down in Provo to see if I liked college life—which I did. But financially I found it quite stressful. I loved the social life, I loved classes, I loved most things about it, but it was a financial burden that made me think I'd better go back to work. And because it was World War II, there were jobs in Utah and California, so when the opportunity presented itself for me to take a trip to California, I liked it too much to return to Utah. I settled in Long Beach, got myself a very good job with the Los Angeles Port of Embarkation. It was good for me, a good living and having an apartment and a nice lifestyle. So I was living in Long Beach through the war until it ended. And at that time, Joe had been a Marine and was coming back to his home town which was Long Beach.

This was Joe Murphy?

Joe Murphy. Joseph Robison Murphy. We met in church because I kept in touch with the church down there, again for social reasons. We met in Mutual.

You were going to church occasionally?

Yes. I'd stop in with an escort of my choosing, some date that I'd had the night before or something. I brought my friends to church with me, and Joe thought I was married. Of course, I wasn't, I was just playing the field. In fact, I wasn't looking for a permanent partner at all. I wasn't looking for marriage. I liked my lifestyle.

Obviously you'd returned to some kind of semi-active ...

Just socially. Not spiritually. It still hadn't met my spiritual needs. I should put it another way. It never did meet my spiritual needs.

You and Joe married?

We were married. We fell in love the summer of 1946, and his intent was to go to BYU in the fall. Because we were in love, the separation didn't seem too wise, so we talked about it, and I decided to leave my job at the Port of Embarkation and come back to Utah. My folks were living in Bountiful at that time. I didn't choose to live with them, but I knew I had contacts in Utah that would be helpful to me. So I left my job, came to Provo before he did, and in the meantime was able to get a job at the Geneva Steel Company in the accounting division and found myself a place to live. In November, during the Thanksgiving vacation, we went to Salt Lake and were married in the temple.

You were married in the temple?

Yes. Then I was able to marry in the temple without really having much of an active membership in the church.

How did that happen?

I don't know. I just asked for a recommend, and they gave it to me. I guess that the idea that if I was going to the temple, they thought I'd be a good prospect for active membership. Perhaps because of my mother's membership in the Bountiful community, good church people, but I hadn't been paying tithing or doing anything that showed my allegiance to the church.

Joe pursued an academic career?

Yes, he did.

And you lived in Provo for a while, and then moved to ...

We lived in Provo for five years. He was a freshman when he entered school here, and he got his bachelor's and his master's here. Then he had a teaching fellowship to go to the University of Nebraska to work on his doctorate. So with our two children—one was born in 1949, and one in 1951—we moved back to Lincoln, Nebraska, for nine years.

During this time, were you active at all?

Yes, we were. We were both active in the mission field. That was a good lifestyle. I liked that. It was challenging. Then again, we were in a city with a lot of Lutherans and a lot of people. The university life was challenging and interesting, so we had what we considered a well-balanced life with family and church and university and community. We also spent our summers in Yellowstone Park. In the wintertime we were in Lincoln and in the summertime in Yellowstone Park, where Joe was a ranger-naturalist. We didn't put off living until the doctorate was obtained. We had a good lifestyle. And while we were in Nebraska, two more children were born, so we were a family with four children when he received a call from BYU saying that there was an opening for a professorship in zoology, and would he fly out and look it over and possibly take the job? By that time, we were in our second new home and had only been in it three months, so I spent a few tears about that decision. I would've been happy to stay in Lincoln or even go farther east. We had had the Provo experience. We knew what it was like, so why not go for something new and different?

Was there anything you didn't like about the Provo experience?

The influence of the church. I had realized by that time that it was a theocracy in this part of the world, more than it was a democracy, and the church had too much to do with our lives. I didn't actually resent it, but it worried me. I wanted more room to move, more room to think, more room to do.

Why at mid-life do you now feel the church doesn't serve some needs, as you indicated earlier?

For one thing, there's no voice for women in the church. If you speak your voice, as I did, in believing that the Equal Rights Amendment (ERA) should be part of our Constitutional rights, then I was speaking in opposition to the church's stand on it. There were a lot of women who felt that the ERA was a good thing because it was in our Utah constitution. And it came out of Congress about the same time that I became an active member in the League of Women Voters. So it seemed to be something that blended with my thinking, rather than being on the opposite side, but the church took the opposite side, so that put me in opposition to the church.

What caused you to come to the point where you felt you could take a stand in opposition to the church?

How could I not take a stand? It was in our Utah constitution, and it was part of my philosophy. How could I not? In the church magazine in March 1971, there was a picture of a man and woman who were in an equal marriage. I thought my church teachings and my constitutional rights really blended, and I was so happy about this article that I made copies and used it for my material.

***This is the* Ensign?**

Yes. I really thought the church would take a stand for it, and when they took a stand opposite, then I could see that they just wavered back and forth, whatever was politically astute for them, rather than for people and for women. It was very disconcerting to me to think that they were taking that stand, but it didn't make me feel like I should back off. I had convictions of my own, and I felt very comfortable taking position for it—all the time that I worked with it through the decade of the 1970s.

With your husband teaching at BYU, you saw to it that your five children were regularly attending church, and you were paying tithing.

Yes, and I was very active in all the organizations of the church for women. I had been in the Relief Society presidency, the Primary presidency, the Mutual presidency, I'd taught the lessons. I was part of the BYU Women's organization on campus. I served in that presidency.

Then you came out in favor of ERA. What kind of heat did you take for your position?

I probably wouldn't have taken any heat if I hadn't asked for a recommend to go to the temple with two of my married children who had not been married in the temple. That was in 1978, I believe. I was a public spokeswoman for the ERA and League of Women Voters. I was well known in the community and was quoted a few times in the paper and on TV and so forth. So because I was a well-known person and was taking that stand, it became a conflict for my stake president to give me a recommend. The bishop didn't give me any trouble. None of my bishops ever gave me any trouble in any of my life activities, but this stake president felt he couldn't approve a recommend as long as I took that position. I disagreed with that. He gave me fifteen minutes for the interview, and I wouldn't leave without my recommend, so we talked for an hour and fifteen minutes, and he finally signed it. Then he rescinded it later.

How did he rescind it?

By letter.

How did that make you feel?

It made me feel sad. It made me feel betrayed. I felt like it was a very political move on the part of the church, and I didn't realize until that point in my life ... It took me fifty years to realize how political the church was. Instead of being my spiritual leaders, they were my political voice. They wanted to be, and I just wouldn't allow it, which meant that I couldn't have a recommend. But going to the temple wasn't the most important thing. My children could still go to the temple if they chose, and I could still be Loneta without a recommend. I just kept going—the same position that I'd taken. I didn't back down.

Were you still active in ...

Yes. I was teaching literature lessons at the time, so I continued to teach until I became so disenchanted with the environment of the church that I gave it up.

When was that?

Probably about 1980 or 1981.

Have you been back at all?

No. It doesn't fill any needs for me anymore. It isn't my spiritual environment, and I've been able to find my own way very comfortably, so I just don't have a need for it.

Do you consider yourself a spiritual person?

Oh, very, very spiritual.

You don't go to another church to meet your spiritual needs?

No. And if I did choose to go back to the Mormon church and be active in it, I couldn't just walk over to church which is two houses away from me. I'd have to go several blocks because of the alignment of the different wards and stakes in our church. They actually make it inconvenient even if I were interested.

Is there any possibility you might?

I can't see it in the future. I'm so comfortable with my lifestyle without it, why bring discomfort to my soul?

Do you get any pressure to become active again?

I've had a lot of pressure, but I just don't acknowledge it. In fact, one of the members of the Seventies group called me after my divorce in 1990—my husband divorced me to marry someone else. So the leadership of the ward took it upon themselves to call on me with the idea of taking care of any needs I had. I quite frankly said, "No, I don't need you and I don't want you."

You have a lot of friends and family.

I have a lot of friends and family, and I have no need for someone coming into my life and checking on me from the church.

Your children, are they active, inactive, a mix?

A mix. I taught them well, so they stay with the church somewhat, but I don't think they have a strong conviction toward it. I think they've come to accept the fact that it's a good social thing to do in a Mormon community—to belong.

You can't imagine becoming active again?

Not unless there're some real changes in the church regarding women and that there's a voice for us.

LONETA M. MURPHY

Can you imagine having your name removed from the roles?

It really wouldn't matter one way or the other to me, and that's why I don't take it off. It doesn't really matter.

It's unimportant to you?

Yes.

If I were a leader of the Mormon church, what would you say to me?

I'd say that you've built a theocracy that makes it impossible for the membership to live in this beautiful democratic country where we all should have a voice. That you make restrictions in such a manner that it isn't an organization of free agents, and that there's no room for a lot of my friends, and probably a lot of members of my family, and unless it changes to meet our spiritual needs as well as our secular needs, I don't seek membership in the church or need it. I do think the Mormon church will continue to bring new members into the church, building its numbers. And maybe that's all it needs—more members and more tithing and not really people who believe in it.

What is your bedrock belief in Mormonism today?

Joseph Smith didn't see God. The *Book of Mormon* isn't a revealed history. It's words brought about by Joseph Smith's personality, and I don't believe that the beginnings of the church are true, and I don't believe, above all, in polygamy. I think that's been one of the worst things that's happened to the Mormon church. So there are many things about its beginnings that I simply don't trust. In fact, I would believe more strongly in the philosophy of a Sterling McMurrin than I would the president of the church.

But there are some cultural ties that are very binding?

For whom? They're binding for my family. They're binding on my past, but they're not binding on my present. I don't need and depend upon the church for my environmental needs or my cultural needs now.

One more question: What do you think happens when you die?

That's a very good question—one that I think crosses our minds daily and probably of every person on the earth, but I don't think there's an answer to it. And that's fine with me. I'd rather believe in the mystery of life than the answers. I don't think there are any solid answers, and for those who say they have the answers, I think they've convinced themselves and they're aligning themselves with groups that also think they have the answers just simply for support. But there are no answers. We don't know, but our life here can be a heaven on earth if we choose to make it so. And if we choose to make it heaven on earth, then if there is a hereafter, that's just another room of that heaven on earth. I really don't know. I hope there's a hereafter, but if there isn't, I've lived a wonderful life and experienced a lifetime of happiness.

I guess if I were to add anything it would be that I'd like to be more instrumental in helping people personally emancipate themselves, even within our church environment, so that they could become whole, wonderful human beings and probably much more sexually satisfied than they are under the umbrella, as we know it, where church has such an emphasis on families and children, and not on the whole human being.

3.

William Mulder

All that is comes from the mind; it is based on the mind; it is fashioned by the mind.

—*The Pali Canon*

William Mulder, retired professor of English at the University of Utah, took his bachelor's degree with honors (Phi Kappa Phi) and high honors (Phi Beta Kappa) from the University of Utah. After service as a communications officer with the navy in the Pacific during World War II, he returned to Utah where he completed his M.A. in 1947. His Ph.D. ("with Distinction") followed in 1955 from Harvard University.

Among his lengthy list of professional activities, Bill was on the editorial staff of the LDS church's The Improvement Era *from 1939 to 1944, edited the* Western Humanities Review, *and founded and directed both the Institute for American Studies and the Center for Intercultural Studies at the University of Utah. He was a Fulbright lecturer in American literature at Osmania University in Hyderabad, India, and also director of the American Studies Research Center there. In 1957 Bill delivered the 25th annual Reynolds Lecture at the U. of U. on "The Mormons in American History."*

Bill has been a visiting teacher at Duke, Brigham Young University, the University of Washington, Sonoma State College, the University of California at Berkeley, and Weber State University. Recipient of a dis-

tinguished teaching award at the University of Utah in 1977, he was also president of the Utah Academy of Sciences, Arts, and Letters and received that institution's Charles Redd Award in Humanities. In 1995 Bill received a Merit Award from the Utah Humanities Council for a symposium he co-organized on the work of Fawn Brodie. He is the author of several books and many articles.

A slender, spruce Bill Mulder greets us at the door of an older, graceful home in the Federal Heights neighborhood of Salt Lake City, not far from the University of Utah where he taught for forty-one years. Bill is trim and looks sixty, not eighty-two. His graying beard is as neat as the rest of his person. He beckons us in. The Mulder home was built by Salt Lake businessman Joseph Rosenblatt as his "honeymoon cottage," and its original dark Philippine mahogany imparts an antique richness to a Renaissance painting hanging against its surface.

Bill's wife Helen (nee Thomson), recently retired from teaching at Brighton High School, serves us tea, graham crackers, and oatmeal cookies in a glass-walled conservatory at the back of the home. The room feels infused with the spirit of a large, many-armed statue of Shiva (the couple spent six years in India on a Fulbright), and there are photos of Helen in the traditional Indian sari. From this and our conversations, I inferred they became very immersed in the culture. Bill settles into a chair. I soon find myself under the spell of his articulate voice, calmly reasoned mind, and beautifully timed language. The family dog—an old Sheltie—wanders in. Bill gently lifts him and carries him from the room. This interview took place in the autumn of 1996.

~

I'm a child of Mormon convert parents from Holland. I was born in Holland. So all my life was conditioned by the Mormon experience from the convert immigrant point of view. And I fulfilled a mission in Holland between 1935 and 1937.

When were you born?

On June 24, 1915. So I'm in my eighty-second year.

You don't look it.

People do say I seem to be well-preserved

And you were born in Amsterdam?

No, Haarlem. I was one month shy of five when our family came to this country. I recently translated and annotated my mother's Dutch diary which she kept on the way over on the trans-Atlantic voyage. And that's going to be published in the fall issue this year of the *Utah Historical Quarterly* with some period photos. So that's a piece of not only family history, but I'd say Mormon migration history. We have many, many nineteenth-century accounts, but very few twentieth-century ones. Yet, of course, the sensations, the anxieties, the expectations, the disappointments are all there in the twentieth century, too. We settled in at Hoboken (New Jersey), where an elder brother of my mother had arranged for our passage and living quarters.

Were they converts when they came over?

They were converts. They met, quite unaware that each was investigating Mormonism, in a small congregation in Haarlem. That's where they met, and they became engaged, finally married. They would've come to the states earlier, I think, because that notion of gathering was still strong in the early part of this century. Dad was a printer, but he had to serve time in the border patrol of the Dutch army. During that period two children were born, myself and my older sister, Ann, who's about fourteen months older than I am. And it's that foursome, plus a younger brother of my mother—eighteen years old—who constituted the family migrating in 1920. We stayed in New Jersey, first in Hoboken and Secaucus, then Jersey City itself for six years and crossed the continent in 1926, when the Lincoln Highway was fairly young, in a caravan of two cars. A sister of my mother and her family who had come over—my family assisted several families when they were in New Jersey to come over, and you know, they kind of leap-frogged. One sister, an elder sister, went on to Salt Lake with her family. But the other sister was still back in Hoboken, and we formed two caravans. My father bought a second-hand Willys-Knight. It was a four-cylinder, just a tiny engine, and a seven-passenger body—a long thing. It looked like a hearse with fold-down seats in the back so that it could accommodate more passengers. Uncle Bill Hooft bought a second-hand Hudson Super-Six, built square. I recall he had tire trouble most of the way across the continent. They were too poor to buy new tires, and they were held up time and time and time again patching his tires. When we emerged from Parley's Canyon, which was then in 1926 just really a narrow two-lane road, he said to heck with it. Took all the tires off and entered the valley on its rims. When we reached the Wyoming-Utah border, Uncle Bill, who had an old army bugle, stopped. We all stopped, and he blew a blast on his bugle for sheer joy. We'd gotten to Zion. These are experiences—I was merely twelve at that time. You can see how embedded the Mormon outlook, the Mormon experience, the Mormon values were in my growing up. I was thoroughly conditioned. I didn't know any cosmos other than what this family, this experience, provided.

You'd lived all of that time in New Jersey?

For six years—from 1920 to 1926. I went to public schools there. My father took us to Bronx Zoo and Central Park and the Museum of Natural History. When I went back years later to those places, I realized that I have very distinct memories of the things—say, in the Museum of Natural History, the Great Warrior canoe that's in one of the lobbies, for example. But there were the ferries, and later when I taught Walt Whitman at the university, I felt I had an original experience of crossing on a Brooklyn ferry. And Fulton Fish Market and so forth. So all of that was part of growing up.

You were exposed to quite a diverse society in New Jersey.

Yes.

What was it like in Salt Lake? Was it a different community?

It was a kind of homecoming. Our sights had always been set on Utah, Zion, Salt Lake City. And it seemed from the very start a home, our community, and the neighborhood where we lived just north of Capitol Hill down on Clinton Avenue was filled with Latter-day Saints from Sweden, from Germany, from Norway, so we were active converts in a group into which we fitted very readily.

Where were you were baptized?

At eight I was baptized in ... I think we went to Brooklyn, the Eastern States Mission, which B. H. Roberts headed for a time. I have very distinct memories of B. H Roberts coming to the Hoboken Branch and speaking. We had a hall above a store, I think, somewhere on Washington Street in Hoboken. But we'd go to Brooklyn for Eastern States Mission conference. I have vivid memories of B. H. Roberts there presiding, and of David O. McKay as an apostle coming to speak. I think they had a baptismal font in that building. They had their own building there in Brooklyn. So I constantly knew of the convert experience in terms of new arrivals. Our family was very active with the Hoboken Branch, multilingual people from various European countries. My mother's diary records going to meetings and seeing so-and-so and so-and-so, and what it meant to her to have this support in an alien country.

The support continued when you moved to Salt Lake.

We identified immediately with the ward, Twenty-fourth Ward. Eventually Dad became a member of the bishopric. Mother was active in Relief Society, Primary, all of these organizations. Of course, I became a Trailblazer in Primary, and a Boy Scout—I don't think I ever made it to Eagle. I guess I got my Life merit badge. And the various quorums and ranks in the priesthood to be a deacon and to serve the sacrament, to be a priest and go ward teaching, and finally an elder. Never went beyond elder. I thought that was a pretty good term in itself. I went on a mission as an elder. The point is I was immersed.

You went to Holland on your mission?

That's right. Of course, I had a pretty good command of the language. So I understood everything and quickly became much more proficient. I really studied the grammar and became a very good speaker and writer. And there were relatives there whom we visited. In fact, in Haarlem, which was my second assignment—my first was in Delft where my father'd been born. We had lodgings with an aunt—a sister of my father. And they, as a matter of fact, converted. I think the greatest sacrifice on their part was giving up their tea and coffee. You know, these external signs, how fully they understood the message I have no clear idea, but it was a commitment. Through them it was also a kind of passage into Dutch ways and the Dutch community. So that was a very valuable exposure. I was a very idealistic young man on the mission. I worked hard, didn't question the cosmos or the cocoon, you might say.

And then?

Now we understand this world that is created in one's growing up—the conditioning. But counter to that, of course, were going to college, reading widely, ultimately going abroad—Okinawa during the war. Seeing how the world wags from a very different perspective, and you respect this. What I found most unacceptable in Mormonism was the insistence on being the one and only.

You were active up through World War II then?

Yes, in fact, on Okinawa when there were LDS boys and women serving in the various units, we were brought together, and I made it a point to attend. It was a tie, among other things, a sentimental and emotional tie to all that was back there. And when you're out there in a quonset hut or a camp on an island in the Pacific, that's the tether. The tether lengthens, but it's still tied to the central post. I was in a first marriage at that time. Among other complications, marital problems and my changing point of view, all of that hastened the sense that I really was no longer at home in what had been this cosmos, this home. You can't mark a particular moment, at the stroke of midnight—freedom at midnight, but a gradual process, because it also involves one's courage, one's sense of whom am I hurting by this declaration of departure from what my parents had given their lives to. But then you realize that they in their turn had made a bold step from their Dutch Reformed period and accepted something new and outrageous in the eyes of others. If you get to the point where you can shed your garments, you begin to see that what you once regarded as fundamental is really peripheral and superficial. And in other faiths, and other beliefs, and other movements, you can see equivalents, so the blind faith in the one and only is shattered. The intellectual separation was easy. The emotional separation was more tangled and gradual. And still living in this community where the people have the LDS label and background ... one does not wish to offend. He wishes to be identified for what he is, but not to offend. And you soon discover there are a lot of like-minded people—closet dissenters, or whatever term you wish to give to them, who simply are no longer intellectually nor even emotionally satisfied with what they grew up. It's a matter of growth. Real simple growth. I'm very interested and continue to be interested in Mormon history as part of American history, Western history; in Mormon letters as a part of American letters, Western letters; and I write, I suppose, sympathetically; that is, I trust, in a way that is understanding and yet critical. I'll have to show you the final paragraphs of an article that appeared in *Dialogue* called, "Telling It Slant: Aiming for Truth in Contemporary Mormon Literature," where I very openly, I think, declared my credo. That may be why the editors of a new collection of critical essays decided they couldn't include it, because it's a very explicit statement as to where I stand. And it's clear that I'm much more of a naturalist than a supernaturalist. It's not just Mormonism and its claim to angelic revelation, but the claims of any other faith about the transcendent or the supernatural. Now I've read a lot of Emerson, and I've read the Transcendentalists and the Romantics, and I understand their sense of an immanent divinity.

Margaret Fuller's ...

Margaret Fuller and so on. But they made wonderful rhetorical use of that outlook, and it had a philosophic base in Kant and other German idealists. In spite of Sterling McMurrin's wonderful essays on the theological foundations and the philosophical foundation of Mormonism, I don't think we can make that case for Mormonism. I just can't accept the Joseph Smith story as theology. It's a unique work in terms of American literature—very creative, very imaginative, and very influential. Think of the names on the land derived from the Book of Mormon. And it still impresses converts who know nothing about the history of the church. I understand nowadays in the mission field they never mention polygamy, for example, or anything in past Mormon history. Richard Cracroft, who for a while was president of the Swiss-German mission, stuck his foot in his mouth when he mentioned polygamy in one of his talks or conversations. The eyebrows raised and a great flurry of excitement. What's this?

There seems to be editing of history by official church sources.

They want nothing that will disturb another perspective. That's one of the institutional annoyances. My disaffection is not as it may be with some—disappointment in the leadership, judgments on their character or unwise decisions. I could boil over when I think of the new conference center that they're going to build downtown opposite Temple Square, but that's not a reason for departure—shedding the dust of your feet on the old. It's much more fundamental than that. There are institutional disappointments. No question. The things that go on in wards, stakes, and church that people carry on seemingly uncritically, mindlessly, can make you angry or disappointed. When it comes to tithing and contributions, there are many other causes to which we now contribute rather than supporting an institution and its ways that we really don't believe in. You know, it would be foolish to do that. Now, to the faithful, there's an element of fear in not doing the traditional. What are the consequences of not conforming? But the people who've been about in the world, and seeing the same commitment on the part of millions to their way of thinking, their way of life, this ethnocentrism on the part of Mormonism seems extremely parochial and it's hard to abide. Very hard to abide. But there are outlets now that there weren't some years ago. The Sunstone symposium is a great way of venting all kinds of talk. My wife accuses it of a great deal of puffery, and I do think there is that. You can take any topic in Mormonism and give it the deconstructionist treatment or the higher criticism treatment or whatever. You throw up these things in ridiculous fashion. But at the same time you're rubbing shoulders with a lot of people you discover also have their doubts, and you can be much more objective about what has been a movement, a dialogue. I'm fiction editor for *Dialogue*, and I feel delighted that I can recommend pieces that would shock the pants off what the *Ensign* or the *New Era* or whatever Aspen Books or BYU Press might want to publish. It's possible in this community now to be absolutely one's own person intellectually. There's a lot of support. It comes not only from the non-Mormons; it comes from people like oneself who owe a debt, shall we say, to a moral upbringing. But at last we arrive where we must stand on our own feet.

Was there ever a time when you left active practice that you felt lonely or isolated?

Not in my case. Relationships formed with non-Mormons were just as supportive. If a person feels guilty, and it's a matter of conscience, I suppose there might be that uneasiness, that wondering. Did you ever see a little piece called "Problems of the Mormon Intellectual"? It was in *Dialogue* many years ago. Well, there's another statement that—and it's not simply my position—but tries to suggest what reconciliations or what steps the free thinker might take ... I think we ought to call ourselves free thinkers ... or maybe a humanist. That's a dreaded term around here.

It politicizes people.

Yes. Polarities result when people declare, "I have the truth." It divides. Look what's going on in Ireland, in Israel and Palestine—all in the name of religion. These are events that also give one pause and say, "Why commit to a religion, a religious institution, which only intensifies the differences and divisions, and which gives an extraneous authority to something that doesn't deserve that authority?" You see, when people invoke—in the name of religion—this belief or that, there's the attempt to give it a sanction that it doesn't deserve. It intensifies division. That's why "the one church, the true church, the only church" business is so offensive.

Have you ever considered asking to be excommunicated?

My wife says I'm a coward, that I should take that formal step, and in all honesty I should because if I'm on the rolls, people in the ward continue to think of me as LDS and then have to judge me as a backslider because I'm not attending church, not contributing financially, etc. It would clear the air in terms of where I stand. And I suppose I'll have to do that.

But the church benefits from your being on the rolls by being able to claim its 10 million members.

I've thought of that, too. And there must be a great many like that. They are not the same. Some will equate the anti-environmentalists with the Mormon outlook. And that's simply not true, because there are ever so many Mormons who are in the environmental movement—no question.

I'm inactive, but by virtue of my birth I'm Mormon. I'm identified as a Mormon by those who are outside looking in, but those who are active don't identify me really as a Mormon. I've been dunked, as a friend once told me, and some would say I have to live with it or get out.

WILLIAM MULDER

If there's some ceremony by which we could be undunked, that might be definitive.

But that makes me sort of schizoid. Part of the reason I'm doing this is because I've never really felt that I fit anywhere.

So this is for your therapy?

In part.

I don't feel schizoid. You know, there's one way to solve problems, and that's to rise above them. And it doesn't bother me. There was a time that it was truly a matter of conscience, but perhaps more a feeling in terms of family and so forth. I have a brother and sisters, some of whom are extremely orthodox and staunch and others who may on the surface be churchgoers and so on, but I know don't have that commitment, and others who simply stepped outside it as I have. I think that goes on in many, many families.

I'm being interviewed by you now. But I'm responding and thinking of my own experience. I felt guilt around my departure from active status, because that tremendous ingraining of the culture and ideals of Mormonism when I was a child, by my grandparents specifically.

Were they pioneers?

Yes. Pioneers, polygamists.

See, this is the Church of the Pioneers. That's another thing. So much is made of that westward trek and, indeed, it preserved a church that was about to go under. Now they're thinking in global terms, but here again is a great difficulty because the thinking is still very provincial and there's an effort to make the Latin American and the Africans over in our image. They even have a mission in India now. And they have a different heritage. There's a wonderful irony. On Latin America, I read an article in *Dialogue* about what's going on in Guatemala. The converts there take the Book of Mormon to be quite literally the book of their ancestors, and they are the true heirs. We Anglos are saints only by adoption. It's a very interesting phenomenon going on in Latin America. Pretty soon, maybe not too long from now, the Latin Americans are going to say, "We are the true church, we are the true heirs, we are the Book of Mormon people; you guys are Johnny Come Lately; now listen to us."

We did, after all, come over in submarines, and landed on the Mayan Peninsula ...

It's something to watch. And, of course, there's something very egotistical or ethnocentric about going into any of these countries of very different cultures and imposing that. The Hindus felt that way about the Christian missionaries who came in the nineteenth century. Again and again I've encountered memoirs and essays in which there's a strong resentment on the part of the Hindu to the proselyting that goes on. The enormity of a Western culture not acknowledging, recognizing the depth and attributes of their own.

It must be offensive to some.

It's terribly offensive. So I think there are parallels here, in spite of this global outlook that is now enabling or motivating the building of temples and establishing stakes and wards where there used to be missions and branches. It's still a very parochial outlook. And that's hard for people who read a lot, who travel a lot, who begin to open up to the values of different cultures and respect them. I'm not the kind of rebel who becomes an Episcopalian or a Hindu or a Buddhist. Sort of equivalent of the feminists who want to become men, really. And that wouldn't satisfy me. I rest in being maybe a continuing seeker. But even the word "seeker" suggests that there's a belief in some supernatural, some monolithic truth that's out there.

Do you consider yourself a spiritual person?

I've never had any revelations. I think sensitivity, aesthetic sensitivity, intellectual sensitivity could amount to a kind of spirituality. I don't think of myself as a materialist, but the opposite of that is being spiritual. I think you're defining elements or qualities that are quite abstract and indefinable but that are very humanistic. I'm going to give you a copy of Wallace Stegner's credo. Years and years ago he was on Edward Murrow's radio program—a series of very short statements called *This I Believe.* I respond to his outlook. This is a very ecumenical outlook. And then I'll give you a copy of a telling paragraph at the end of my *Dialogue* piece "Problems of the Mormon Intellectual," which people tell me, who have read it, helps them locate themselves.

You don't believe in a higher power?

I'm afraid not. There may be intuitive things. How does intuition operate? We are at this moment all that we have ever been—the result of all the experiences, internal, extraneous, that we have ever been. Louis Zucker, one of my hero professors at the university, said something like "human nature is biological in its root but spiritual in its flower." You see? We are of this earth—earthy. We have to feed, cultivate ourselves in a material sense. We ingest and we evacuate. I mean, we are living organisms, but at the same time, we have minds—however you define mind, whether it's a mere mechanism or not—that are capable of entertaining dreams, ideas, hates, loves, and so on. That's spirituality, you know. All that is not material and has to be then, I would say, of that kind which you might call the internal as opposed to the external. But that means that I simply dismiss all this angelology. Whether it's Joseph Smith's or Islam's or anyone's. It takes a big burden off my system of beliefs, because then you begin to realize you don't have to blame a supernatural power or deity for what's happening to you. It eliminates an awful lot of misery—the kind you hear at funerals. Why this had to happen or that had to happen. The question doesn't come up, because you see it as an inevitable consequence of natural causes—or psychological causes—but causes that are palpable. It's a big relief. That's a bigger relief to me than stepping outside of a ward ritual. Now maybe in some people that could make them callous. They might raise the question, "Well, that's going to lead to Nazism and uncontrolled behavior toward others." If your system of ethics isn't supported by a divine belief, that could lead to terrible atrocities—treating human beings as simply atoms or natural products. But I don't think so, because a person growing up with humanistic sensitivities and beliefs isn't going to behave like that. So that's the burden of my relief. Let me tell you this. My long association with Sterling McMurrin has been an important prod in the direction of this kind of thinking.

Were you a member of his ... What did they call you?

The Swearing Elders. The last thing we did together before his death was make a presentation at the Sunstone symposium in August 1995 on the Swearing Elders. I have a copy of my part in that. I didn't record Sterling's. But there is a record. Sunstone puts everything on tape, and they'll have an index of all the sessions and so on.

Sterling was the kind of person who kept a façade in terms of good public relations with the community, but he was a heretic. I'm still not able to pin down what his ultimate fundamental philosophy might be, except perhaps personalism—something he got when he was at the University of Southern California under Pepperell Montague. But I recall in one of our Swearing Elder sessions, a very important one, when Bruce McConkie defended Joseph Fielding Smith's creationist point of view as opposed to the evolutionist. I think it was there. And someone accused Sterling, "So then you have no hope of resurrection?" Sterling answered, "That's exactly all we have is a hope."

Speaking of that, what do you think will happen to you when you die?

Go back to Mother Earth, to be honest. Now, there are religions which say these atoms will reform and recruit those who believe in reincarnation to come back again in whatever form your karma deserves. But that's a form of the supernatural which I can't accept. But to snuff out a candle, it's snuffed out. That's it. Self-realization is a very important element in many Oriental religions—the Buddhists, the Hindu. And I think that element is there in the Mormon notion of eternal progression. Mormonism is really very eclectic. It wasn't just Joseph Smith who pulled it together. There've been a lot of theologians since—John Widtsoe's *A Rational Theology*, Talmage's *Articles of Faith*, and so on. But that idea and the idea that the glory of God is intelligence—these are very attractive ... We're attracted to the early intellectuals like Lorenzo Snow. In a century that was very biblical, literal in its biblical belief, these positions made a lot of sense. But if the Bible is not the literal Word of God to you—that's great literature—then you can't accept it as a basis. To double the jeopardy, Mormonism gives not one book of scripture but two or three. And even some very enlightened people down at the BYU, among my friends in the English literature department, continue to have this sense of the division between what man says and what God says. It's *all* what man says. A Hebrew proverb says, "The law speaks in the tongues of men." And when anyone, the brethren or the people at the Y or wherever, talk about the literal word of God, they forget the medium.

The tongue of man.

Right.

WILLIAM MULDER

You've left Mormonism, but obviously you're fascinated with it.

Sure. I'm fascinated with Americana. I took a degree at Harvard in what they call very pretentiously the History of American Civilization. Well, that's very inclusive, but it does suggest that you approach the life and institutions of any culture in a multidisciplinary way. You think of what the sociologist can give you and the psychologist, and the anthropologist, and the literary critics, and on and on. And use all of these the way a carpenter uses a set of tools to get his work done. And to be hung up on any one of those approaches, whether it's Marxist or classical or biographical, is to limit yourself in the same way that the dogmas of a given religion hamper themselves, hobble themselves. The nice thing about interdisciplinary approaches is that you're unfettered. There's a danger in that, to be so eclectic that you're like a sieve full of holes and have no methodology. But you can work out a methodology, and it allows dissertations that couldn't be honored in a given traditional discipline. In my case, I taught forty-one years in the Department of English, but my dissertation at Harvard was really a historical thing. The Mormons from Scandinavia, the migration of the Mormons from Scandinavia, which the University of Minnesota Press published as *Homeward to Zion*. And it's still the definitive work on that particular migration. Being of Dutch birth and having lived in a ward that was full of immigrants and so on, it was a natural attraction. I did a Master's degree at the University of Utah on immigrant writing, immigrant journalism as both an aspect and instrument of immigrant culture, and that got me into Scandinavian sources, German and Dutch. The Scandinavian sources were so rich that when I carried my M.A. thesis to Harvard and had an interview with Arthur Schlesinger, Sr., the historian, wanting to get into his seminar, I showed it to him. He said, "You should build on this." In his seminar on immigration, I looked much deeper and wider into the history of Scandinavian missions and migration, and it eventually did become the dissertation which became the book. And then with A. Russell Mortensen, at the same time—because we were at it for several years—we produced the anthology that you may be familiar with called *Among the Mormons, Historic Accounts by Contemporary Observers*. Well, it's back in print, in full format at Sam Weller's. I'll show you the original. But it's held up, you see, since 1958; it went through three hardcover printings with Knopf, then the University of Nebraska Press picked it up in their

Bison Book Series. And now Sam Weller ... I negotiated with Knopf to get the rights, and Sam Weller, under his Western Epics imprint, has brought it out in full format, has taken that wonderful cottonwood scene of the Mississippi as the paperback cover. It was the jacket in the Knopf work. Well, I cite this to suggest what you call a fascination with Mormon history and Americana, and to treat them, I think, with objectivity ... It's not the kind of approach of a Mrs. Ferris or a Charles Kelly or people who are out to undo and to *get* the thing they are writing about. We provide the documents and narrative connections and introductions to the document with a lot of history in them. And people can judge for themselves. Without question, it was a major episode in that whole wester- ing. We've just seen this big series on the West on TV, and this book makes available fascinating documents.

Bernard DeVoto is one of those who was out to get somebody. I felt that way when I reread recently some of his work.

In his early essays, he had a very particular ax to grind. Ogden, Utah, was not the cultural center of the universe, but he had his growing up there, and he did attend the University of Utah for a time. He's someone who really bit the hand that fed him. He had an ax to grind—several axes to grind, several chips on his shoulder. There's no question about it. In 1926—this is all fresh in my mind. I don't think I have a photographic memory. I just gave during the governor's conference a keynote address on Utah's literary heritage, and towards the end I quote Bernard DeVoto for my own purposes. In March 1926 the *American Mercury*—H. L. Mencken's *Mercury*—published an essay by DeVoto called "Utah." It's a long catalog of illustrations, denunciations of the aridity of Utah culture. Stegner refers to this in his *Life of Bernard DeVoto*, and in Stegner's case, it was a very interesting personal episode. He was a student at the U. at the time—1926—had just started. One morning the young Stegner came down a hall. A door opened and George Emory Fellows, ancient history professor up there from Maine—he'd come West—tossed out a magazine onto the floor of the hall. Stegner picked it up and discovered that there was an essay there by Benny DeVoto called "Utah" that was really hateful and scurrilous in terms of Utah culture since the Wild West. In effect, Devoto had said: "With an effort, some people in Utah might be able to sign their names."

DeVoto did burn some bridges, didn't he?

He wrote a centennial essay that was just about as bad. Nineteen-thirty was the Mormonism centennial. They didn't appreciate him, obviously. He mellowed, you know, toward the end. He really mellowed.

You mentioned passing on to heaven. One of the practical difficulties is the Mormon belief of family reunions in heaven ... To think of the different ages at which people die, and—the resurrection—at what stage are these people going to be resurrected? Children continue to grow, not really knowing grandparents, certainly not great-grandparents. Doesn't that present an irresolvable problem about family life and the hereafter?

4.

Levi S. Peterson

A verse may find him who a sermon flies.

—*George Herbert*

With degrees from Brigham Young University (B.A. and M.A.) and the University of Utah (Ph.D.), Levi S. Peterson teaches at Weber State University where he is a professor of English. He has served as director of the school's Honors Program and chair of the English department. His articles and stories have appeared in such publications as Western American Literature, Utah Historical Quarterly, Dialogue: A Journal of Mormon Thought, Journal of Mormon History, Ascent, Sunstone, *and on National Public Radio. His books include* Canyons of Grace, Greening Wheat: Fifteen Mormon Short Stories *(editor, with introductory essay and a story),* The Backslider, Juanita Brooks: Mormon Woman Historian, Night Soil, *and most recently* Aspen Marooney.

Levi holds honors as a recipient of the Distinguished Service Award in Arts and Letters from the Utah Academy of Sciences, Arts, and Letters. He also has received numerous awards for his work, including the David W. and Beatrice C. Evans Biography Award, a Best Book Award for 1988 from the Mormon History Association, awards from the Utah Arts Council, and a first prize in the short story category from the Center for the Study of Christian Values in Literature at Brigham Young University.

He's a big man with a mustache and an easy, genuine laugh. He greets me in his office at Weber State University, and the first item I notice in the small space is a coffee maker. A cross of cholla cactus and yarn hangs on one wall, and on another is a photograph of a small white house in winter in a southern Utah setting. The back wall is solid books—Levi's own Aspen Marooney *and other titles mixed in with Larry McMurtry's* Lonesome Dove, *Plato's* Republic, *Herman Melville's* Mody Dick, *and* Refuge, *by Terry Tempest Williams. Levi sits beneath a large set of bull horns mounted on the wall. He wears a blue shirt, red-and-blue tie, and khaki pants. He pronounces the word "ward" with a broad Utah "a."*

~

When were you born?

On December 13, 1933. So I'm sixty-three right now.

Where were you born?

In Snowflake, Arizona. It's about as far north as Flagstaff, but it's a full 100 miles east of Flagstaff. So north-central Arizona is about where you are—toward the center of the state. A little toward the east side of the state. But it's on the Colorado Plateau, and the terrain there has a lot in common with southern Utah rather than the Sonoran Desert where Phoenix is. That was foreign country to me. I lived in Mesa my senior year in high school and didn't like it at all. I felt like a foreigner in the desert down there.

The red rock is what's in your blood?

The country around Kanab—there's a fair similarity with Snowflake in that. Junipers and canyons and rocks.

Snowflake was a Mormon colony like St. Johns and some of those others?

Even more so. In fact, Snowflake really was the key Mormon settlement of northern Arizona, and the first stake president in northern Arizona, Jesse N. Smith, kept his headquarters there. As far as I was concerned in growing up, I was in the center. I had no concept of being far away from anything that was important.

Your active Mormon roots go way back?

Absolutely, you bet. My ancestors on both sides—my father's side and my mother's side—were pioneers, pre-railroad pioneers. My grandparents from Sweden came by wagon before the railroad. And my mother, both her father's and mother's ancestors go back to Joseph Smith's time. In the gathering on the Iowa prairie between 1846 and when the Saints moved out to Salt Lake Valley in 1847, I had twelve ancestors there. Three of them died. The other nine made it. Five more crossed the plains by wagon before the coming of the railroad in 1869. So I had a lot of ancestors—grandparents, great-grandparents, and great-great-grandparents who were active.

Maybe that's something of a record.

Well, there's a lot of them there.

Snowflake was 99 percent Mormon, wasn't it?

Oh, yes, largely Mormon. There were some non-Mormons. There were some railroad section hands whom we called Mexicans. They were Hispanics, spoke Spanish, and they were Catholic. And most people were church attenders. There was a liberal dosage of Jack Mormons. The word Jack Mormon to me didn't mean anti-Mormon. It was just somebody who didn't obey the commandments, who didn't go to church, and who smoked and told profane stories at the post office, and things like that. I had plenty of disapproval of them because my mother was Bishop Savage's daughter. My Grandfather Savage was bishop of Woodruff, Arizona, for twenty-seven years. And being his daughter, she conveyed very strong sentiments about people who wouldn't go to church. A bottle of beer was terrible. I remember empty beer bottles in the street and looking upon them as instruments of the devil.

Clearly, you were very active as a youngster?

Yes.

Both your parents were active?

Oh, yes. My father, in fact, was counselor in the stake presidency from the time of his marriage to my mother until 1939—fifteen years—and about four years before he died. My father was quite a bit older than my mother. Nineteen years older. In fact, he had been her teacher in the local academy. But he had six children when his first wife died. And then my mother had two daughters and divorced her husband. Later they married and had five sons together. So there were thirteen total children between them. I'm the last of the bunch. My half-brothers and -sisters were basically adults before I was born. I knew they were my brothers and sisters. Many of their children of course are my close peers, and I grew up with them. Even though they were my nephews and nieces, they were also brothers and sisters to me. I had a very close relationship with most of them, and still have a very cordial relation with them when we get together. I come from a very large family now. I have innumerable relatives. The vast majority are faithful Latter-day Saints, and they're scattered all over the West, but the largest number still congregate in Arizona. A fair number still in northern Arizona, but I suppose the majority of them now are in the Phoenix-Mesa area.

You stayed in Snowflake how long?

I left at age eighteen to go to college. In reality, I left a year earlier. My mother took me to Mesa. She needed to finish her college, so I did a year at Mesa High School. I felt like an alien there. Then went to BYU. I hadn't even turned eighteen when I arrived at BYU in the fall of 1951. I spent four more summers at home, but basically I've lived in Utah most of my adult life. I had a three-year period out to go on a mission. I went to the French mission serving in Switzerland and Belgium from 1954 to 1957. And my wife and I went over to Berkeley one year between a master's degree at BYU and a Ph.D. program at the University of Utah. So we had that one year in California, but otherwise I've been in Utah for my higher education. Immediately upon graduating with a doctorate in English out of the U in 1965, I came here to Weber State College. And I've been here—it's been my only employer these thirty-two years.

Stable.

Yes, and pleasant. I've not regretted that. I've never had any reason to regret coming to Weber State. It's been a good place to be, in fact. Pleasant and reasonably good support for my writing and my scholarly activities.

You are the writer-in-residence up there pretty much, aren't you?

Well, I do a lot of writing, but my colleague, Gordon Allred, publishes quite a bit. He's more acceptable to the mainline Mormon reader. He publishes with Bookcraft and Deseret Book.

At some point in your life, from what I've gathered, you became less active. How old were you? How did that happen?

My first three years at college, before I went on a mission, were a period of perturbation for me as I ... I really grew into a mood of doubt in that period. And I suppose I would've been well advised not to go on a mission, but the doubt hadn't quite jelled, so I did go on a mission. But I hadn't been out, I suppose, a month, and it struck me this was pretty poor business. There were a lot of reasons why I doubted, but I had no fervor at all for feeling like I had something all these people needed. And they very obviously didn't want it. That was evident from the first knock on a door. I sheltered myself from the difficult situation I was in by being a junior companion for seven months—up in Switzerland, which is a nice place to be even in the winter. In the summer of 1955, I'd been out about seven months, I was made a senior companion. I learned French fairly fast, and I think I spoke it quite well. I'd had a year of it at BYU, and I went down to Belgium and became a senior companion. It seemed to me that it was a question of dishonesty now that I was senior companion and could no longer retire and just be an observer as junior companion, which I had been for seven months. I made quite a concerted effort to come home the summer of 1955. I didn't get any encouragement anywhere and finally decided not to. The mission president conversed frantically with me a number of times, trying to persuade me to stay. I finally did stay. I went to a psychiatrist very briefly in Belgium who said, "My advice to you, Mr. Peterson, is to stay here. You're not hurting anybody. You know that?" He said, "You might even do somebody some good; nobody's going to believe you that doesn't need it." And so I finally decided on the basis of that—given that I saw nowhere to go when I got home, nobody who would welcome me—I just stuck it out. I never bore a testimony. I never told anybody I believed it. I just said this is the doctrine. And, yes, a number of people were converted and baptized, either directly or after I'd left. That was a difficult period of time, and I came back still angry at having stayed out. And in retrospect, I grant it was probably the best thing to do. I can still get angry feelings about it if I really think hard. But I came back with a kind of vow to myself that I was never again going to do anything in the Mormon line that I did not personally want to do, and I wasn't going to pay a penny of tithing. And I've paid only ten dollars, and that was one year I decided to make my mother feel better if I could tell her I was a partial tithe-payer. So that's how much I've paid since 1954 when I went on my mission. Anyway, I married a gentile—Althea. She's still a gentile. I met her at BYU. She's one of that 3 percent of gentiles who went to BYU. I was very lucky to find her. She adapts totally to Mormons. Her roommates were Mormons. She's just turned sideways to the wind all these years, the gusts of conversion. You know, there've been innumerable attempts to convert her, and she just deals with them graciously and tactfully.

I've never been able to make a total, clean break. I just don't have the motivation to do it. I've always worn garments. In the hot summer I don't. It doesn't bother me not to, but if the weather is comfortable for it I wear them. And I went many years—far longer than you'd expect after becoming intellectually independent—saying my prayers. Well, I personally don't believe in prayer. I don't think the architect of the universe is going to alter the gears for individual prayer. And yet I'd been so conditioned to get down on my knees at night. It was like breathing to me to do it. Gave it up, but only slowly. And when I got back from my mission, I never failed to look up a ward any time I moved. After I got married, for three or four years I was fairly alienated. We'd go to church not too often. Actually, the year at Berkeley was better, being out of Utah. I had more motivation. I was a scout leader over there. I was fairly active as an explorer leader. But all through the U of U period—the four years at the U—I was an infrequent attender. Up here, I started attending because we had a little girl, our only child, Karrin. Althea said: "You know, your relatives are going to make her life impossible if we don't at least do the external things, Mormon things, with her." So she was blessed. I blessed her, and she was baptized, and I did that too, and she grew up a Mormon. And she's really liberal, but she's still in it. I mean, she's still attached. She had me bless her little boy. She's married to a gentile, and I blessed her baby here a year and one-half ago, which was quite an adventure getting permission to do that from my bishop.

But you got it.

I got it.

You weren't married in the temple. But you got your endowments, so this must have been after your mission or before?

Before my mission, well before my mission. Missionaries get their endowments. For a while when Karrin was little, both Althea and I went to church quite a bit to give her a model. Even Althea did, and she doesn't particularly like going to church. She's not Mormon, but she did. When Karrin got to be about twelve, she lost interest in going to church. We went through a period of four or five years where we did a lot of sports-like things on Sunday. And hunting season. She wanted to hunt. She took the hunter safety course. But when she got into junior high, she fell in with Mormon kids, and she kind of had a conversion and she started on her own to go to seminary and to church. Althea and I were in support of that. When she no longer wanted me to do things with her on Sunday, I started going to church on my own. For quite a few years—fifteen maybe—if I'm in town and I don't have anything interfering, I go to a sacrament meeting on Sunday. And I sleep. That's not a joke. I make a joke out of it and people laugh, but I sleep with almost total reliability. Once the sacrament's been passed, I'll sleep through two-thirds and sometimes the entirety of the sermons. And I go away refreshed. Much spiritually rejuvenated by having been to church. People ask me why I go, and I say, "Well, this is a place you can sleep knowing no one will rob or murder you." But there has to be an explanation for why I like to go to church, because I do like to go to church. Obviously, I can't stand dull sermons, but if I can sleep through most of them, I don't mind waking up to listen to part of the sermon. And that's just about right—my sense of proportion.

I think I know what you're talking about here, because there is this soothing kind of Mormon liturgy, the way things are phrased, that flows over you. I've noticed this in funerals. When I go to a Mormon funeral, I become very comfortable and sleep could come very easily. I think it feels womb-like and safe and warm.

Yes, I think that's good. And see, I don't fight it. I just go to sleep. I recognize connections with my parents. Going to church is what I was conditioned to do as a child, and there's some sense of doing what they want me to do, and some of the same effect as if I were still able to sit by them. As I say, I have no problem with that. I'll do whatever I'll do but I won't do more than that. I've been a home teacher the entire thirty-two years that I've lived in this town and in this same ward, the Thirty-third Ward, and I'm a reasonably conscientious one. The vast majority of months I get my home teaching done, which consists of just visiting. I don't pretend to give a lesson. My latest companion I really like—because he's very reliable and willing to go—is the ward records clerk—I don't know just what they call him. He runs the ward computer and does the counting of who's there, etc. When he first joined me five years ago as my companion, he wanted to know if we should pray in his car to be ready to go on our first outing. I said, I don't mind, but you'll have to do it. I don't even remember whether he did, but if he did it that one time he never did it again. And when we arrived, he said, "Should we give a little lesson in here?" I said, "I don't mind if you do, but you're going to have to do it; I haven't given a lesson in the fifteen years I've been meeting this family." I've had the same four families for probably twenty years, and once in a while a group leader will want to change me, and I'll just say to them, "Look, you'd be well advised to leave me there, because three of those families are rank Jack Mormons and it took me five years to get in with them, and you'd just better leave it alone." And they have. They've left me with those; the other family is a very active family but our chemistry mixes very well. I get along with that couple and have pleasant times with them. So this present partner's got enough sense and tact to just go with the flow, and we go in and have good long talks. Sometimes we'll stay an hour at some of the places, just conversing. I'm willing to do that. And when they get in a real pinch at the high priest group—I teach a lesson maybe once every three months—I'm not a high priest, but they crowded me out of the elders quorum because I was getting old. And I was still an elder, because I'm not worthy to be ordained a high priest. They don't know that. They've got me on the records as a high priest.

They're going to know it now.

Well, I don't care. It doesn't matter to me. All I know is off my latest record sheet it still calls me a high priest, so I just got ordained. Maybe it was a computer that did it.

Clearly at some point in your life you had some kind of conflict with the church. What were those conflicts, and are they still there today?

I regard myself as a liberal Mormon, and I define liberal as one who wants to see things change. There are a lot of things about Mormonism that I'd like to see changed. That's as good a reason as any to stay in it. For example, its attitude toward historical truth; it doesn't have to try to re-edit itself into a history it never had. It could survive without doing that. So I feel pretty strongly on that. Its treatment of women—though you've got to admit that most men and women accept it fervently and they will condition their daughters to accept it. But it strikes me that women are kept unnecessarily in an inferior role, and they don't need to be. The church would survive, probably flourish, if they change their attitude. I think they ought to have a different attitude toward homosexuals, alternate lifestyles. I think the church ought to have a much less serious attitude towards sexual sin. I think it's okay to define some moral standards and say that premarital sex isn't good and extramarital sex isn't good. And yet I think the church would be well advised not to make as much of it as it does. Deal with the sinner much more gently, and I think they'd probably have no more sin than they've got anyway—since they've got plenty of it. The big thing that I'm against is this requirement that if you're called, by damn, you've got to do it. Even if it isn't to your taste, even if it's inconvenient, you've got to accept every call. I think that's a very bad attitude. I'm against it. I say what little I can against it any time I can. So, yes, there are things, a lot of things, I'd like to see changed.

What about the doctrine? What about the basic bedrock tenets of Mormonism? Joseph Smith and the gold plates?

If you're a deep doubter that God is personal, all that's irrelevant—this other stuff you're talking about. I'm not an atheist in any sense. I think I'm a very reverential person. I find a lot of reverence in me, but as to describe God as just merciful, so concerned with human beings that he prescribes what they eat and wear, etc., etc.—no, I don't. Intellectually, I simply am a doubter.

I like being attached to a community of believers, and I like being attached to Mormonism because it has its own history that comes out of the American West and out of the American frontier. If it's no better than Methodism or Presbyterianism, it's certainly no worse, and it's no crazier. Anybody who points out the lunacies of Mormonism, just let them identify their religion, and I'll point out their lunacies. Human beings have their lunacies no matter which organization they're in, and you just hope there's some good people who try to rectify them in each organization. See, unlike anti-Mormons, who somehow think if you can stamp out this wicked thing called Mormonism, then you're going to have this wonderful thing called born-again Christianity, which is just as loaded with irrationalities and craziness as the thing they're trying to stamp out. I'm not anti-Mormon. I'd like to see Mormonism flourish. It's got a wonderful history.

Most of the people I've interviewed are not anti-Mormon. They embrace a portion of it. I've had a growing feeling that one of the reasons we tend to embrace it and continue to embrace it even in the face of disbelief is because there's this tribal hold on us that goes way back. I mean, the sacrifice of the ancestors and all of that.

You're loyal to it. By damn, you're loyal to it.

You bet. I've asked a number of people who don't believe and who have even denigrated the church why they don't ask to be excommunicated. And when we finally get down to it, it has to do with some very deep psychological ties to the past.

Sure, I wouldn't want to be excommunicated.

If I were the president of the Mormon church, what would you tell me? What would you say to me if I were sitting here now and said, Brother Peterson ...

I'd say, for hell sakes, reinstate Lavina.

Lavina Fielding Anderson?

Yes. It seems like I ought to ask for something bigger, shouldn't I?

You could.

I focus on Lavina just because she's my friend and I did a paper on her, read it at the Sunstone symposium and all. But it all seems so ironic that she really *believes*, and she's excommunicated. And it hurts. I look at it and I think how ironic that I'm glad to be in and don't want to be excommunicated. But somebody like her who really *believes* and is excommunicated. No, I think what has happened to her is the essence of what's wrong with Mormonism. Its fear of history, its fear of women. Maybe that would be the right thing to say to the president of the church—get yourself square with history and you'd get yourself square with the women if you'd reinstate Lavina. That's what I'd say.

In your book* The Backslider, *guilt and shame cause terrible problems. You have a wonderful feel for that guilt and shame. Why does Mormonism seem to generate those feelings in some of us?

I feel that Mormonism is a very stern religion. Some of my good friends think that *The Backslider* isn't even a Mormon book; it doesn't describe Mormons. It describes some crazies, you see, who don't belong to Mormonism. I think Richard Cracroft, a very good, close friend of mine, just feels that the people I'm talking about in *The Backslider* aren't typical Mormons. I'm not addressing typical Mormons with that book. And I can't argue with him, but I do see people in my ward who seem very happy, very complacent, and maybe guilt's not a problem with them. But I know an awful lot of Mormons for whom guilt is a problem. And yes, I was addressing among other things the tendency of Mormons to make an excessive demand on themselves and on human nature. If Christianity has any genius, it's in its acceptance of atoning sacrifice, for heck sakes. If there's anything that's positive about Christianity that would be it—that you've got a safety valve for human guilt in this atoning sacrifice of the deity. It seems to me that Mormons would blithely ignore that.

I suppose the roots of *The Backslider* lie a long way back. In my adulthood, but my young adulthood, I became aware of blood atonement in the Mormon background. Nothing I knew about as a child at all. I was shocked by those sermons that you read of Brigham Young and Jedediah Grant in the early publications. And the history of blood atonement which was almost always more a theory and a possibility than an actuality. It was as if everybody—particularly those leaders—was toying with the idea. Then maybe the Mountain Meadows Massacre drove Brigham Young back from it, if nothing else brought him to reality about what could be happening. But it resonated with something in my childhood—a sense—and I will pin it on my mother without the slightest bit of personal blame. But something I grew up wondering about is that my mother extolled the mercy of God, and yet I could see in her a profound doubt that she was saved. I saw in my mother fear of damnation. I saw in my mother a guilt that hadn't been purged. And she's a terribly good person. I mean, anything you want to name by way of a Mormon virtue, my mother had it. And it just weighed on me quite early. Why is Mother afraid of God when she's, as far as I can tell, doing everything God demands? But into her old age, my mother could be brought around to doubting her salvation—if you asked her the right questions. You know, if you said to her, "Is God merciful and forgiving?" "Oh, you bet." She'd go off into a good positive line. But if you asked her about her own sins and led in that direction, pretty soon you could get her pondering whether she really is going to be saved, if she's going to be in the highest heaven.

Is there an underlying self-esteem question about her own life, do you think?

There could be. She had self-doubts and all that, though she was an awfully sturdy woman. When my father died when I was nine, she took over as the bread winner and continued raising her four sons. Just a fine, stalwart human being. But it seemed to me that the sense of unpurged guilt and the doctrine of blood atonement that says that human beings are beyond the pale of Christ's forgiveness ... there are sins that it doesn't have any effect on; you've got to pay for them by letting your own blood. That resonated with something in my childhood and focused on my mother. But not my mother alone. I mean, there's plenty of others for the evidence. I wrote *The Backslider* very consciously as against that kind of guilt. And if most Mormons don't have it, then that's wonderful. You know, if they don't need it, the book won't mean anything to them. But basically all the book adds up to is quit harassing yourself over trifles, and if you've got a doctrine of a deity's own sacrifice to save you, well, rely on it.

Do you think we have no mechanism for purging ourselves of this guilt? Catholics seem to be able to use confession effectively for that. Nonbelievers go to psychiatrists and psychologists. What about going to the bishop and ...

Some do. We have evolved a confession system I think in my lifetime. When I was a boy and a very young man, it wasn't thoroughly in place. I think a lot of young people now get into it. My daughter would tell me of her friends. You know, you trot in to your bishop over maybe things that don't need to be confessed, but ... I think it's a very common experience for Mormons, very active, good Mormons, to feel themselves different from all those others they're sitting in church with. Even though they don't know it, the others feel the same way; they feel different. Somehow they're not measuring up. I do think there's a perfectionist ethos among Mormons that's beyond human nature, and you're bound to feel guilty just because it's beyond human nature.

What happens to Levi Peterson when he dies?

Well, I have my doubts, but in my essay "A Christian by Yearning," I say why not buy into it? The hope. You see, you don't lose anything by it. I suppose intellectually I'm a natural animal. To me, resurrection would be a stunning miracle. It seems to me that most of my fellow Mormons accept it as such an everyday fact that it's hardly meaningful to them. And, of course, that's what that essay was about. That was an interesting essay to write. I'd been asked to deliver it at Sunstone's "Pillars of My Faith" session in the late 1980s sometime.

I'm very close friends with a number of believing Mormons. In fact, I'm in a writing group—have been from the early 1980s. The group first consisted of Bruce and Donna Jorgensen, and Dennis and Valerie Clark, and Linda and John Sillito(e). Bruce and Linda and Dennis and I would produce a piece of writing in turn each month. One of us had the turn, and then the others would come to the house for dinner and then discuss the piece of writing. In time, Linda evolved out of the church and out of the group—became uncomfortable with the group. John Bennion and Karla Bennion joined, and then Gene and Charlotte England joined. So now there's ten of us—five couples—and we meet once a month and the writer in each of us has a critique every five months. Each of us must have something produced. Usually it's the five writers, but once in a while one of the spouses will do something. The Sillito(e)s excepted—all the others are like Lavina. They're inside people and they really believe. They're not like me. They're not in there only on their emotional connection; they're in there on an intellectual connection. You know, they're liberal Mormons, they really believe. And how am I going to write something that doesn't get me in trouble with my good friends whom I'm so close to? How am I going to do something with this "Pillars of My Faith" assignment? And it worked out. The audience really liked it. There was long, loud applause, and I've had lots of compliments on it. But best of all, my close friends, they bought it, and it didn't drill me out of their fellowship.

Another fact that I probably ought to mention is that the acceptance of my Mormon fiction by Mormons has had a big impact on me. I didn't start writing Mormon materials thinking that it would somehow help certain Mormons remain Mormon, but that's what happened. Fairly early, I realized people were coming up to me and saying to me, "What you've written makes it easier for me to be a Mormon." That was rather astonishing to me. I guess it hasn't been too hard to become a Christian by yearning or a Mormon by yearning, see. What I would desire to be substitutes for what I intellectually believe.

5.

Business Woman

In every cry of every man,
In every infant's cry of fear,
In every voice, in every ban,
The mind-forged manacles I hear.

—William Blake

The interviewee is attractive and smartly dressed in a suit and scarf. She is well-known and highly accomplished in her profession. Arranging for this interview has taken time; she was reluctant and insisted upon complete anonymity. She lives and works in Salt Lake City.

~

Where were you born?

I thought we weren't going to ask that.

Okay.

However, I've lived here most of my life.

Most of your life in Utah. And your parents, were they active?

Yes. A hundred percent.

Both of them?

Yes.

You were one of how many siblings?

Three.

The oldest or youngest?

Oldest.

You attended local schools?

Yes.

Were you a regular attendee at church services from earliest memory?

Yes.

And your parents, were they married in the temple?

Yes.

What about their parents? Were they also active and pioneer stock?

Yes.

You were baptized at eight like most of us were. And you lived basically a life of an orthodox, young Mormon child?

Totally. Absolutely. Yes.

I regard any church, but especially this one, as sort of like a train rolling on its way to Paradise. And there's all these people on this train, and you're on this train, and everything's fine, and let's just stay on the train and we'll go straight to heaven. The only trouble comes is when you fall off the train.

So at some point, something happened to your train.

No, the train is still going on as usual, but I fell off.

And why did you fall off?

The thing that happened to me was divorce. So there I was off the train. You're not going to heaven.

Why did this divorce cause you to fall off the train?

Because it's all set up. You don't have to worry about what you're supposed to do in life. You know.

If you're active?

Well, yes, you're just on the train. You know what that means, you know the rules. But if something goes amiss, such as this—you get divorced—then you have to rethink everything.

Why is that?

Well, you have kind of messed up. You know what you're supposed to be doing, and getting a divorce is not part of the plan.

But is anyone that perfect that they can't deviate from the plan a little bit?

You know what we're talking about. How can you get a divorce and stay on the train? You can't. Now what do you do?

What does the church say about divorce?

The official statement? The whole point of being on the train is that you don't have to worry, that you're somehow protected from bad things happening in your life if you're good. You stay on the train, you do what you're supposed to. Divorce is not supposed to happen. If it does, you'd better look to see if something's wrong with you; you made a misstep.

Have you been treated as a third-class passenger since you got divorced?

Of course.

How? Can you give me some examples?

Suddenly you're no longer invited to dinners with all the couples.

Did the bishop outwardly change in any way toward you?

Well, I moved.

You moved.

Yes, it was entirely different socially, economically, every possible way. Suddenly I was socially sort of an outcast.

This occurred in the past ten years?

Yes. So you look at what your choices are. What if you can't get married again? What if you can't replicate that? What if you can't find somebody who also has a ticket on the train?

In other words, temple-worthy.

Yes. Then you have to go in, cancel what you did ...

What do you mean, cancel what you did?

... and do something else. Well, what you did was supposed to be irrevocable.

Oh. So you've got to get a temple divorce?

Yes. And the new person you've got has to cancel whatever he was in. Then you put together this kind of melded family, and theoretically you can now be on the train again.

In your mind, even if you could do all that, would you feel like you were worthy of a first-class ticket?

Worthy—leave that up to God's judgment. But see, what happened is you fell off; you didn't go the distance.

The difficulty for you in all of this is while you may not be active right now, you have a deep faith, it sounds like.

I feel that human beings are evolving, that we're not like we used to be, that we have actually learned from our heritage and we've grown and we've expanded. And we're now in a period of accelerated evolution, so that we're learning and growing and expanding very much faster than we ever have before in the whole history of mankind. We're not Stone Age people.

In some respects organized religion is like training wheels on a bicycle. That's all humanity can handle at first. And the basic structure that I got from the church, living a good life, not stealing, not cheating, being kind, being good, being compassionate—being very Christ-like—that's deeply embedded. Somehow you have to get basic teaching, or you grow up adrift. Once it's there you can ride your own bicycle. But the church always wants to make sure that you need that organized structure called the church. So it's always set up that you need them to get to your destination. You need somebody and you need something that they have to offer that you can't get on your own. When you begin having a direct spiritual experience with no intermediaries, you might start thinking, "Hey, heaven is for everybody, not just the people on this particular train." It's whatever exists for all—how many—six billion of us?

Do you consider yourself a spiritual person today?

Oh, yes. Yes, I'm a really spiritual person and I always have been.

Do you pray to the same God you did when you were active?

Well, it's the same God. God hasn't changed. We just don't have a very good understanding of what God is; we just don't know. Our human minds have not really come up with a good way to comprehend it. That's so enormous.

Do you think during your divorce you were treated any differently than your husband was treated by church officials—your bishop, whomever?

I don't know because we split up. I do think it is easier for men.

This is that nun's existence you talked about.

I don't have any statistics for this, but the feeling I get from women is that they just can't find good people to marry and get on the train with. This is putting us in a difficult situation. If there just aren't enough partners to go around, what do you do?

Is there any possibility the church would ever change or modify?

How could it? How can they modify the man, woman, children, nuclear family thing? It's this great chain going back to eternity—hands holding hands all the way back through time.

Maybe they could recognize that the nuclear family is not what it has traditionally been. In the real world, we are not forever and always a nuclear family.

But that is exactly the opposite of what the church teaches. The whole point of doing all this is so that you will stay together as a family forever.

That's right, that's the ideal.

Not the *ideal*—that's *it*. That's the whole ...

But look how exclusionary that is when the reality is that the ideal doesn't exist for a large number of people who have been baptized.

See, I don't even want to believe that. I would like to believe that all these wonderful families are going to go on forever happily through eternity, and that just a few people have fallen off the train, like me.

If divorce isn't supposed to happen, how did it happen to you?

I can't tell you. For purposes of anonymity, I can't.

Okay. During this divorce did you seek counseling from your bishop and church officials?

Yes. But they had no answers.

BUSINESS WOMAN

It's not supposed to happen.

What could they say? Here were two really nice, terrific, wonderful people—what could they say? They just didn't have any answers.

Did you go for any other kind of help, therapy?

Yes.

Did they have better answers? Did it hold some promise; was it helpful?

No. There were no solutions.

Did it enable you to better cope with what had happened?

I didn't cope at all well. It was the greatest disappointment of my life that my marriage didn't work out. Because that's the one thing I wanted most growing up. I was going to be the one to do everything right. I was going to make no mistakes. I was going to marry absolutely the right person. I'd absolutely followed the rules perfectly. So I was really upset when it didn't work.

At that point, did you become inactive? Did you stop going to church or do you still attend regularly?

I kept going for a while.

So you continue to try to get onto the train?

No, I've accepted that I won't get on it. It's going on without me.

What's going to happen to those of you who aren't on the train when you die? Where will you go?

The train is going to Sandy [a Salt Lake City suburb]. When you think about it—here's the father and a mother and the kids together forever. So they have to have a house to be in and a yard and a dog, and that's Sandy. Right? So that's where they're going. Now the trouble is everybody's going to be twenty-five years old for the next billion years.

Now obviously, the view of heaven as a giant Sandy with all your animals, kids, grandparents, everybody all together doesn't work. If we're all twenty-five years old, all looking good, all healthy, all equally powerful, all the same age, then you have nothing but peers. You don't have parents and children anymore. This takes some figuring out.

But what happens ... Will you go the celestial kingdom having been divorced?

You will if you do two things: Get married again to somebody who can get on the train, or don't get a temple divorce from your first spouse. You can get divorced just as long as you don't break that bond. And still follow all the rules.

So then you wind up in Sandy with your first husband, even if you marry again?

Right.

Oh, wretched reunion.

But you'll be perfect; you won't care.

You won't care?

You'll be able to love anyone. Right?

How does this make you feel?

Obviously, I don't think it's going to be like that ultimately. But wouldn't it be wonderful if we might be able to get whatever heaven we believe in? And the belief, the faith, will create it? And that's a possibility. I can imagine that a lot of people in different parts of the world—if they ended up in Sandy they would be miserable. They don't want to be there. They wouldn't love it.

Some people don't want the heaven that the church has outlined. They wouldn't be happy in it. A lot of people have been monks all their lives; they never married. They don't particularly want a wife and children to go through eternity with. I do believe in God. I just think the most amazing thing is that we even exist.

I agree.

And why is there *something* instead of *nothing*? I mean, all reason says that there would be nothing here—that you and I wouldn't be sitting here talking today. Reason and logic say there can't be anything—especially not people. Especially not thinking, evolving people. There can't be ... [She pauses.]

The idea of sentience?

Consciousness.

Yes, it's pretty amazing, isn't it?

We can't exist, but we do. I think the very fact we're here talking about this, thinking about this—and even have the consciousness to think about it says, yes, there was a creator, there was a plan.

Would you like to add anything?

I think we've lost sight in America of what makes people happy. And what makes people happy is loving each other and being with each other. People are all that make life worth living—not a job, not a career, but each other. That's what we care about. When we think about the end of the world, when we think about a war, bombs dropping—Where's Marge? Where is Ezra? That's what we care about. That's what our hearts care about. The rest of this is peripheral, extraneous. So it's our human relationships that matter. Having a community of people who are trying to do good and trying to live good lives ... Our American society is falling apart without that.

I think the reason for our existence is to love and be loved.

And it's absolutely true. Such a basic truth, and the minute you learn that, then the train feels a bit narrow. It's too small. Because if you really know that, you don't have to love only people that are just like you. You can expand that. And this is what I mean about accelerating evolution. You can expand that love to encompass the whole world. I think I'll stop there.

6.

Stewart L. Udall

Rule will show the man.

—*The Seven Sages*

Shortly after being elected to his fourth term as an Arizona congressman, Stewart L. Udall was appointed by President John F. Kennedy as the nation's 37th Secretary of the Interior—a position he held for eight years under both presidents Kennedy and Lyndon B. Johnson. It was under Stewart that the seeds for the ecological revolution in America began to flower. It was Stewart who arranged for Robert Frost to read poetry at the inauguration of President Kennedy. It was Stewart who, as Secretary of the Interior, brought live theater back to Ford's Theater in Washington, D.C., after more than a century.

Stewart has authored a number of books, including the best-selling The Quiet Crisis *(1963), in which he advanced the "proposition that men must grasp completely the relationship between human stewardship and the fullness of the American earth." An updated version,* The Quiet Crisis and the Next Generation, *was published in 1988. His other books include* 1976: Agenda for Tomorrow *and* Myths of August: A Personal Exploration of Our Tragic Cold War Affair with the Atom. *He co-authored* The Energy Balloon. *A 1987 work,* To the Inland Empire: Coronado and Our Spanish Legacy, *celebrated Hispanic contributions to American history (reissued by the Museum of New*

Mexico Press as Majestic Journey). *King Juan Carlos of Spain conferred knighthood on Stewart to show his country's appreciation for the book.*

At the time of this interview, Stewart was living in Santa Fe, New Mexico, not far from St. Johns, Arizona, where he was born. In Santa Fe, he does legal work helping uranium miners and widows to qualify under the federal Radiation Exposure Compensation Act. He is also at work on his latest book, Western Settlers/Western Myths: Reflections on the Warping of Western History.

When I spoke with Stewart by telephone, snow had fallen in Salt Lake City. "We just got your storm," he said, after picking up the receiver. We'd corresponded before talking; he'd sent me a file of yellowed newspaper clippings and articles on him and his family. It contained everything from stories about his high school basketball successes to clippings from the Congressional Record. *The file also contained a letter written by LDS church President Heber J. Grant. It was dated June 24, 1929, and in it Grant explained why he strongly opposed naming a new bridge over the Colorado River at Marble Canyon the "Lee's Ferry Bridge."*

> *The descendants of John D. Lee can't be any more anxious than I am to have no reference made to the Mountain Meadows massacre. I can assure you that no one of the General Authorities has any desire to do anything or say anything to wound the feelings of the descendants of John D. Lee. We know that some of our choicest and best citizens are members of the Church as his descendants. I believe that you do our people a great injustice when you say that "Church members seem to take great pleasure in bringing it up and telling about it in gossip."*
>
> *I remember distinctly the interview with your father and others to which you refer in your letter, and I have never changed my position from that day to this. I am in favor of allowing the entire matter to die, and in no way could it be resurrected any better in my judgment, my dear sister, than to have the bridge over the great gorge at Marble Canyon named Lees Ferry Bridge ...*

I honestly believe that in the years to come all the descendants of John D. Lee will thank me for the part which I took in seeking to have the bridge not named Lees Ferry Bridge.

In our interview Stewart speaks about his mother and about the massacre, and his part in bringing about what he hopes will be a symbolic healing of the pain inflicted on his family by an historic event. We arranged a date and an hour when I could reach him at his home. He measures each word carefully.

~

What year were you born?

In 1920, so I'm getting in the "old timer" category. I was born in St. Johns, Arizona, a Mormon settlement. My grandfather was one of the founders, and the first bishop, and the first stake president. And my father was born there; so that gives you some roots.

You have some illustrious names in your Mormon background, names that would be familiar to all Mormons, I think.

Well, the names that are most famous, or infamous [he laughs] in one case, John D. Lee of the Mountain Meadows Massacre. Another is Jacob Hamblin. Another of my great-grandparents was Levi Stewart; he was a prominent merchant in Salt Lake, close to Brigham Young, and was sent down to be the first bishop of Kanab, Utah. Almost all of my great-grandparents were sent south by Brigham Young. Juanita Brooks once wrote something where she said that "it was a kind of a Siberia." You know, we were sending them off to the far end and they would never have a chance to enjoy the cultural advantages in Salt Lake City. So they were all dutiful and accepted it. But all of them—all of mine were sent south.

It sounds like your ancestors were very active in the Mormon church.

That's correct. To add, my other great-grandparent, a Udall, was a little Englishman who came across in 1851 and went down to Nephi and lived there all of his life. That's south of Salt Lake, but it isn't that far south. My grandfather, whom I knew as a boy knows a grandfather, was the first the bishop of St. Johns, and then when that was made a stake in 1887 he became the stake president. You know, in those days there were probably only thirty-five or forty who held that rank. He served until 1922, when he was succeeded by my father who was stake president until he was elected to the Supreme Court of Arizona in 1946. So they had that long stretch, and I grew up in a religious family, a strong family. My mother was a granddaughter of John D. Lee, but that's another story.

Were you active as most children of active Mormon parents were?

I was the oldest son and my father was the religious leader and I was very dutiful as a young man. I participated in church activities and then I went on a mission. I was the only one in the family who went on a mission, by the way.

Where did you go?

To the eastern states.

So you were active up at least through your twenties. Did you enjoy church activities? Or was it more out of a sense of duty?

No, it was not all dutiful. There was conveyed by my parents a strong allegiance to the church. I was interested in the beginning in church history; I absorbed a lot of that. That still is a fascination of mine today and that's my current book ... a part of it grows out of that. I participated in the church activities for young people, and I look back on my missionary experience as fruitful experience. I got a lot out of it, and I came away with warm feelings toward the church. I got all of my education at state schools. I was at the University of Arizona before the war, and then I went on my mission in 1940 to 1942; the war started in the latter part. I came back and went into the service for three years, and then I went to the University of Arizona law school.

You were in the service during World War II?

I was in the army air force. I flew on bombers out of Italy; I was an enlisted man, a gunner. I was in B-24's, long-distance bombers.

Did you fly to that godawful Ploesti?

Several times.

That must have been a terrifying experience. Did the war strengthen your faith?

I don't think it changed it much. Because of my missionary experiences, and a young Pennsylvania-Dutch minister whom I met while I was on my mission, I was moving in the direction of being a pacifist and a conscientious objector. I was toying with this while I was on my mission. I didn't say much to anybody about it. But then, of course, with Pearl Harbor that was the kind of event that sharpens decisions and makes you decide what you really believe. While I was in the service, I did a lot of reading and spent a lot of my time—you know, army time is 90 percent wasted waiting—and I spent most of my time in libraries. I'd done some of that on my mission; I began being a very wide reader in terms of religion and literature and history and so on.

Shortly after the war, you married. Were you still active at that point in your life?

My wife is LDS from the same kind of background—old, cohesive families. It turns out we had pretty much the same experience and attitudes with the church. We ended up having six children; four of them in the mid-1950s when I was in Washington as a congressman. But neither of us was ever devoted church-goers; we maintained our ties but didn't participate very much.

So by the time you were back from the war, you weren't a regular attendee at church. Is that fair to say?

Yes and no. Two of the influences in my life were at the church institute at the University of Arizona. Before the war, one was Lowell Bennion. A lovely man. I participated a great deal at the institute. I didn't at home. But, of course, an institute environment is different. After the war, it was Sterling McMurrin, and we became dear friends for life. Both of them had an influence on my thinking, I think Sterling more than Lowell. But after the war, I participated in the institute activities. Of course, after I left school, I didn't.

What did your parents feel about your inactivity? Was there any pressure from them; did they say anything?

Oh, sure. My father, being a judge, was very fair-minded, very judicial. He was also a church leader. He made it clear to us he was pained at why we weren't being more active; and one of the reasons we maintained ties and did church things was what we used to call "parent pleasing." But there was more than that, I guess, in my case. My mother—I guess because she had the Mountain Meadow massacre hanging over her—was more liberal and tolerant. But the church was very important to them, and it was important to have as many children as possible and to maintain their ties and be active, which most of my sisters were, but not the brothers.

Your brother Morris, a former U.S. representative, wasn't active, but your three sisters were.

[He laughs.] Morris, my brother Mo, at the age of twelve or thirteen was thrown out of Sunday school class. He was always a free spirit.

Why was that?

For making fun of his teacher and his sense of humor. Among our three boys, I was the one who was most active, so I guess I got more credit for that reason.

As you raised your own children, did you make any attempt to give them a religious upbringing? Did you take, or send, them to church?

The older boys in McLean, Virginia, where we lived, fell in with Mormon kids, and they went to Sunday school for a while, but we didn't press it hard, and that sort of petered out after a while. So our children haven't had strong ties with the church, but they haven't drifted over to other churches.

They're still Mormons?

Yes. Four of them were baptized.

Among the papers you sent me, I found an interesting one written in the 1960s, "An Appeal for Full Fellowship for the Negro," by Stewart Udall. You were a Democrat, a liberal, and Secretary of the Interior. Obviously you were high on President Kennedy's list. Were there at this time political differences you began to feel with the church and was this part of why you became inactive?

That was part of it, very definitely. During all of my reading during the war, I developed what is now called pejoratively a "liberal conviction." I was politically drawn to Franklin Roosevelt. I also became politically active early. And I developed strong convictions about civil rights early. I joined the NAACP while I was in the army, which will show you something. When I was a young lawyer, there was a statewide organization formed—I was one its organizers—to repeal the Arizona segregation laws. So I took part in that. And as a congressman and a member of the cabinet, I had liberal views on most everything, but particularly on civil rights. I just felt blacks and other minorities were human beings like the rest of us and should be treated accordingly.

I was increasingly dismayed by the rigidity of the church's position, and I used to talk/correspond with Sterling McMurrin that this wasn't justified on the basis of church doctrine. It was very harmful when Brigham Young University became a focus of demonstrations during the 1960s—their athletic teams and so on. I thought this put the church in an awful light that was sort of like South Africa. It implied that we favored apartheid in our own way. The first year that I was in the cabinet, I was seen by the First Presidency and had a pleasant visit with President David O. McKay and others. But I held my peace until finally in 1967 I just said to myself, "Well, I occupy a national office. They'll have to listen." And I wrote that piece which I am very proud of to this day. I think Sterling McMurrin or somebody helped me get it published. The national press was increasingly picturing the church in a very bad light, and I thought that maybe I could have some influence. Maybe I did; but I got very stern rebuking letters from Spencer Kimball who was an apostle and from Apostle Delbert Stapley, the two Arizona apostles. They were upbraiding me. Those letters are in my papers at the University of Arizona. I got a lot of hate mail from Mormon people and it was painful; but I didn't reply to the letters. I said, "Well, I made a statement, a statement of conscience," and there it sits. Then, of course, when he became president a few years later, President Kimball, whom I consider the most inspired Mormon president of this century, did the right thing, and I've been enormously pleased by it.

What has happened to your belief in Mormon theology? Do you still have a testimony? Did you have one in your early years?

I did have when I was a missionary. As I read more and more widely, I became a kind of free thinker, and that encouraged the side of me which is to be free and non-conforming. And as a result of that—it was a slow drift—I began having more and more reservations about doctrine. It was painful for me, too—partly because of my parents but partly because of my attachment to Mormon history and Mormon culture. I wanted to maintain my ties. I say proudly today that "I'm a Mormon" and always have been and I'm proud of that heritage.

You've never considered asking to have your name be removed from the rolls?

No. I'm Mormon born and bred, and it's inside me, and I still have elements of faith in some things. I prize my Mormon heritage and status. I've never had any desire to sever any ties; in fact, some of them have grown stronger these last years.

Do you believe the story of Joseph Smith and the gold plates?

I have a strong mind; I have a very rational mind; and I'm a free thinker, as I've said. I don't go out of my way to wrestle with that—the kind of thing that to me is not the heart of Mormonism.

You were quite instrumental in organizing a reunion between the Lees and the Fanchers, both names associated with the Mountain Meadows Massacre. Tell me a little about that.

I want to preface this by saying that my mother, who was a very strong person and very important in my life—as important as my father—was a granddaughter of John D. Lee. Back then when she was a young woman, back at the turn of the century, this was a burden for those people to bear and the church kind of laid it on them. The Sunday school lessons taught it was the work of one evil man.

John D. Lee.

Yes. That didn't affect Mother's faith or her feeling about the church as a whole; it affected her thinking that the church leaders doing this (allowing Lee to be a scapegoat) were wrong- headed. This hung over her life and she talked to me about it later. Juanita Brooks who wrote the book [*The Mountain Meadows Massacre*] was a heroine to her, and as a result of this I got acquainted with Juanita, and corresponded with her. That got me emotionally involved in a way that my cousin, the late Rex Lee [former U.S. solicitor and BYU president], for example, wasn't, because his father died before he was born. My views were known and two wonderful people, Vern Lee, who lives in California—he's a good Mormon—and a Fancher descendant began talking in about 1988 about whether it was possible to bring the families together and, in effect, bury the dead and bury the issue. They brought me into it, and I was glad they did, and I went out of my way to help. I made trips to Salt Lake and did other things, too, to see if this could be done. President Gordon B. Hinckley received us. I don't know what he knew about me or how he viewed me at that point, but he was very gracious and we talked about it. I remember telling him, "The families can close the book. The church cannot. The families can do it, but we want you there."

If I were president of the Mormon church, what would you tell me now?

I wouldn't venture to be so presumptuous as to start telling people what to do. I think the great traditions of the Mormons, of our people, are to me one of the great American stories. And I'd say, "You're doing a pretty good job." You know what they've done at Nauvoo and other places. Preserve that story and be true to it. Release some of the old records; the church sometimes is as secretive as the CIA, you know. There hasn't really been what historians would regard as a first-rate biography of Brigham Young, for example; and he was one of the great men of this country, no question about it. I don't know why they don't let bona fide historians get the records and tell the true story. All of us are human, nobody's perfect, including leaders of the church. We have our personal flaws, and I think the church certainly has a higher status today than it did twenty, thirty years ago. I'd also say, be more ecumenical. You've elicited out of me why I've become very ecumenical. One of my dearest friends here in Santa Fe—he just died a year ago—was a Franciscan priest, an historian, and an artist. We became great friends when I was working on a book on Spanish history. I've become an expert on the Spanish part of our history which also laps over with the Mormon. I think religion is terribly important.

Are you a spiritual man?

I don't know that I'd characterize myself as spiritual, but I think that I have a feeling for humanity in that sense. I keep asking myself, "Where would the world be, where would this country be, if the churches weren't there?" In terms of maintaining ethics and values and order and so on. I tell some of my friends who don't hold that view that they ought to think about it; that they're wrong. So I value much of what the church does today. I think it makes a good contribution to humanity and to the lives of people.

Can you see a situation where you'd return to active status?

I'll just say I haven't closed that door, but I'm seventy-seven.

What happens when you die? Do you still feel there's a celestial kingdom awaiting you?

I've had a long, rich life, and I have my own intellectual doubts and reservations, but I don't let that completely dominate my thinking. I'm more open to things than I might've been earlier. You know, I've never been in the category of what people would call an atheist, an agnostic at times, I'd say, but I don't know that those labels cover me.

Do you ever feel any conflicts over your beliefs?

I'm at peace with myself. And I'm at peace with the church in the frame of reference I'm telling you about. I have strong feelings when my relatives and friends die; I give funeral speeches in the Mormon church. And they're more tributes, of course, than sermons. I'm fortunate, I guess, in that I don't feel strange. But I want to maintain my relationships and esteem that I have for the church. I was fascinated, not surprised, that President Hinckley would receive me, not as a Mormon in good standing, but as someone whom he respected. I like that.

I hear people talking about "good Mormons." What makes one a "good" Mormon, and is that term offensive to you?

No, I guess it isn't. It could, but I sort of floated above it. I guess that's one of the reasons I strayed: the orthodoxy, "here's the catechism, here's what you must believe, now repeat it back to me." This is something that I just intellectually can't adjust to, and, therefore, I know what you're talking about, if somebody said, "Well, Udall's fallen away; Udall's not a good Mormon." That doesn't bother me. I simply say, "Well, I'm my own unique kind of Mormon and I'll stay that way. So don't you pass judgement on me, and I won't on you."

How do you think you're viewed by active Mormons?

I haven't had unpleasant contacts. We don't receive ward teachers and so on. I have a cousin who's a bishop, and I'd say there are people there and I counsel with them and they're good, prominent Mormons, and so on. So don't press me, please. Rex Lee and I were looking through some correspondence we had. He was much younger than I, but we had a very fine, warm relationship the last twenty years. I'm proud I had a hand in starting his career. He was one of the first law clerks for [Supreme Court] Justice Byron White; he was one of my friends.

I'm not boasting of this in a family way, but it's one of the things that says to me what inner strength the church provides for people—"inner strength," not just in a spiritual sense. I grew up in this little town; there were probably 600 or 800 Mormons. This one little place produced—and neither one of them had a chance to go to law school—two justices of the Arizona Supreme Court: my father and my uncle. It has produced a lot of judges and lawyers—Rex Lee who was the solicitor general, president of the Brigham Young [University]; Shumway, the president of Brigham Young in Hawaii, is from St. Johns. My brother, a candidate for president ...

And yourself, a congressman and Secretary of the Interior ...

All out of one little town.

Maybe it's the water, Stewart.

I think the church had a lot to do with it.

7.

Scott Burton

There is no substitute for talent.

—Aldous Huxley

Owner of an avant-garde furnishings store in downtown Salt Lake City, Scott Burton lives in a spacious and inventive apartment that is part of his store. It's a dramatic and delightfully off-key setting where we settle to conduct the interview. Three zany dogs, all large, suddenly enter like a circus-come-to-town, roaming among chairs upholstered in unmatching but harmonious fabrics, prancing across handsome oriental rugs, sliding against raw birch wall coverings. Scott patiently calms them.

Framed pictures are in abundance, including a large 1890s organizational chart with photographs of the "Zion Leaders of the Dispensation, Past and Present." Rolls of leopard-spotted fabric stand next to a dozen lamp pedestals; panels of bright fabric hang as drapes over his windows. A kitchen island overflows with votives, and rolls of paper, vases, and even an animated Santa bank sit atop tables. An amateur painting presents a good likeness of Wallis Warfield Simpson, the late Duchess of Windsor. Scott has owned and operated a number of retail stores in Salt Lake City, where he was born in 1958.

~

You were born here in Salt Lake?

I was.

Did you come from an active Mormon background?

I came from a very active Mormon background; my parents were quietly devout. I like to think they didn't scream and shout religion, but they were very active themselves. They did temple work and they did church work and participated on a lot of different levels, but allowed their children to choose how they would approach it.

You say they were "quietly active." Did they attend church regularly?

Very regularly.

They paid tithing?

Oh, they paid big tithing. You know, they've always had temple recommends ... worked in the temple. That was a part of all of that I grew up with, and it was a very normal part.

You went to church every Sunday with them?

I went to church probably through my early teens, and then began to lose interest, partly in the structure and partly in the content. It just didn't *take* for me. I remember several times trying to do the things you were supposed to do to get a testimony or the spirit of it. I went through the motions of it, or at least as I understood them, and it just never quite jelled for me as a concept. For me, it was a very narrow structure. The lack of diversity was very difficult for me.

When you say "lack of diversity," what do you mean?

I don't have a strong background in a lot of the historical rhetoric or doctrine of Mormonism. But early on I feared the whole thing about being like everyone else. Is it the very best you can be to be like your neighbor? That's what everyone wanted. I was really disturbed by that.

You used the word "fear." Are you saying you feared it?

At that age I knew I was gay and I knew that being gay was a bad thing. I wasn't willing to accept a doctrinal belief or group of people who arbitrarily chose to make me a bad person because of something I truly knew I had no control over. I think it's an absurd perception that somebody picks their sexual preference or that it's changeable. I knew that early on. So that was a big problem for me. Then you can extrapolate from that a lot of other issues of lack of diversity.

You knew being gay was a psychological and physiological part of you.

I'd guess that's by far the most typical response you'd get from someone who's fairly comfortable in that part of their life.

What did you hear in church about this?

Growing up in the neighborhood I grew up in, there wasn't a big difference; I mean, you knew clearly everyone was Mormon. I can't remember too many people who weren't. So the crossover between the prevailing social climate and Mormonism got very skewed, at least in my time, and I think certainly that's different in this city now to some degree. But within the social class and structure of the neighborhood I grew up in, if you weren't Mormon, you weren't good. So there was a real clear line that you were either an insider or an outsider, and as I've met people who've grown up here outside of that, it's been fascinating to know the other side of it and how strongly they felt ostracized for being Catholic or having some other faith. I found that disturbing. I felt that I saw early on the hypocrisy of the difference between what people said was right and what they did, and that was disturbing. But clearly to this day, I think at some point the hierarchy of the church will have to figure out how to de-demonize homosexuality because in my view it will come to a point where there's clearly some genetic link. Therefore you can't make a moral judgment against it. I think they're going to have to figure how to backtrack out of that, and I'm not sure how you do that in terms of getting a vision from God or whatever their process is. I think they're in the process of softening the hard stance, but at that point it was clear that: (a) I had made a choice, and (b) it was a bad choice. Being gay was the second worst thing to murdering somebody, or so it goes within the church. I chose early on not to listen to a lot of that because I was tremendously disturbed by it. I truly felt that I tuned it out.

You must've had real guilt and conflict ...

I have to say I have suffered from a lot of guilt or conflicted feelings. I went through electroshock therapy from, I think, age thirteen to fifteen which was at that point a very vogue treatment specifically within the Mormon church to "cure" homosexuality.

This was an attempt to make you heterosexual?

It was. The way it came about is that my parents through a series of events found out about my orientation. They must have sought some advice because one day I came home from school and my dad was sitting on the porch and I could tell he was upset. He said, "Is this something you want to change? Do you want to work on it?" I thought they were very smart in finding out what they were going to approach me with. They gave me a choice, so I thought, "Sure. I might as well attempt to change." I wasn't threatened by change at thirteen. So I agreed to do it. I have to say I never believed that they knew exactly what the procedure was. I think they would've been tremendously alarmed had they known [he laughs] what actually went on, and it was never discussed with me present that they knew.

What was the procedure?

At thirteen, with a Mormon psychotherapist, I was shown heterosexual pornography films and homosexual pornography films. It was the first time that I'd ever seen any of that [he laughs], so it was a pretty interesting thing to get thrown into. This psychotherapist was one of the big people treating it. He had a huge practice in it. I knew the first time I met him that he was way out there and had some strong issues floating around of his own, as I came to find out from someone who was ten years older than I was who was being treated as an adult by him at the same time.

Anyway, electrodes are placed on your wrists and then a meter is attached to your penis to gauge the arousal. I'm this thirteen-year-old kid thrown into all this stuff, and it had a rather surreal quality to it. When I call up that memory, it's this strange quality of doing this really absurd thing which from day one I knew was bogus. The whole patterning thing is absurd, and I figured out how to work within the system and simply didn't look at the gay stuff so I wasn't aroused. I tried to arouse myself through the straight stuff. I was playing into what he wanted as the end result. I remember going home at night for dinner. It had never been discussed in my family, never been brought up to the rest of my family, and I would have burn marks on my wrists from this shocker thing. The shocking never worked for me either, because I have a fairly high pain threshold and it was very unmoving. I can't imagine how it would ever get you to change your behavior. One of my clear memories is going home and wondering if my siblings had any understanding or recognition of what was happening—if they'd question me about this burn. There were these two very clear, round burn marks on my wrists. It was the extraneous things like that that are the memory parts of it. I was magically cured when I told him I'd been elected student body president of my junior high school. He deemed me cured because he perceived me as an active member of a social order. It cracked me up and taught me, very early on, that regardless of what we want it to be it's often how you're perceived and how you present yourself which matters in the world. In a lot of ways I feel like what I learned there was quite positive and useful. I made a real conscious effort not to be overwhelmed by it. I could've chosen to really be angry at my parents about it, or I could've chosen to become antisocial. A lot of people are really pulled down by stuff, and I chose to look at it as a thing that happened. I didn't realize until my mid-thirties when I was going to a counselor because of a relationship break-up that there was a whole part of that stuff inside of me still. It didn't take too much work to get it out or at least give it a voice. But it was interesting when I finally decided to try and pull it up and get it out. There was a lot more there in terms of raw nerves or damage or whatever you want to call it. It's interesting from that perspective how an element like that can take you to "another place," if you will.

After your "cure," did you return to church?

By that point I might've gone through the motions of it and I might've attended off and on and probably to some degree for the social aspect of it. But in my heart-of-hearts I knew that it was never going to work for me. The biggest thing is I simply refused to have anything to do with a group that tells me I'm a bad person for something I know in my heart-of-hearts I had nothing to do with it. I guess I continue to have a lot of anger with people who can tell me that they know for sure because it's written somewhere that it's a choice I've made and God will punish me.

Out of my four siblings, only one of them is an active Mormon. I had a discussion with the active one—my brother—and it was absolutely fascinating. He's forty-eight and a very bright guy. He's a judge and hopefully well read, but he still maintains that it was a choice I made. Then I convinced him that it wasn't a choice, and for him it became an obstacle that God had put in my way that was supposed to make me stronger. I said, "So that means I'm supposed to die at eighty-five, never having had any significant relationship or any kind of primary relationship because that's what God wants?" I was trying to convince him that that is an absurd concept. I think I got him past that, but he absolutely refused to believe that there was any genetic sense to it because he said it made it too easy (to be gay). He said to me, "You know I've really never thought about this, but this is what I'm supposed to believe." That says so much to me about the people who are successful with their Mormonism. Many choose not to think it through too much, because there are too many loose ends to it.

Did you ever have a bedrock belief in the Book of Mormon?

It was a social thing to go to seminary in the ninth grade before we went to school, but it was also the social thing within my group to lie about reading the Book of Mormon. [He laughs.] So we all lied, and I've actually never read it. I guess I've read parts of it. The basic concept of someone in the nineteenth century, a fourteen-year-old, finding the real and only true religion in an age when starting your own religion was a big deal? It was quite a fashionable thing to do in the nineteenth century.

I guess the absoluteness of it is what I find objectionable. I think any belief in a system in which God creates a better world—why we're here and where we're going—is great. But I can't imagine how centuries of people who've lived and died and believed in a diversity of faith have all been wrong, and a 150 years of Anglos living in Salt Lake City, Utah, are right. It's certainly spread beyond that, but the concept of the rightness and wrongness of it is very troubling to me. Many people are drawn to that—that they are the "right" ones, and everybody else gets to be wrong.

Have you ever thought of asking to have your name removed from the records of the church?

I've thought about that and I'd probably do it if it was easy. I guess I do have some issues being counted among "the numbers," although I certainly haven't been tracked like a lot of my contemporaries have been. Somewhere along the line I was dropped, and I don't know if that was something my parents had something to do with and said, "It's not going to happen there." A lot of my friends who've been very removed from the church for even twenty years still get people trying to pull them into it. I find the church a curious organization, but I'm not drawn to antagonize it. I guess I don't particularly want to give anybody the thrill of excommunicating me. I don't have any need for that finality, because I think I relate so much to my personal heritage, my familial background which is very tied to Mormonism. That's very comforting, and I like that part of my history. I've been able to separate that, enjoy it, and remove it from my own personal sense of what should be. I really have a tremendous amount of respect for my parents' sense of faith. But my parents also gave me the ability to find my own place in that, which has a lot of power to me. I've seen so many parents who don't do that. I feel extremely lucky to come out of a basic conservative Mormon background without a lot of the baggage—guilt being part of that baggage that a lot of my friends have.

Would having your name removed cause your mother a lot of pain? I know your father's dead.

I don't think it would. My mother is aware that I have a sister who converted to Catholicism as an adult, and she's very aware that out of her five children only one of them is active. My second brother had a situation with his young children—four and six and an infant at the time. They were being sexually abused by Mormon neighbors, and the reason the Mormon element is important in it was because the acts were very much contained or structured within that environment. The way these people worked was through the church "format." It's a very complex story. It's a group where men are given all the power. Traditionally nobody else has a voice, so it's a perfect setting for it to happen. Certainly for political reasons they don't want it to become public that we have this problem. But it was interesting to see them go from absolute belief to "this can be a very destructive element in somebody's life." They actually do some work in trying to bring about change by being on panels, working within the community. They're not just sitting there saying it's a bad thing. I think some day the church will have to address that problem, too. But those kinds of things build little layers of stuff where you see this organization whose most basic tenet is to protect itself.

Survival?

It's survival of the church's positions politically and socially, and so often times it gets more and more inwardly directed. I'm fascinated to see where that will land, where that will put them.

What's good about Mormonism?

I think any religious teaching that helps us to do good things in the world or to be better people or live a Christ-like life is good. "Christ-like" can take on a lot of different meanings, but a more charitable, giving life is a very good thing, and I do believe the church does that for a lot of people. That's a mechanism in which they work well at reaching out to others and doing good works. It's very valuable that way. I think it brings a lot of peace to people. One of my favorite memories of my maternal grandmother—one of the last times I saw her in her house—was when she'd just turned ninety, and I went to see her for her birthday. She was sitting on her sofa reading the Bible on a Sunday afternoon. She was very content to move on to the next life; the church really worked well for her. It was like she wanted to turn ninety and then she was ready to go. For her it was such a clear path from where she had come to where she was going. I thought that was a beautiful thing to have such a clear sense of this life and an afterlife. I think that's a very valuable thing for anybody to have. I think there's a sense of peace that it can give people, a sense of structure that a lot of people need and is very powerful. You know, I think anything that tells us to be good, to do good things, is a good thing.

Let's backtrack for just a moment. Why do you think some of us simply seem unable to have the faith that the church is true?

I believe that I have faith in things that I can't touch, feel, see, explain. I don't need everything proven to me. But my whole issue really revolves around it being a much bigger picture. I have a real belief in an afterlife. I think the element of a supreme being is something to do with the collective good energy, not one "divine" soul. I don't think it's a "guy" because honestly I'd be disappointed if it was just this "guy" and women could never be the "guy." Men are not inherently better than women or more "godlike." I'm not happy with those kinds of dynamics of Mormonism where the guy gets to do it, the women don't, so deal with that. I'm fascinated with how it's a religion that was designed by a white man for white men of influence and it's always been that. They have done a good job of protecting their power base. As for the element of faith, I think it depends on how you define "faith." For me, the historical and social aspects of Mormonism were interesting and comforting, but as a doctrine, as a belief system, I just never could buy it. It's fine in the context of other religions, I suppose, but the absoluteness of it is what really has always struck me as being totally off-base.

Do you consider yourself a spiritual person?

I'd like to think I am. The night my father died, I strongly felt that I was experiencing him leaving his ... I could feel a spiritual being who was leaving this physical body and it was very comforting and it was very real. It had a comforting quality. We're made of certain molecules and energy, and then there's a kind of energy that has to somehow go somewhere. I was very close to my dad and he was a great guy. I feel connected to him, and sometimes it has a very strong message-quality to it, as if his "soul" is still present. It's like trying to listen or build on what we learn as we go through life, and we're all going to make mistakes, but hopefully we'll figure out how to do it better the next time.

You mentioned that you almost felt your father's spirit leaving his body as he died. Is this your Mormonism still tagging along?

I can call that memory up pretty clearly (the memory of his death). I'm a pretty bad memory kind of guy, but it was such a strong quality that for me it didn't have a religious overtone and certainly not a "Mormon" one for me. Death is culturally so removed from us. I was driving to my parents' house because my sister called in the middle of the night and said he'd died. I knew I could react really badly. It could be very traumatic. I was really surprised how comforting it was to see him after he died. It had a really strong sense of the process we go through entering and leaving this world.

A spiritual thing?

Yes, it was. It wasn't like Mormonism versus whatever. I'm so removed from the patterning of Mormonism that it doesn't come up in many images of what that is.

When was the last time you were in a Mormon church?

For my father's funeral three-and-a-half years ago. It was interesting because it was in the chapel I went to as a child. I hadn't been in one for a very long time. So it was interesting because it does call up a lot of memories. His funeral was a very strict, traditional Mormon funeral. I really didn't need that closure for me personally because my whole thing with my dad was very separate from the public goodbyes. It was fascinating on one level to see the comfort, especially to my mother, of the structure, and it made a ton of sense to me why people are drawn to it. There were people there whom my dad had gone to grade school with—he was that kind of guy. People remembered him and he was well regarded. I met a few people who'd never entered my life before, and it was fascinating to see how overlapping all our lives can be. That's the result somewhat of culture, somewhat of this city being as small as it is. The sense of community was so strong, and I think that's a very good thing for people.

Could you foresee any way that you might return to an active Mormon life?

No. [He laughs.] I think off and on about trying to become more connected to something more structured because I do think there's some good to allotting a time in a day of the week to focusing on it. I think you can get so lost in everything else. I really do think that the structure, the go-to-church-on-Sunday thing, has a lot of positives. But I don't think it would ever be Mormonism for me.

You could see yourself in another religion?

Maybe, and it would probably be some religion or philosophy with looser definitions of what's right and wrong, good and bad. One of the most poignant examples of the rigidity of it for me was when my niece had been abused. She was six and was in the car with me one day. We were looking for a new place for them to build a new house because they left the old place to get the kids out of the neighborhood. She was a very serious six-year-old kid. And she turned to me and said, "You know, Scott, my dad said that you drink coffee." I said, "Yeah, I do." I couldn't figure out why she was saying that. But one of the ways they—the perpetrators of the abuse—manipulated these kids was to make them drink coffee. The kids had always been taught from day one that drinking coffee was a very bad thing. The abusers made the kids drink coffee and said, "If you ever tell that we did this (the abuse), we'll tell your parents you drank coffee." So in a kid that age, that threat has more negative power than the abuse. I'm a bad person because I drink coffee? People drink gallons of Coca Cola. There are basic health tenets that we should all live by. But the concept that you can take one element out of the bigger picture—as in coffee versus Coca Cola—and focus on it to the point where it manipulates people's lives so dramatically is very troubling to me.

If I were the president of the Mormon church, what would you say to me?

I'm not sure. I don't know how I would relate to someone so removed by life experience from me. I'd like to believe that the expressions of compassion and reaching out that you hear from these guys are true. So my desire is to believe that they have good intentions about what they're doing. I have respect for the institution and understand that to maintain that you have to have certain guidelines. My personal sense of things is that they'll have to adapt to the next century. They'll have to figure out a way to make it okay for women to respect themselves if they go to work, because otherwise they're "not being good mothers." They have to allow women to take more power in general. That one baffles me to this day. Most families now—young families—have to have two people working. But at least there's a subliminal message, if not an active one, that says a mother should be with her children, which obviously most mothers, if they could economically afford it, would do. It would be great if men were given that same option socially, which I know within the culture (Mormonism) is not thought of as being up-and-up. Those are the things I'd like to see change first because I think they cut a deep wound in people. In all of the people I know who survive in Mormonism, there are pieces of that which don't really go away; the doctrines don't fit anyone's life completely. Everyone has their own way of dealing with where to place that. I guess my statement would be: Come to the party (as in, get with it), come to the year, come to the day in which we live and then figure out what works. They're very old guys and they've lived in a different time; so it's very easy to make these rules and lose focus on how poorly they may work. I guess the other thing is that Ezra Taft Benson at one time said he couldn't believe that anyone could be a good Democrat and a good Mormon. I was so appalled by it. It's like, have a little respect for a difference of opinion. That's the kind of thing that troubles me dramatically, because if that's the message people hear, it's not going to work.

SCOTT BURTON

I certainly feel a part of the bigger thing—heritage or history—and again partly that's my familial heritage. My great-great-grandparents were killed by Indians in Ephraim, Utah, during the Black Hawk War. I just recently found a memorial for it (their gravesite); and it struck me how amazing their lives were and what they gave up. He was a sailor in Denmark, came to Utah, and was sent to Ephraim by the powers that be to be a farmer. He was very ill-suited for that. It amazes me that we've become so removed from giving up anything. I think of people who lived through World War II, lived through a hard time, and knew what giving things up was. They struggled for a "greater thing," and now we have this generation which I belong to where you had expectations of getting things the easy way. I was really struck by the color of the day in Ephraim and the setting where these people led this life and worked really hard and then died and were buried in a common grave with seven people because they just couldn't deal with digging single graves. It fascinates me how difficult those times were and how people survived it all.

It still binds you to the church?

Yes. I don't know if it's cultural or "the" church, but the church is the culture today and it certainly was then. There's that binding, and I think it'd be fascinating to go back in time and feel a sense of what that was like. We have a pretty easy and comfortable life even at its hardest, you know. So those kinds of things I have a great appreciation for, and I'm appreciative of my parents for speaking of it (my "Mormon" heritage) and giving me a heritage because a lot of people my age don't have a sense of where they came from and of their family history.

8.

Met Johnson

Virtue is like a rich stone—best plain set.

—Francis Bacon

A two-term Utah legislator, Met Johnson is known for his straight talk and opposition to the federal government's management of western lands. His leadership in the Western States Coalition, as well as his business activities, keep him hopping.

Met's in business with his sons, and they make a living buying, improving, then selling ranch properties in the intermountain states. Trying to reach him at his home in New Harmony (south of Cedar City) proved difficult. At last, I got a call.

"I can meet you in Antimony," he said. "I'm putting in an irrigation system in a ranch right across the street from the store."

"Which store?" I asked.

"There's only one here."

We met over Easter weekend; the air was cool, the cottonwoods were beginning to bud. A big man in Levis left a front-loader at a headgate and pushed back his Comanche Canyon Horse Company cap as he greeted me. We went inside an old outbuilding Met's already refinished into pleasant—if temporary—living quarters. He'll stay here until this ranch is ready to market.

He invites you into the only chair, and pulls an upended bucket to sit on. On a table are cans of chili, cut green beans, and soup. A two-burner camp stove sits nearby. No women here.

Met's a barrel-chested man with a voice like a shotgun. He's got an unaffected, natural way of phrasing that warms you to him. His sense of humor is sometimes alarming. When he first began working on the Antimony property, he posted signs telling the community he was going to build a hog farm. After citizens got over their shock and realized Met was teasing, they came to love telling the story as a joke on themselves. In southern Utah just about everyone knows and likes Met Johnson.

My brother Joe accompanied me on this trip. As I was packing my recording equipment after the interview, Met was talking to him. When we stood up to leave, Met said to me: "You know, I been talkin' to your brother Joe here, and we both agreed we didn't like you." Then he let loose one of his belly laughs and a wink. Maybe you had to be there, but Met Johnson knocks me out.

Met graduated from North Sevier High School where he was student body president. He attended Pasadena City College in California on a basketball scholarship until a knee injury took him out of play. The knee healed and he played basketball at Southern Utah State College in Cedar City, where he was also student body president, a drum major, and took part in track events. He eventually earned a bachelor's degree from Utah State, graduating in English ("I needed 178 credits to graduate and I had damn near 300 hours. I just liked everything," he says). He then taught school in Japan and Okinawa. After returning home, he started running the family farm and continued to teach.

Met attended an auctioneer school and eventually left teaching to go into the auctioneering business. He ran the livestock market in Cedar City for L. W. Gardner for several years, until he bought him out. Met was elected to two terms in the Utah State Legislature representing Washington County, where he made his home in the town of New Harmony. He was active in the Western States Coalition, a non-partisan political organization seeking more shared jurisdiction for management of public lands. About 1995 he left Utah politics and moved to Wyoming for a short time, but now lives in New Harmony, Utah.

~

When were you born?

In 1941.

Where?

In Salina, Sevier County. Redmond, actually.

You come from a pioneer line; your ancestors were active Mormon?

I wouldn't say active. Participating maybe is a better word.

Were you participating from an early age?

I went to Primary, I think, regularly, and Sunday school from time to time, but my father also ... He worked for the state road, but he always was in agribusiness and bought little farms and would fix them up and whatever. Then he got in the bishopric. He wasn't very active before he got in the bishopric. Then I would run the farms, I'd say, probably, when I was twelve or so. I'm not complaining. That was fine, but a lot of times he'd have church obligations and I'd run the farms or pastures or whatever. And I was happy to do that. That was an obligation I had or an opportunity to do his farming chores when he was participating as a bishop.

You were baptized at eight, like most of us?

Yes.

Did you have brothers and sisters?

I have a younger sister and a younger brother.

What does Met stand for? Is that short for something?

Yes, it is, but we'll just leave that alone. I'm like the Johnny Cash song—"A Boy Named Sue." But Met's been my name since I was twelve. In fact, when I was three or four they called me Met just for short. I don't have anything that's in my real name, any property or anything, nothing. It's just been Met. The bonds, the livestock market, the ranches. Licenses. Everything's just Met.

Was your mother or father more active? Or were they equally active?

No, my father was more active.

But your mother was Mormon?

Oh, yes.

Was there ever any discussion between them about being more active in the church?

No, never.

Were you a Boy Scout?

An Eagle Scout.

You had to be active in the ward to get that?

I wouldn't say really active. There was another young man who wasn't LDS at all. He participated with us. Salina is a different community. Of course, it's a Mormon community, but it's kind of like a non-Mormon community in a way because the railroad was there and the turkey plant and the carrot plants, the beets, the mines—the coal mines, the salt mines. There was a mix of people who all got along whether they were Mormons or non-Mormons. You know, I lived in Salt Lake and I've gone to school at different universities and been in lots of circumstances, even when I went to school in Pasadena. The Mormons and the non-Mormons—I wouldn't say they were at odds, but there seemed to be an antagonism, a slight one maybe that you'd hear in church about the non-Mormons, that they haven't seen the right way, or too bad for them, and we have the only church. And then the non-Mormon people, when I'd be around them, they'd cuss the Mormons for being pious. I couldn't see the point of either side taking issue with the other over things like that. It didn't make sense to me. They're both good kinds of people.

You were active in church?

I wouldn't say active. Semi-active—in my younger years, yes.

Was church of interest to you? Boy Scouts must've been of interest. But what about actually attending a Sunday school class?

That all depended on the instructor. Some instructors were fine and used anecdotes, and others were condemning, if you will, in a way—maybe didn't condemn those of us who were in a class, but condemned other people or condemned other ways of life. I don't know that they actually condemned other religions, but were critical of it. And that seemed to bother me some.

You'd seen other people and the way they lived in Salina?

Yes. I worked for other farmers, too. We didn't have a lot of machinery, so if we needed to borrow a baler, I'd go haul somebody's hay so we could borrow the baler. Consequently, I worked with lots of adults as a young man, and a lot of those adults were antagonistic towards the Mormons, and some of them were very pious Mormons. To me, they were both good guys. And why they had this friction—now I'm using the eccentrics in Salina. Ninety percent of Salina got along—Mormon or non-Mormon, no big deal. But these two ... What shall I say?

The fringes?

Yes, I guess the fringes. I liked to work for both guys, and why they didn't like each other. You'd hear "SOB Mormon" or "SOB gentile." I never did understand that. Hell, they both treated me fine. And for all I knew, they always paid their bills and those kinds of things—the ethics were above reproach with both gentlemen I'm thinking of. It confused me as to why they should use standards of the church or the Word of Wisdom, let's say, more than anything, as a way to judge someone.

Later when I was a senior in high school, my father had an opportunity to go run a ranch in the corner of northern California, Oregon, and Nevada. You could just throw a rock from the ranch house and damn near hit either of the other states. Anyway, this was a really remote area. That's my point. And the church there—it was a community church, and it was run by a guy named Nat—a little short guy. He had a traveling circuit that went up into Oregon and out in all these remote areas, and out in Nevada and then northern California. When I say northern California, it's more like Nevada and Oregon than it was any part of California. Anyway, so we went there, and it was nonsectarian. Everybody went to church there but Catholics. Of course, they had a church of their own not too far away, meaning sixty miles or so. So here I am with the Presbyterians ... heck, I don't know, they were every denomination. But the sermons there, to me, are probably what changed my attitude a lot and set me on a course of being noncommittal to a specific set of doctrines. Let's call it that. I went to the church for an hour and listened to the sermon, and sometimes it was on Monday night and sometimes it was on Thursday night. About every ten months it would be on Sunday. Maybe because they rotated so you could have it once in a while on Sunday. When it was during the weekday, the evening, I'd go to church. When it was on Sunday, I didn't go, because usually I went fishing or raising hell somewhere.

Anyway, the whole sermon as long as I was there was the same. Well, not the same sermon obviously, but the same general idea. It was "peace and goodwill towards everybody," and like I said, "friendship and trust the Lord and have faith" and those kinds of things. They never, never did get into any criticism at all of anybody. There was always praise for people who were good people and the challenge for us to be good. If you sin, fine, but repent. See what I mean? It was positive. That's the best word. Everything was positive, and I really enjoyed that. Then, of course, you go on to college and that whole scenario. Of course, I drank beer and smoked and raised hell. They probably didn't want me to come to church. I don't know.

How old were you when you started to smoke?

I was in athletics in college.

Football?

No. Track and basketball.

How tall are you?

I was six feet five then. Probably six four now. Anyway, I was a very good athlete—no brag, just fact—so I trained hard when I was in athletics. Then when I was out in off-season, of course I did what all my roommates and all my friends did. Probably I was the leader, probably led some astray. It was a long time ago. Wouldn't be proud if I led anybody astray. And I still chew tobacco. I probably am the first house member in the Utah State Legislature that ever chewed tobacco the whole time I was in the legislature. People would say, "What's that in your pocket?" I'd say, "Oh, it's my boot polish." But I have no criticism of the Mormon religion at all. In fact, I would recommend ... Well, and this is the funny thing, I think, in my life. Lana [his wife] and I went to the Orient with the military as instructors.

Anyway, we were around people, of course, who probably hadn't met somebody from Utah. So the first thing is, "Are you a Mormon?" We'd say, "No, Jack Mormons; we won't deny we're Mormons, but we certainly aren't practicing Mormons or orthodox." So if they ever criticized the church, I'd be the first to defend it. Do you see what I mean? If they have misunderstandings, that's unfortunate because I think the Mormon religion—let me put it this way—is more a way of life. If I could wave a magic wand over the world, I would have everybody be a Mormon. And then take a few of the bad Mormons out of the clergy. I think if people would follow the Mormon way in raising their children and the health standards, it makes a lot of good common sense. It's surprising to me that the government is trying to not impose, yet legislates more ethics and morality that the churches are already preaching. Do you see what I mean? I won't go into politics, but there is ... I just believe that if everyone was a hell of a lot more Christian, we'd have a hell of a lot less problems. Period.

Like the young men who go on missions. I help a lot of them financially if I know that they're having a struggle. And happy to do it. I'm not trying to promote a specific religion as in Mormonism, to put people in a forced belief. I think they're just out there doing good and maybe giving people faith and hope and those people—especially those folks in those countries that are so ... well, third world countries, let's put it that way. Hell, they need some kind of a lift. And if these young men and women are there doing it, I'll help them. Damn right.

You don't attend church anymore?

No.

When was the last time you were in a Mormon church?

Probably if I was to a funeral or spoke at one.

Do you pay tithing?

No.

But you do help the missionaries?

Yes.

Does being inactive and living in rural Utah in any way affect the way that you relate to your friends and neighbors? Do you feel that you're ever treated differently, being an inactive Mormon in the town of Antimony?

No. Or even in New Harmony. New Harmony is smaller than Antimony. No. I mean, our very dearest friends—they're elderly people. They were assigned as our ward teachers. I don't know if they call them that anymore. But we're delighted to have them come once a month. If they're ill or if it's cold or whatever, we go down to their house so they don't have to get out. You know, to accommodate. But I'm tickled to death to share a half hour with those folks. But there are non-Mormons in New Harmony, and non-Mormons here in Antimony. I'm friends with all of them, but they criticize each other, and that's what irritates me. The Mormon church doesn't irritate me. The non-Mormons, they don't irritate me. But why they have that damn rubbing-salt-in-the-wound deal, that's what I don't understand. I never discuss religion with anybody, ever, but that always makes me scratch my head. My hell, just leave it all alone. If he's a good guy, he's a good guy. Period. If he goes to church, great. If he doesn't go to church, great. I guess speaking a little theologically, in my opinion, the Lord is the only judge there is. Of course, we'll find out when we get to heaven—if we go. But anyway, so to judge each other on our own values, I just don't buy that.

What's your basic belief? Do you believe in Joseph Smith as a prophet and in the story of the golden plates?

Well, I'll put in percentages. I'd probably give it 50 percent yes and 50 percent no, just because I've never read the Bible totally, and I've never read the Book of Mormon. So I have so much respect for some people who say they have a testimony and they believe it, that it's like if somebody says, "Well, Met, I've seen the sun and I've seen blue sky and I've seen water," and maybe I'm blind. Do you know what I mean? But they're credible people—I'm going to believe what they tell me. And these people that I'm referring to that I have so much respect for, bishops and stake presidents and whatever, when they say that, there's no way that I'd say, Oh, hell, I don't ... I just don't deal with it. So do I or do I not? I don't know. Never studied that in my mind. Of course, I've never studied it in literature either. So ...

Do you have children?

Three sons.

How are you raising them?

Just like I am. Even if I tried to do it differently, they'd probably ... Anyway, how am I going to say, Do what I say, not what I do?

Are they active?

No. None of them.

And your wife?

No. Same as me. We have the very same philosophy, I think, about just trying to be good and leave that other, those friction things, out of it. If we can be good people and honorable and live the Golden Rule, then probably that's the religion we practice.

What happens to Met Johnson when he dies?

The hell if I know. The only thing I can handle right now? I can handle the way I live. That's all I can do. If there is a judgment day and I pass, fine. And if I don't pass, I guess that's my problem. So that's all I can tell you.

I don't know if you knew, but I owned the livestock market for thirty years, so I dealt with thousands of people every year. And some of the worst deals I ever got in was with some of the so-called best-go-to-church Mormons. Now I'd be in other bad deals with people who'd lie and cheat, etc., you know on weigh-ups or weights or quality of cattle or whatever it was. But if they weren't a Mormon, I found myself saying, "He's just a no-good son of a gun." Now, if they were a Mormon, "He's a no-good son-of-a-bitching Mormon." That's not fair for me to say that. I was using the church because I happened to know that he went to church or he was in the bishopric or the Sunday school something. And I really wish that I'd never done that. That wasn't the church's fault, for hell sake. If there really is a church, and all that really is true, the Lord is going to be more in judgment of that no-good sucker than I was, probably. Do you see what I mean? So that's again just judging, and I shouldn't have done that. But I did that probably on four or five occasions. Just get so damned mad about something that I say what I don't like people to say. And I said it. So I don't do that again, but it happened a time or two.

Do you agree with the church's politics?

I'm complimentary to the church's politics in the fact that I think that they pretty well stay out of it, meaning the organization of the

LDS church. Let's just use the legislature. Then I think there were times that legislators as individuals—not maybe representing the church—I don't think have any authority to represent the church. But because they represented their values or what they thought, I think, they tried to impose church values on legislation. Do you see what I mean? But I don't think the church felt that way. Let me give you a very good example. I think Mel Brown [a Republican legislator and former speaker of the Utah House of Representatives] is probably the most religious, honorable man that I know. Neil Nielsen is a bishop, and I went over when their church burned down and we raised $30,000. Hell, I don't know if I smoked or chewed then. Anyway, I was his good friend, an auctioneer, and he asked me to come help, and I said I'd be happy to. And I did. Anyway, so you take guys like that—and I could name a thousand ... But Mel Brown is so honorable, not only with religion and the way he practices it, but with everyone else that he'd never propose in the name of the church or in his own beliefs. Do you see what I mean? That's the admirable character about him being, I think, a very pure Mormon. In my mind he is one of the greatest guys ever, and he'd never impose his religious values in legislation. Then there's others who sometimes did. See? In the Mormon church as in any church there's all kinds of people. Some of them are great, and some of them are good, and some of them are not so good, and then there's a few stinkers.

If I were the president of the Mormon church, would you have any suggestions about how I should run the church or how I could do things better or worse?

The current president ... I've listened to him a couple times, you know, on the radio in my pickup or something like that. Of course, I've never listened to many of the presidents, but this gentleman ... I saw him interviewed on TV one time, and I have so much respect for him and the way he articulates things and the way he seems to be all in good balance that I'm very, very impressed with his leadership. And my criticism wouldn't be of him if I had to say something to him. It would be of the people who maybe misinterpret what the doctrine is or what he says, and then leverage it against another human being. Maybe a church member and/or maybe a non-church member. That's where I think the friction is between the Mormons and the non-Mormons. It's not the church or the non-church, it's the people who ... well, I don't know what a good example would be. But the church doesn't do the wrong thing as an organization, but the people in it misinterpret and then use it in the wrong way. I mean, they use church to do business or to leverage things, you know, like from the bank—I'm just using this as an example—and/or from their neighbor or brother so-and-so. Church should be practiced, in my opinion, personally and/or in Sunday school or whatever the meetings are. I don't think it has a place in the business world or in the political world. Do you see what I mean? So I can clearly draw the line because I don't participate in church, so I don't have any leverage that way, but I see others who do. That bothers me a little bit that they do that. But I'm not the judge, so I'm just telling you what bothers me.

Is the Mormon church the only true church?

I have a problem with that. In fact, not to reiterate what I said—and I shouldn't say everybody should be Christians, because the Japanese ... Of course, that's the only culture I lived in that was really dominant of either one of the two religions that aren't Christian. But, damn, it's all just if you're good or bad to me. So the only true church? Well, I can't disagree and I can't agree. So I just don't ever make an issue out of it.

9.

Helen Bowring Ure

Wisdom outweighs any wealth.

—*Sophocles*

Helen Bowring Ure's service to Utah education began with a tentative commitment to the Libbie Edward Elementary School PTA in 1951 and eventually resulted in her becoming the first woman to chair the Utah State Board of Education, where she served two terms. She was president of the Utah State PTA, president of the Utah Public Health Association, chair of the Governor's Committee on Children and Youth, chair of the White House Conference on Children and Youth, chair of the Utah Head Start Committee, vice chair of the Salt Lake County Board of Health, president of the Women's State Legislative Council, president of the YWCA, a member of the board of directors of Planned Parenthood, a member of the University of Utah College of Nursing Board, and chair of the Salt Lake Commission on Youth.

Helen was also vice president of the National Congress of Parents and Teachers, vice president of the National Association of State Boards of Education, member of the board of the National Committee for Children and Youth, and a member of the board of the American Public Health Association. She was a delegate to two White House conferences in 1970, one for children in Washington, D.C., and one for youth in Estes Park, Colorado.

She received the University of Utah's Distinguished Alumna Award for Meritorious Service to the University and Community presented by the U. of U. Alumni Association. She is a recipient of the Susa Young Gates Award, the Merit of Honor of the U. of U. Emeritus Club, the Beatty Award of the Utah Public Health Association (first non-professional to receive it), and was named Man of the Year in Education from Phi Delta Kappa Educational Fraternity, University of Utah Chapter. She also served nineteen years as a member and chair of the Advisory Council to the Utah Department of Employment Security, for which she received a special citation from Utah governor Norman Bangerter. She is the author of several publications on health and education, and is a member of the Salt Lake Council of Women Hall of Fame.

It's August 1996, and Helen is seated at the kitchen table in the modest home she and her husband, Jim, bought in 1942. It's on Salt Lake City's east bench, in the Mill Creek area. Helen was born in 1913 in Salt Lake City, and her alertness, trim figure, and beautiful thick hair suggest a woman twenty years younger than her eighty-three years. The benefit of mellowing through the years and the security of retirement from an active life in the community have in no way tempered the direct, sometimes indignant, view of the way things should be. She's quick to respond. There are moments of anger that rise in her voice, especially regarding her defeat for a third term on the Utah State Board of Education.

Interviewing one's mother requires discipline in formulating questions, especially if you think you already know the answers.

~

Do you attend Mormon church services?

Never, anymore.

What about funerals? Christenings?

Well, I go to funerals if they're held in Mormon chapels, but I wouldn't want mine to be held there.

Where do you want yours held?

I think the best place is over in the Wasatch Lawn [a cemetery with a chapel], because I have many friends who aren't Mormons. Some are good Mormons, too. But they kind of lost me during the 1960s.

Do you consider yourself a Jack Mormon?

I've thought of myself as a Jack Mormon, but I haven't mentioned it to anybody. I think most of the people who know me well would classify me in that way.

You were born to parents who were active LDS?

Very, very active. As a family, we used to go to all the Sunday meetings. Until the older girls got a little bit wayward themselves, we'd all go together—Sunday school and sacrament meeting, the works.

How many siblings do you have?

Six.

Was either of your parents stronger in the faith? Or did they both seem to share equally a zeal?

I think probably Mother was more unshakable, but Dad had traveled a lot and been in a lot of little timber towns and small towns in the West. Although people would ask him to stay at their homes and preach in their wards, he was sort of taken aback when he'd come home ... Of course, he hadn't been around usually for eight or nine months, and he was welcomed, but he wasn't given any special job to do. They'd always ask him to pray, and he made a lovely prayer, but I think he felt a little bit rejected, according to my brother who talked to him about it. I think he felt that they should have made a little place for him when he was home.

Did you ever hear him complain?

No, I didn't.

So nothing anti-church was ever said by either your mother or your father to your memory?

No, although I think Dad was better-read than Mother, and he'd mention certain things he'd learned as a child. He was brought up as a

Catholic and went to Catholic schools. His mother was a Catholic before she came to Utah, and then she joined the church. When her husband married another woman in polygamy, she left. Dad, I think, had a jolt there.

He told me about the pope's cap and the writing on it. There was one that looked like 999, but it was interpreted by Mormons to be 666, which was the devil's number. He told me about little things like that, which I don't know whether he told any of the others in the family or not.

Was he raised a Mormon? Or did he convert along with his mother?

His mother married a Mormon, and he was born and raised as a Mormon when he was young. I know he had brothers and sisters from the relationship between his mother and original dad. But Dad's father went to Brigham City to live with his new wife; his dad's mother was really hurt, and she was kind of spiteful about it. She married a Mr. Black whom Dad didn't like. Everybody thought he was sort of a bum. He didn't work, he didn't have a nice home for her, and she didn't have the things his dad had given her.

Was Mr. Black Mormon?

No, he wasn't. My father's mother joined the Catholic church again after that, and I think that's why Dad was sent to the Catholic schools. They did call it St. Mary's on First South, and it was more or less downtown. He did get, I think, probably some indoctrination. Maybe he had more of a questioning mind than mother.

He went on an LDS mission, didn't he?

Oh, yes, he did. He went to Oklahoma Territory.

What are your early memories of going to church with the family?

In the good weather, we'd usually walk to church from our place. Highland Park Ward was first just a little cottage-like ward, and then they built the new ward, and that was more or less a show place. That wasn't too far—several blocks—but we'd usually walk in a group. Then Edith and Maureen [older sisters] kind of dropped out.

Why?

I really have no idea. They moved in quite a high-class social life.

Was this in contrast to the way you felt the family was economically?

Sort of. Edith went with the mayor's son, and Maureen went with the governor's nephew.

Why do you suppose they went with these people?

I think they liked the things they did, and the kind of high falutin' life they lived, and the places they had access to, and their lovely dinners that they went to.

Did this seem different from the Mormonism that pervaded your life?

Yes, it did. It felt out of my reach. Oh, Maureen would come home with some new ideas for dinner. The first time I ever had artichokes, she'd had them up at the governor's mansion for dinner, or at her boyfriend's mother's house. They had some beautiful homes, and they did a lot of entertaining, which we seldom did.

Did you envy that?

I didn't think of it in that way, but I thought it was pretty neat.

Did you ever feel any guilt or any conflicts between your actions and what the church taught?

Oh, yes. Growing up I did. We'd always listened to conference, and some of the speeches of the apostles used to scare me to death. I thought for sure I was on the wrong track and I was going to go to hell for some of the things I did. It was a different era for me than for them. I just didn't see their way of looking at things. Things were being modernized. And the flappers were coming in, all the dances and all the kind of wildness that everybody accused them of. That was all part of my life. I was a little younger than the flapper age, but I could do the dances that my older sisters couldn't do. It was just natural, being a little kid you'd pick it up. I'd have to teach them how to do some of those intricate steps. It was always kind of intriguing to me, but I did feel that I was kind of a fish out of water in my family, because all of them—even my older sisters—were really back into that last generation before the flapper age. They didn't quite fit in.

You were the youngest of seven.

Yes.

And your sisters were in their twenties when you were just a sprout.

Yes. Edith was fifteen years older; Maureen was fourteen years older.

And they belonged to the nineteenth century? The Victorian to the Edwardian era?

Yes, I think essentially. They did finally get the flapper haircuts like Louise and I did, but I don't think they were at heart into that. They'd just do it because it was being done by others they knew, and they thought they looked good.

Of the seven children in the family, how many would you call Jack Mormons or Mormons who became inactive?

Certainly Edith. Really Maureen, although she tried to sort of pretend to keep a connection with the church by being in the Daughters of Utah Pioneers and things like that, but she never went. She never really embraced it, I don't think. Jarrold was kind of a Jack Mormon until he got married, and then Elsie changed him. Ed wasn't a really good Mormon when he left home at eighteen and went into World War I. He was a deep sea diver in the navy, and settled in San Francisco after his stint was over, with some others—I think four or five other fellows whom he knew—some from Salt Lake. But I don't think their main interest was going to church or Mormonism. They had their own apartment, and they were out of the navy and raring to go.

So it sounds like four of you came from very devout parents and chose to walk the inactive road rather than become active. Did it take time before you became inactive?

After Jim and I were married, we both had jobs in Winder Ward. I was a teacher and so was Jim.

You both were still active in 1938?

Right. And beyond that, I was activity counselor—that's what they called me. Then we kept our fingers in it, but even at that time I felt like they shouldn't have asked me to be a teacher. But I didn't really have the spirit, I didn't have the heart to insist on certain things when I was teaching. I'd skim over things I didn't really believe in. So I didn't feel totally immersed in the religion, even though I was active. We went to Mutual Improvement because we were teachers in that organization. Then when we moved up here, they asked me to be a Sunday school teacher and activity counselor in the Mutual, and I did that. I also began smoking, probably just to show my independence, that I wasn't going to be wholly taken in by the assignment. I was always a little bit rebellious.

Even as a child?

Oh, yes, even as a child. I remember going to all the organizations—Primary, religion class, and Sunday school. I remember my Sunday school teachers getting after me quite often for not being attentive or absorbing what I should be.

Were you interested in what they were teaching?

Not particularly.

Was it poorly taught or basically very dry?

Some teachers could get into it better than others, but most of them were so implacable and inflexible that you felt like you didn't have any say in whatever you were doing. We just took orders and had to live with them. I think that's probably what made me a little bit rebellious.

The demands of the church—did they seem rigid to you?

I thought so.

And you rebelled against that?

I did. And in Mutual we had a man, a Mr. Harmon, one of the builders in the city. He read the bumps on our head. I'll never forget that night. I wasn't being very cooperative, but anyway he wanted to read the bumps on my head. He did, and he said I was a leader in whatever I did, but I didn't want to be. He said you do it reluctantly, but you're a leader. I don't know whether he was trying to put something in my head that I should be a better example for others or what, or if he could really read bumps. I have no idea.

So you're married, you have children. What were your expectations of your children regarding Mormonism?

Really, we didn't have any expectations of their being good Mormons. Neither Jim nor I did. We could always see a little different angle. For instance, the two-and-one-half minute talks, Jim would always think of something that was a little off-beat and might challenge the Mormons in the talks. I can't remember exactly, but he did introduce some terms that maybe would make people wonder what he was thinking. I don't think we ever thought of having you indoctrinated in the Mormon church. It was convenient for you to go, and we sent you. We didn't go with you, but we sent you because all your friends were going.

Was that why? Or was it to make sure that grandparents were pleased?

That was partly it, too. Yes, that was the reason we went through the temple. We knew that Jim's folks and my folks would be utterly devastated if we didn't. So we just thought, Well, it's better to keep peace in the family and make everybody happy, and it doesn't hurt us. So we went through the temple. All of them were really quite religious. I think Will and sometimes Mabel [Jim's parents] had some small doubts, because when Pop died, he said, "I wonder if I'll ever see Mabel again."

He was a bishop, wasn't he?

Yes, he'd been a bishop in Ogden for years, and he was working in the temple when he got sick. We both thought that was quite unusual, because that's a part of Mormonism that you'll be with your wife, married in the temple, and have your children and everything. And to have him question that on his deathbed was a shock.

You were married in the temple. Your husband was physically handicapped. This was difficult?

That was one of the most difficult things we ever did. We were married in the Salt Lake temple, and if they had an elevator, we weren't informed about it. Jim had to climb stairs. You have to do a lot of that to go in different places and different rooms, and then come back down and go back and forth. And you had to change your garments or your hat that men wore. You had to change those around when different ceremonies were performed. He was just in a sweat the whole time. His dad helped him, but it wasn't a pleasant experience for Jim at all. And as a result, it wasn't for me, you know, just being worried about him. We didn't get anything spiritual out of it. Even when they washed your body and told you all about your garments and things like that. And they gave us secret names, which I guess I shouldn't feel sorry, but we didn't keep secret. We told each other. Now I'm not sure what mine was. But it wasn't an impressive ceremony, not at all. The words that they used sounded kind of silly to us. It just didn't make a good impression on either of us, partly because of his condition and partly because our hearts weren't in it.

At what point do you think your faith was shaken?

There were several points. In fact, when you—my oldest boy—were in Sunday school and the teacher talked to you in some way that made you feel like your dad wouldn't go to heaven because he smoked. That infuriated me, and I thought it was too narrow-minded, and his teacher should never have said it. And there were little things like that in the other children's lives that were said and done that I didn't like. And then when you kids got into your teens and were more independent—all of you more or less changed your lifestyle. And your hair was long. I thought it was just a way for you to show your independence from the church. But the fact that the church wouldn't accept kids who had long hair ... They'd always be riding them. And kids who smoked, they weren't good. And yet people who drank—closet drinkers or anything like that—could go to church and be accepted as fine members. I thought the church did the opposite from what they should. I was quite active in community youth affairs by then, and I thought they should've accepted them and made them feel welcome. They lost a lot of kids in that era. They certainly lost me. I'd go to church, not very often, but I'd go into Gospel Doctrine class and I'd have questions. I'd raise my hand and ask them, and they all seemed so startled by my questions. I didn't feel they ever answered them completely or even partially. I got disillusioned and decided it wasn't worth my while. I didn't think they liked to see me come, and I certainly wasn't getting anything out of it, so I quit going.

Did you ever consider actually having your name removed from the church roles?

It occurred to me, but that's about all. I thought, "I don't want to go through that trouble." They make it so miserable to get your name removed from the church roles that I figured it wasn't worth it.

HELEN BOWRING URE

Is there any advantage to appearing to be a Mormon?

Oh, I think so. In the political end of my life, I don't think I would've been so easily elected if I'd made a point of not being a Mormon. I didn't stress it at all, but I think people just thought I was and were surprised when eventually they found it out. I was a Mormon still, but I wasn't a good Mormon.

When you say "good" Mormon, how do you define "good" Mormon?

A person who goes to church and pays tithing and obeys the Word of Wisdom and does what the bishop wants her to do.

Did you pay tithing at some point in your life?

We did for some time, and the fast offering, as well. In fact, we had to to get in the temple. It didn't last at all. We didn't have within us the feeling that it would bring any blessings like some people thought, and many people still think that if they don't pay their tithing they'll be condemned and held back for some reason or other from getting to heaven. That just didn't enter our minds.

What about your basic faith in the Book of Mormon and the teachings of Mormonism?

I had a hard time accepting the story of Joseph Smith and the way he translated the Book of Mormon and how the angel appeared when he was so young. How he even understood what was happening, I don't know, at that age—fourteen. It all seemed more or less like a fairy tale, and I have an impression of the pictures that they showed of Joseph Smith receiving the plates in the forest. But it's not a picture that I revere. It was just there. I had a hard time accepting Joseph Smith.

Did you ever wish you were stronger in your faith?

I don't believe so. The only time it even crossed my mind is when someone would die who I knew was a Mormon or lived intimately with Mormons. I thought, Oh, it would be nice to feel that safe and secure just knowing that you're going to be all together and be in this wonderful place.

Did you ever have any open conflict with active Mormons?

I have no way of identifying them, because it was always done in secret meetings. But just before my last try for elective office [to the Utah State Board of Education in 1974], when I wasn't elected, I had reliable reports of a John Birch meeting up at the Mill Creek Library. A person called after a Saturday night meeting there and said, "I don't know you, but I voted for you all the way along." She said, "You wouldn't believe the things they said about you." I know a lot of Mormons were followers of the John Birch Society. The president of the church, Ezra Taft Benson, and his son Reed were. So I'd imagine there were a lot of Mormons at that meeting. But at that meeting she said they accused me of teaching about sex. I'd taken a stand on sex education in the school, and they accused me of going into the schools and teaching the kids while I was naked. That just blew my mind. It was Saturday night before the election, and there was really nothing that I could think of to do. Besides, I was informed from one of our good Mormon elders at the board of education that his wife had been called and they had a chain call going on in Granite School District urging people not to vote for me and telling them some of these lies. Chain calls are so expansive and so fast, they can get through a ward in a hurry. Afterwards a lot of people told me they'd been called by either a bishop who'd been a Republican party chairman or somebody of that kind in their ward—"Don't vote for Helen Ure." So that kind of turned me off to the church. In fact, it turned me off completely. I was furious about it, because they didn't tell the truth and they got me defeated.

You're sure this was church-driven?

I'm absolutely sure, because the wife of one of the assistant superintendents in the state office got the call. He told me what happened. And Duane Cardall at KSL attended our meetings and we did an interview before the election. He said he went to work the next morning at KSL, and his question was, "What happened to Helen Ure?" One of the men up there said, "Well, I know what happened. We got called by several people to not vote for her." So I feel sure that it happened, and it happened with Mormons leading the cause. Another board member, she was the wife of a stake president ... I liked her a lot, too, but she told me they had a Republican party gathering the night before the election, and they were all discussing politics and everything. She was running for the state board, too, again. She'd won one term. She asked one of the men who was there ... She said, "Of course, Helen Ure will get it." And he said, "Oh, no, she won't." And she said, "How come?" He said, "The word's gone out from 47 East South Temple" [LDS Church office headquarters at the time]. He was as sure as he was standing there that I wasn't going to be elected. I had little reports like this from several different good Mormon people who worked in the same circle I did.

Politically, where do inactive Mormons go in terms of a party in Utah, in your opinion?

I'd assume they go to the Democratic party.

Does the Republican party seem to be a home for active Mormons? Does it seem to better fit their philosophy?

It seems so. They embrace the same kind of thing that the Mormon church preaches, and the Mormon church keeps going along those lines. And that reinforces being a member. I think that's the main reason we have so many Republicans in the state. There aren't too many people who want to take an open stand against the church. It's too scary.

Did you ever feel any stigma from being a Mormon?

Yes, sometimes at national meetings, national conventions. People would look at you a little differently, and they usually never said anything. But if they found that I smoked, they were astonished, because Mormons didn't smoke, you know. I did for quite a while. I think, as I said, it was sort of in defiance to show my independence that the church couldn't own me and couldn't run me.

Have individual active Mormons ever created any animosity in you because of their religious views?

Yes. I remember being resentful of some things that they were saying and clinging to, but I never made an issue of it. It's not my way. I don't like to create trouble.

Were you ever confronted by an active Mormon about your degree of faith?

Yes, after I got notice of this meeting at East Mill Creek by the John Birch Society, I had several calls that night and the next day by Mormons who questioned did I go to church regularly and did I believe this or that, and was I a good member, and different questions. I could tell they were Mormons and they were questioning the plausibility of my being a good Mormon. I never claimed to be, but people just accepted it because I had been. I never used it in any of my elections. I deplored that. I deplored having men saying they were active in their priesthood and had so many children, and their wives were active in the auxiliary organizations and things like that. I thought that was dirty pool.

What do you like about Mormonism?

Well, I think Mormons more or less are honest. They're faithful, and they do a lot of good in a neighborhood. I think they give a lot of their time to helping kids and arranging entertainment for people, and I suppose old folks, too. They give of themselves a lot in the church, but they're not very willing to give of themselves outside the church.

Why do you think that is?

I think their time's too taken up with Mormonism. I don't think they have time to even think of anything else, and they don't read enough to broaden themselves, they're so involved in the church and the church work and the church books and the church magazine, and just doing what the church tells them to. I don't think they have the time. They don't give it much thought. They think they're on the right track, and that's that.

What do you think the church could do to keep more of its members from becoming inactive?

I think if they weren't so authoritative. If they'd involve people in questions of community, of church, and of philosophy, I think people would be more interested, but they don't. You just feel like you're being told by someone on high, and you don't feel you're really involved. You read what you're supposed to and pass that on to whomever you're supposed to. I don't think there's enough chance for interchange or any discussion of things that are in question. Intelligent people have things that they question about the church that the church can't tolerate being asked about them. They just cut them off. Get rid of them so they don't have to answer any hard questions. And yet we've seen a lot of things come out in the church—stealing—like the guy out in the prison who tried to sell church writings and killed a couple of good church members.

Mark Hofmann.

Yes, Mark Hofmann. I don't think they tell us the truth about those things. They probably don't even say it to themselves. They just cover it and think everything will work out, and they have the power. I just feel there are lots of things that intelligent people in the church have asked and have not been answered.

What about women in the church? Is this an area that troubles you?

It does bother me. I think they're losing half the population who could give them leadership and direction and challenge their minds if they'd use women in the right way. But so far as I've seen, women have always been under the thumb of the men in the priesthood, in the church. Relief Society was under the direction of the men, and the auxiliaries also. You didn't have any authority as an organization. You had to go through the hierarchy, and I think they haven't used women to their advantage at all—or to the women's advantage.

Any chance you'd consider becoming active again?

I can't think of any right now. It just doesn't hold any interest for me. I'm more comfortable being with different kinds of people. In fact, I get more out of going to the Unitarian church and listening to their programs and their wide-ranging discussions than I ever did at the Mormon church.

Do you ever feel isolated?

Yes, I do, sometimes. There are things going on in the neighborhood that are sponsored by the church that I get invited to. I usually decline because I don't want to go. We just don't seem to speak the same language. They're so involved in every church thing that's going on that you do feel a little isolated, but I'm also not interested. I find this true especially going down to the PTA conventions these later years in Provo at BYU. That's the only place that's big enough to hold the convention, so they always go to BYU. There are usually four of us in a car—three of them are active Mormons. And that's all they talk about—what they're doing in the church, and who's doing this, and who's doing that. I think, my gosh, they don't know anything that's going on in the world, but they know everything that's going on in the church. It's almost like a little gossip society, but it turns me off. I'm sure they think that I'd love to be involved. And that's the hitch. Actually, I don't. I don't want to be, and that's the truth.

The Mormons have a superior way of clinging together and keeping out other people who aren't Mormons, especially children, and that grieves me. I think they could spend some discussion on, and explore, that feeling that's just embedded in the Mormon culture that if you're not a Mormon you're not as good as they are. And you can't be as good if you don't go to the ward for the scouts and meetings and ...

There's the implication you can't achieve anything like a spiritual afterlife if you're not Mormon?

No, you can't. And even the scouts. Your nephews, for instance. But they make so many announcements in church for what the Boy Scouts are going to do this or go there or do that. And a Boy Scout outside the church just never hears about some of the things they're doing or some of the things they should be doing. The Mormons, I think, could spend a lot of time working on that subject, because I think it's wrong to hurt the kids. They don't even know why they're being ostracized—little kids. It just burns me up. Kids living in Mormon neighborhoods and being ignored or worse—actively rejected. I think that's terrible. That's one of the worst things they do. And some of the times I don't think they even know they're doing it, it's such a part of the culture.

Do you believe in God?

I really don't know. I sometimes think somebody has to be directing an orderly world, and yet when I look at the world I think it isn't very orderly and maybe it was just happenstance that it all came together and we have human life on the planet, and we've just evolved because we had to. Maybe I believe in nature. Some natural thing, but I can't quite believe that there's an omnipotent person who pulls strings or affects my life personally. I can't quite believe that's happening. And I think that if there were such a person, he wouldn't be like the God of the Old Testament. He'd be more like the God of the New Testament, and be more understanding and more kind and more friendly, and he wouldn't deliberately put things in your life to make you unhappy or to make you sick or put obstacles in the way of your attaining something. I just can't imagine that there'd be a personal

God who'd take that much interest in every person in the world. It just doesn't seem logical to me.

What about an afterlife? Is that a possibility?

That keeps coming back in my life, especially at this time because your thoughts go back to your fundamental beliefs and the way you were raised. And I find myself thinking along those terms and thinking, oh, it'd be nice to see Louise [a sister] and it'd be nice to see the folks. And yet I think, gosh, if it's the way it's supposed to be, I won't be on their level. They all have to come down to the other kingdom to see me. I told Louise to be sure to do that. Your mind just reverts back to the fundamentals that were drilled into you for so long. And then I come to and think, "Oh, that's ridiculous." I don't know whether there'll be anything or not. I have no idea. I have no inclination, no revelations have come to me, and no people have appeared before me. And I just wonder where your dad is ... if he is or if he isn't. And there was a time that we talked about that. I guess it was about in the 1970s. I asked him point blank if he believed in God. He said no.

He told me that, too.

I waiver about it. In my mind now I think no, there isn't, and yet I find these thoughts from way back just creeping into my mind when something like this comes up ... and thinking of some of the ways I used to think, about the family and how they're going to be able to all be together if there were three kingdoms, and some of them were married in the temple and some of them weren't, and some of them were divorced—how's that all going to work out? I just can't believe it. But it just creeps into my mind. I think about it once in a while, and yet I don't really have any reason to believe that there's a God.

10.

Betty Condie

A child said *What is grass?* fetching it to me with full hands.

—*Walt Whitman*

Betty Condie's list of accomplishments is lengthy. She has degrees from Utah State University (B.A.) and Arizona State University (M.A.), and has taught in public schools in Utah, Hawaii, and California.

She first became active in the Cache Education Association and today is associate executive director of the Utah Education Association. She was twice elected president of the UEA where she was a policy leader and a spokesperson on educational and professional issues. She was also UEA vice president for two years.

At one time she developed a two-volume course of study for LDS schools of the South Pacific. She has been active in National Education Association activities and has headed three professional exchange delegations of educators to the People's Republic of China.

Recognized as woman of the year by the Utah Business and Professional Women, she has been a panelist on numerous television and radio programs. In addition, she has served on the State of Utah Income Tax Recodification Task Force, the Utah State University Council on Teacher Education, the Governor's Reform Steering Committee, Utah

Federation for Drug Free Youth Advisory Board, the ERA Coalition of Utah, Mortar Board Alumnae, and the Women's Legislative Council.

In an office decorated with oriental rugs, cloisonne boxes, temple rubbings, and paintings from her travels to mainland China, Betty sits amid banks of looseleaf binders with titles like Education on the Internet *and* The Team Building Process. *"I've developed such a passion for the Orient, and I've not been able to accumulate enough Chinese art," she says. Both a computer and typewriter rest at arm's length. Her blue eyes and sandy hair are set off by a scarf of black, white, and tan worn over a tan sweater and slacks. She wears large gold earrings. On her desk sit a Brackman Brothers coffee mug and a teacher's brass apple. Her hands are at rest on her desk top and remain there throughout the interview.*

~

May I ask when you were born?

I was born in 1932, in Brigham City, Utah. My grandmother lived there, but I grew up and my parents lived at the time in southeastern Idaho. Preston, in Franklin County. So, you know, that orientation is toward Utah. It's like being a native Utahn to be born in southern Idaho.

Were your parents active in the LDS church?

Yes. I come from a family of very active church people. My mom was really active; my dad was; my sister is. I have only one sister.

Did you attend church as a child?

I did. I was married in the temple. I was all those things you are supposed to be when you are raised a Mormon woman.

Now you're inactive?

And I have been for approximately twenty years.

What were the circumstances of your becoming inactive?

When I look back on it, I think it was a long, gradual process. It took a lot of accumulation of data—maybe even a subconscious process that I wasn't aware of until the 1960s. I remember exactly what caused me to start consciously questioning Mormonism. It was reading *The Feminine Mystique* by Betty Friedan. Has anybody else told you that?

No.

When I read that book, I realized Friedan had put into words many of my own thoughts and feelings. I didn't know until then that anybody else had that perspective. [She laughs.] It went from that into questioning a lot of church teachings, principles, and doctrine, basically surrounding equity, both gender equity and racial equity. Reading *The Feminine Mystique* heightened my sensitivity to feminine issues, sensitivities which I think were always dormant, somewhere in my thinking and in my mind. I started thinking about the church's stand on women and the church's stand on blacks. I said to myself, "I don't think God is a chauvinist and I don't think he's a racist," and to belong to a church which has what I interpreted as chauvinistic and racist doctrine didn't square with me. I was quite uneasy about it and it really caused me to question. I started to question some of the things that I'd always been taught from that kind of a perspective.

It was a difficult emotional and intellectual thing to go through. It was a questioning process which lead me to feel unsure about things I'd always believed or thought I believed or pretended to believe. It was a very conflicted process, I think, because I was saying, "I don't believe what my parents believe. I don't believe what my grandparents believe. I don't believe what my sister believes. I don't believe what my husband believes." That's a difficult kind of a thing to go through—rejecting those things—when all your family and most of your friends believe otherwise.

Were you able to talk to your family or your husband about it?

You know, I didn't. I didn't ever talk about it. And I'm not sure why. Perhaps it was because I didn't think they would understand and it would be too hurtful for them. It was really a very internal process for me. I didn't talk with my mother or my sister or my husband. Gradually I began not attending church meetings. My ward teachers commented on my absence, as did my husband, but it just happened without any real open discussion about it.

Was there any pressure to become active again?

I guess I've always felt there was pressure. Not a lot of pressure, but the people who were home teachers to my family during part of this time were really good personal friends and they did directly say, "Betty we've noticed that you're not attending church." They may have asked, "What's the problem?" But I felt that I really didn't owe them an explanation. I guess I felt I didn't owe anybody an explanation, because I never gave one to anyone.

Did this isolate you from friends and family?

I'm not sure I felt isolated. I guess I did. When you're active in the church, basically all your friends are people in your ward and people who are active, especially when you live in a predominantly Mormon community. And I was living in Smithfield at that time. I think that feeling a bit isolated is what led me to become more active in the Utah Education Association. I took a role and sought elected office in my local association and then state association, as well, because I found there some relationships and some friends who weren't active Mormons. I think I substituted that activity and those relationships for my church relationships and activities.

Were these people you could talk to about your feelings?

No, I never talked about that, although I felt a comfort level with them. There was a void there. When you've been doing a lot of church activities and then cease them, you fill the void with something else. It's transferring attention and focus from one thing—the church—to another thing—in my case, the education association.

Eventually the energy you redirected toward education took you to a high position.

I ran for and was elected president of UEA. I became more involved, not only with the state association but with others around the country. The position has a national focus. There were lots of meetings and conferences with my national counterparts. That gave me a whole group of acquaintances and friends who had something in common with me. In that way I really filled the void that leaving the church created.

What happened to your relationship with your family?

My relationship with my husband deteriorated and eventually led to divorce. It was nothing really overt, it was nothing angry, it was nothing that was really awful at all. It's just that he was—is—a very devout Mormon who needs an active Mormon wife to be happy. When we were living in Hawaii, on the BYU Hawaii campus, he was president of the student branch. That's equivalent to being a bishop. And he's a high priest. He's all those things that come with working your way up the priesthood positions in the church. He needed a wife who'd do these things with him and go to church with him, but it wasn't something I was comfortable with. So it left him really out there. Hanging in the wind, so to speak. It was his desire to have a mate who'd be an active church member that led to our divorce. My inactivity had a huge impact on my marriage. In fact, it basically was the end of it.

Hadn't you been married in the temple?

Yes.

How did this resolve itself?

I really never dealt with that. My former husband did find an active, devout woman whom he married a few years ago. I got a letter from his stake president, saying your former husband is going to be married in the temple. I can't remember the details of it, but basically it told me that if I had anything to say about the marriage which was going to take place, I should contact him. I didn't do anything about it; I just ignored it. In retrospect, I should've written back saying it was wonderful that he's getting married. He's a kind, wonderful, generous man who deserves to be happy.

There was no temple divorce?

Not that I know. But I think doctrinally he can be married to more than one woman. So it's my assumption that he's married to me and he's married to her and plans on living with both of us in the hereafter. But I don't know.

Which brings me to the question, what happens after you die?

That's a very good question. I guess I don't *disbelieve* in the hereafter; I don't think I do. But I can't define it except to say that I believe life on this earth is not the end of existence.

You don't think it's celestial, telestial, terrestrial?

It could be, but I doubt it. I don't know. I've never been interested in doing theological reading and research to define that. I guess I'm comfortable not knowing.

What about your basic belief in the tenets of Mormonism.

I've never had a strong belief in those tenets. The things I learned when I was young, growing up in the church, are not totally erased, but they've faded. There's a portion of it still there. But, basically, I never had a testimony of the church.

Some individuals in the church have been blamed for interpreting doctrine in a way that drives some away. Was that ever a problem—the lay clergy?

Yes, I think it was. It's one of the many things that accumulated over the years to cause me to disbelieve. I know there are a lot of people who profess to be good Mormons who are not. Who may be criminals, in fact. Who may be liars and who may be cheats. But they go to church on Sunday and profess to live the gospel. I remember, when we were living in Hawaii, leaders in the church weren't very inspiring people sometimes. When I had to go after a temple recommend, I remember being asked personal questions about my relationship with my husband and I thought, you know, I just don't think this is necessary. It struck me as being not the right thing, and not an obligation I had. Did God want me to have to be interrogated by a person whom I didn't consider to be any more spiritual than I am? Why should this bishop who is no better than I question me? It was also a feminist thing. It was the whole male authority thing with the church.

Are you a spiritual person?

I don't know the answer to that question. I have non-religious friends who follow spiritual leaders or gurus not affiliated with organized religion, but I don't do any of that. I don't go to other churches, and I don't really seek out something else to believe in. I guess you could say I don't know if I'm spiritual or not. It depends on how one defines spirituality.

You seem to have a lot of serenity.

I feel comfortable with myself, my values, and my beliefs. I'm okay with whatever is. If there's a hereafter, it's okay. If there isn't, it's okay.

I don't feel stressed out by not knowing and by not having something I deeply believe in terms of a hereafter or a God. I think I'm spiritual in the sense that I believe there's a higher power. I don't reject God. I don't reject Jesus. I don't reject Christianity. But I'm not sure about the efficacy of strong religious beliefs unless one is also a truly good human being.

Did you have children?

Yes, I have four children. And my experience with them growing up in the church also contributed to my leaving the church. I could see gender-bias operating. I have three boys and one daughter. The Mormon church provides significant opportunities for men and boys throughout their lives. From Cub Scouts to priesthood programs to intramural athletics. My boys were always involved in camping and jamborees and all sorts of activities. The church basically provided nothing for my daughter. That's part of my feminist objection to the church. Males and females are acculturated in the church for the roles the church perceives they should fill as men and women. I just felt so strongly that my daughter was short-changed as a young woman in the church, while my boys were catered to. Programs were very strong to turn boys into leaders and prepare them for the priesthood. And for girls the message is: you know your place, Relief Society. Even Relief Society decisions have to be sanctioned or approved by male church leaders. That was part of the gender-bias I saw.

For example, when I was active in Relief Society and was a counselor in the ward, a couple of things happened which confirmed this for me. I went to a meeting at the home of the Relief Society president one afternoon. There were just the two counselors and the president and we were doing some planning. I wore pants. It was before the church really approved of women wearing pants, and she [the president] asked me not to wear pants again. She said that as a Relief Society counselor, I ought to set a good example and not wear pants. That struck me as weird. Another instance I recall is a musical program for the centennial of the Relief Society organization. They asked me to be in charge of the program called "Melt Down My Pewter." It was a program that came from the church. No doubt it had been approved by the priesthood. It was supposed to be produced in every stake in the church. It really was quite a good program. It included music, dance, and drama. So I produced this program. We presented it one evening and it was really very good. In fact, it was so well received that afterward people wanted to schedule a second presentation so others who hadn't seen it could come. I remember the Relief Society president saying, "Well, I'll have to check that out with the bishop." She checked it out with the bishop, and he felt one performance was enough. I thought, This is so crazy to have an auxiliary organization for women (which in itself signifies inequality) and they can't even make their own decisions about their own activities without getting priesthood approval. So there again was that authority/power problem. It was another example of the status of women in the church—subservient.

Do you expect any changes regarding women in the church in the future?

Perhaps, in time. Just as it became impossible not to recognize that blacks are equal to whites, perhaps gender equality will some day prevail. It's obvious that doctrine changes as social and political climates change. We've seen that what is "truth" at one point in time may not be "truth" indefinitely. Gender-equality is a problem in many churches, as you're well aware. Some churches have decided that women can be priests. But real equality is something that's going to be slow in coming. I listened to some of the last LDS general conference sessions. I notice the authorities of the church still say to women, "Now, don't work outside the home unless you absolutely have to. If you're a single mother, you need to provide for your children, but not unless you really have to should you work outside the home." That kind of persistent mantra tells me doctrine is not changing very fast. I certainly don't expect that doctrine regarding women holding the priesthood will change for a long, long time. But I think eventually it will have to.

If I were president of the Mormon church, what would you say to me?

I guess I'd say that before I really want to participate in the church, I'd have to feel more comfortable that this church didn't have practices and doctrines that discriminate against certain people. Of course, right now, it's mainly discrimination against women because the racial issue has been dealt with.

Back to your children for a moment. Are they all active?

My oldest son is active. He went on an LDS mission and he remains a very devout and active member of the church; so does his wife and so are their five children. My other three are not. They're just like me. [She laughs.] Sometimes I feel, Oh, gosh, what if I've made a mistake here. I've been an example to them and they've followed me and there may be a hereafter and we're all going to be some place we don't want to be because I was wrong. [She laughs again.] So I have moments of thinking I may have botched it up for them. But that's assuming the responsibility that they aren't active because of me and I don't accept total responsibility for their choices.

How do you deal with your active son and his wife? Do you support them?

Yes, I do. When he was made a bishop, I went out to California where they live because I knew it was really important to him. They just understand that I'm not active and I understand that they're active. There's mutual respect for our differences. I often go to church with them when I go out there, because I respect their beliefs and want to show my support for them.

Do you have any conversations about this?

No. I basically don't have conversations with anybody in my family about my inactivity and my beliefs and disbeliefs. Partly I think because I feel like that's an individual decision, and I really don't want to impact others' personal beliefs too much. We do have some pretty heart-felt conversations, but it's rarely about the church. It's like avoidance behavior with my active son. I believe that old axiom about not discussing politics or religion because you just end up angry. The relationship's better if we just avoid the topic.

Is the same true with your inactive children?

No. With my inactive children, we're more on the same wavelength, and I know I won't say anything that offends them because they have the same belief system that I do about the church. So we can talk about it from time to time, but we don't spend a lot of time discussing religion.

What would you guess actives think of inactives?

My guess is that they're sorry for us because they believe we've gone astray, and wonder how we could do that after knowing the truth. I really believe that they feel pretty bad for us. And they're pretty constantly trying to save us from ourselves.

BETTY CONDIE

How do you deal with that feeling of pity?

Sometimes I wonder if the attention active members pay to me is based on anything except trying to activate me. I have some very good neighbors who've been very friendly to me since I've lived in the neighborhood. They're all very active members, and they've been very good friends to me. I wonder a little bit about that attention. But whatever the motivations are, I appreciate their attention. I have a wonderful neighbor who does home teaching. He brings his son over and we have some good conversations. He's a great guy. I like him a lot. So the ward has been pretty civilized, so to speak, about how they approach me. I've had the Relief Society visiting teachers also call and say, Could we come and visit you? I know they're calling because that's part of what they're expected to do, but they're great. I enjoy talking to them, and I enjoy their friendship. I'm not hostile to active members or to the church.

Do you get anything out of your meetings with them?

Yes. I think they like me and I like them. We're interested in each other and our neighborhood. I respect and adore them and I like visiting with them.

Have you remarried?

No.

I saw your ring and wondered.

Oh, it's just 'cause I'm so used to wearing it. I feel kind of naked if I leave it off. Sometimes I wear a ring. Sometimes I don't. My actual wedding rings were stolen a few years ago, so when I wear a ring on that fourth finger, left hand, it's not sentimental, it's habit.

Can you foresee ever becoming active again?

You know, I think I can. Although I can't define it very well. I've sometimes wondered if as I grow older, and I feel a need for support, and I no longer have a job, and I'm retired—if, in fact, I won't need something else to take the place of what fills up almost twenty-four hours a day for me right now. So I can foresee possibly a time coming when I'm retired and I'll want to have some kind of activity. Perhaps it could be church activity. I don't know. I think it's a remote possibility.

Never say never.

That's true. But I'd be very surprised if that were based on anything I could perceive happening in terms of my belief in the principles of the church—my belief in the truthfulness of the church. Because one thing I used to resent a bit was that a church could say, "We're the only true church." Such a small percentage of the total population of mankind belongs to "the true church" and there's only one such church? That bothers me quite a lot. It seems preposterous to me that any church should proclaim itself "the true church." There must be a lot of truth in a lot of churches. It's pretty egotistical to think you have a corner on all truth and light. And it's just a bit of a problem for me that a church would claim that.

If it is "the true church," I ask how is it possible for injustices to occur? Take the Mark Hofmann incident. In another state, selling his bogus documents would've resulted in a trial. Why didn't that happen? It would have been embarrassing to many of the high officers of the church. Often, when somebody else commits a crime, if they're not tied into the church, or it doesn't reflect badly on any of the officials in the church, they throw the book at them. It seems to me it's pretty corrupting to have a theocracy, which is basically what Utah is. The church has always seemed to me to have two different kinds of sinning. One is financial sinning, or white-collar crime, and that's not a big deal. You can be a counselor and cheat your ward members out of half a million dollars, and it doesn't cause the ripples one would expect. Financial sinning, fraud, or scam occurs quite often and sometimes involves pretty high members of the church. It's either swept under the rug or they're sent away to be a mission president. The other, seemingly more serious, sinning is sexual indiscretion. Good people are disfellowshipped for these sins. "Sin" is not treated the same. [She pauses reflectively.]

You know, when you asked did I ever talk to my mother and my family about my inactivity? My mother knew I was a feminist. Do you remember when the Sonia Johnson stuff was going on? Sonia was from Logan, Utah, and I'd gone to school with her brother (actually they were from Preston, Idaho). So I had a special interest in that. And either Sonia or some of the NOW [National Organization of Women] members went down to the temple and chained themselves to the temple gate or something like that during a conference session. My mother called my sister and said, "Was Betty there? Was Betty one of those women?" [She laughs.] So, you know, she knew, even though we really didn't talk about it. She considered me pretty radical.

11.
Richard Brown

All we know is still infinitely less than all that still remains unknown.

—*William Harvey*

Richard Brown practices internal medicine in Sandy, Utah. He's an active outdoorsman and a volunteer doctor at Alta ski resort.

~

When you were born?

On June 10, 1943.

In Salt Lake City?

Yes.

Where? On the East Bench?

Yes, my folks lived on 19th East, just right by the country club and Highland High School. My mom still lives there.

Were your parents active LDS?

No, they weren't. It's an interesting story. My father's family were all from Draper. In fact, his great-great grandfather was Ebenezer Brown who was one of the Mormon Battalion and founded Draper. But his father wasn't very active. And Dad said he was active until he was twelve. He said he went out fast offering collecting one Sunday and didn't get any response from anybody and he said, "That's it." And he never went back to his church. So he was inactive all his life.

My mom's family was from Chicago, and her dad was very anti-religious, really. So neither my mother nor her sister had any religious training. It's a very complicated story because her dad's wife died, and he ended up marrying a Salt Lake woman. The woman he married was my father's aunt, and there were three sisters, and the one sister was my father's mother who died when he was young. The second one sort of raised my father, and then the third one was the spinster who ended up marrying my mother's father. So my dad and my mother ended up being cousins by marriage, and that's how they met each other. His family was a prominent Mormon family, but they were all inactive also.

Were you at all active when you were a youngster?

No. It's interesting because we live half a block down from the ward house—the old Rosalyn Heights Ward house, which is now in the Parleys Stake. I'd never gone to church at all. My father never went, my mother had no religion. But socially, when you're growing up in Salt Lake in those days, the church was your outlet. A lot of the kids my age would go to church, and so I started going to Primary, I guess, probably about age twelve—well, before then actually. I started going to Primary more as a social event than anything else, but I'd never gone to church until I was twelve.

Of course, the Boy Scouts were throughout the church. So when we graduated from Cub Scouts into Boy Scouts, the troop was affiliated with the church, and they used to meet on Mutual night. One of my friends was very active, came from a very active family. So he just started talking to me about the rest of church—that, "Gee, you ought to be going to Sunday school and priesthood meeting." You know, so you can get your Duty to God Award and all those kinds of things. So I started going to church with him. I think that was the first time I'd ever gone to Sunday school, and I remember going to priesthood meeting the first time. You know, they said for all the deacons to stand up, and I stood up. The bishop looked and said, "Who's that guy?" They'd never seen me before. I'd been baptized, by the way.

You'd been baptized?

Yes. I'm not sure why. I think it was actually my mother who kind of arranged for the baptism. I'm not really sure why we were baptized.

I think when you were eight, everybody else was, and Dad had been a member, although he wasn't active. I know I was baptized.

You remember that?

Yes. I do remember getting baptized, but I don't remember why. It was just sort of what you did with your friends. That was typical in Salt Lake. What's interesting is our family ... Dad hadn't gone to church, Mom wasn't even a member. My mom and her sister, brought up without any religion, had this deep desire for religion, which is really interesting. I think she's the one who pushed and said, "Well, you ought to be baptized." I'd never gone to church before until this twelve-year-old incident. So I started going to church. Once again it was a social thing, more than anything else. But I was conscientious enough that I listened to what they were saying and started believing it.

One thing about Mormonism is it has a very rational appeal. They do have an explanation of why we're here, and what we're doing, and where we were, and where we're going. It's not mystical like ... You know, maybe even Catholicism can be a touch mystical at times. So the more I listened, the more I started believing this. Then my mom took a great interest for some reason. About the same time she started listening to what I had to say and started going to church and reading. She had the missionaries come in and was converted, and she was baptized. Just as an aside to explain a little bit about that, her sister who lived in Seattle had married a Catholic person who was inactive. But my aunt started looking at the Catholic religion, took the instruction, converted, and became an extremely devout Catholic. My mother became an extremely devout Mormon. She's almost fanatical. She started dragging Dad to church, and he became active and went through the whole thing, and worked all the way up, and then they were married in the temple. I remember going down and being sealed to my parents, because my mom really went wholeheartedly. We're still not quite sure about Dad. I think he did it for Mom. I don't know how much he really believed.

Is he still alive?

No, he died twelve years ago.

Is your mother still alive?

My mom is still alive, but she's sort of in poor health now.

Was she active as long as her health ...

She was very active until she broke her hip, and then just stopped going to church. But she's still very devout, very upset that I'm not.

Let's get back to that in a moment. Do you have sisters and brothers?

A younger brother. He was three years younger than I. He'd been baptized also, and I guess he would've been about nine when I started going to Mutual. So he started going to church, too, and just kind of followed a natural pathway.

Is he still active?

Quasi-active, I guess. He ended up going to West Point, and did a military career. Now he's a lawyer living in Texas. He married a girl who's not Mormon. I don't think his kids were ever baptized. He goes to church; I think he's sort of a believer and sort of active.

Let's get back to you now. You're twelve, thirteen, fourteen, you've become active. You're a conscientious Boy Scout and you're enjoying scout activities, I presume. This continues for how long?

I went whole force, was very active in church, and went to seminary, and wanted to go on a mission, and finally went on a mission at nineteen. I joined a fraternity in college, and I was really straight. In fact, I was the designated driver for everyone. We'd go to the parties and they'd always try to get me to drink or try the beer or whatever. I had no interest whatsoever. I was extremely devout, I guess. So I went on a mission.

Where did you go?

I went to Argentina. I was with one of the first groups that went down to the Missionary Language Institute in Provo, which was an excellent language training program. I'd taken some training in high school—three years—but I don't think I'd learned a thing. And this was an excellent training program in Spanish. I spent four months there because my visa took a long time to come through. I really went down to Argentina with a very good knowledge of Spanish. So I served the mission.

I was thinking a little bit about what I was going to say today. And these are some of the ideas as I reflected on my own feelings about things and why I'm where I am now, and I think a lot of it is the provincialism in Salt Lake. You grow up with the church, and that seems to be all there is. In those days particularly, you didn't really have any other view of what was going on in the rest of the world. I think we all sort of thought that the rest of the world was just like Salt Lake—everybody thought the same, and everything was the same.

It was for me.

I think my first real awakening was going to Argentina. Talk about a completely different society, where religion had a completely different meaning to the people there. They're nominally Catholic. The joke was they only went to church three times in their lives—when they were christened, and when they were married, and when they had their funeral. But they were devout Catholic. You know, religion to them meant going to church those three times. They probably really had very little understanding of the doctrine or what Catholicism was, but would never think of anything else. Catholicism was their religion, and it was very much a part of their whole life. In Argentina, not to be a member of the Catholic church was very unusual. It meant a lot to you in society. You were looked down upon or not accepted the same way if you weren't Catholic. I think what this did for me is I started realizing there's another way to look at the world. These people were living quite happily and doing fine without really much of religion. It gave me another way to look at the world and life.

As for my approach in the mission field, it was extremely logical, and I really enjoyed teaching the lessons. I knew the language quite well, and I just enjoy teaching people, because the appeal to me was still the very logical explanation of the spirit world and why we're here and the Celestial Kingdom. As you talked to people, you'd sort of think, Well, they understood it. But to become a member, what does this mean to these people? It's a complete change of their life. A real change in how they're accepted in their society and what people think of them, and why they have tithing and the Word of Wisdom, and going to church, and all these things. I started realizing, Boy, this is a real sacrifice, a real change in these people's lives. I saw a lot of people embrace the idea of Mormonism, but the ritual became a real problem. I started seeing that a little bit, wondering, Gosh, is this really worth it?

You were on your mission at a time when you were probably expected to be as devout as you'd ever be in your life, and yet you were seeing something else. You were being opened up to another vision of the world.

I think so. You start realizing that there's another way of looking at things. So I started thinking about that. I think it was really not 'till later though. I was a pretty successful missionary. We had a lot of baptisms. I don't know how many of these people remained active. My feeling was, Well, you teach them the principle or show them what's going on and then turn them loose. I don't think I was a very good fellowshipper. I'm afraid I was more on the intellectual level of the doctrine. I always wonder how good a job I really did after they were in the church—keeping them there, helping them through all these doctrinal rituals. So I came home and sort of just jumped right back into school and the fraternity and all my friends. Of all my friends, none of them were active. I was always the odd one out. When I came back from my mission, I was twenty-two. I'd buy the beer for them all, because I could do it. But I never drank it. I'd buy them the beer and drive, and they could have fun. When I came back, I was fairly active, but I started noticing things. I was just real bored. You know, you'd go to church and be bored.

This was a change, then, from before your mission?

I think so.

Why do you think that was?

Was it that I thought I knew it all and didn't have to sit and listen to this, or had I gotten to the point where ...? That's when I started thinking maybe there's a different way to look at this.

I'll tell you one of my big stumbling blocks, and this may be getting into theology. The whole crux of the Mormon doctrine is that you're presented the gospel, why we're here, and you accept it, and then you do whatever you need to do to get into the Celestial Kingdom. That's all well and good for the million people who live in Utah. But when you start thinking of how many people have lived on the earth—countless millions of people who never even heard ... First of all, probably never heard of Jesus Christ. Or the whole story of the gospel. You start thinking, Gosh, if this is the whole reason we're here and it's so important to do all these things to get into the Celestial

Kingdom, why is only one one-millionth of a percent even hearing about it. It just doesn't fit. If this is the real reason we're supposed to be here, everybody should be hearing about it. Of course, the Mormon answer is, "Well, that's what the work for the dead is; and we've got the Millennium to teach all these spirits." I think that's a bit of a cop out. If the whole reason we're here is to learn how to live and make the right choices, why is such an infinitesimally small number of the populace involved? It doesn't fit. And I started thinking about it; I think that was the beginning of the end. Then the experience of seeing a whole society in Argentina that had lived all their lives without hearing about this and were doing just fine, thanks. In fact, we were probably causing more problems. Their life became much worse, seriously, after being involved with the church. It became a real ... they were very different people. And that's fine. That's the Mormon way, we are a different people. But you know? Maybe we're way too different. We may be out in left field some place. I thought, Gee, this just doesn't fit.

I guess the next big step was marriage. I married a girl who had come from a very inactive family, quite a prominent family. This woman had been brought up somewhat with the knowledge of Mormonism but had never gone to church. So she and I dated and fell in love. I sort of insisted that we be married in the temple. I was in that period of still believing, still wanting to go through all the motions, but wondering. She was very good, did what she needed to do, went to church, and we were married in the temple. And she still holds that against me, because her parents weren't able to go to the ceremony. But I don't think she was ever convinced. I think she was just doing it for me. She refused to wear garments, period. I quickly decided I don't think I need to either.

When we moved to an apartment, I think we went to church about two or three times and then just stopped going to church. We didn't know anybody, and she certainly wasn't interested. Then I did my [medical] internship in Los Angeles—never went to church in Los Angeles. In fact, Sundays were about the only days we'd have off, so we'd go to the beach. After that I went in the air force, and we were stationed in England. I never went to church there, was contacted by the local Mormon people in the air force, but I wasn't interested in going to church at all. Then my next downfall, I guess, was discovering great

German beer and fine French wines, and all of a sudden realized what I'd missed all these years.

Had you tasted beer or wine prior to that?

A little bit. My parents drank until my mom converted and my dad became active. I guess I was probably sixteen when that occurred. My dad loved to drink and probably kept drinking the whole time, although he used to hide it from Mom. So I'd tasted it, but I really never had any interest at all.

Then in England ...

But then when you're living in England and Germany ... and I just started. It was really good, and I enjoyed that part. My wife did, too, so we got into that—the enjoyment of that part of life. Then came back to live here and sort of picked up with all my friends, and now I was really more like one of them. You know, we'd go fishing or golfing and drink. Sunday morning was no longer a day to go to church. It was that you played golf in the summer and you skied in the winter.

Did you notice any change in attitude toward you from your inactive or non-Mormon friends after you decided that French wine and German beer were a part of your life?

No, I think they were just glad to have another person to enjoy things with. It's really never come up. We joke about the fact that I used to be the designated driver and that now I was having as much fun as anybody else. I think they all think, You finally saw the light. Nobody's ever said that in so many words, but these people just think the religion is a bunch of bunk. I think they're glad that I came around to the correct way of thinking.

How about your mother? Was she a witness to this change?

Oh, yes, she was. This has been really hard on her. Of course, she's very upset about this whole thing, and I've never tried to hide it or anything else. I remember one time she said to me, "Now, tell me, Rick, you're just on vacation from the church for a while, right?" I said, "Yes, that's right, Mom." So she still thinks I'm going to come back. And she's always asking, "Do you still believe in this? What do you think?" She was always very disappointed in me, I think.

What do you tell her when she asks you that?

She doesn't ask me anymore. I used to just say, "Well, yes, I don't know where I am, Mom."

Is that the way you feel now?

I really don't know where I am. I still go back to my basic tenet that made me get started—it doesn't fit. If this doctrine and what you need to do to get into the Celestial Kingdom is so important—the whole reason we're here—why does such a small number of people ever hear about it? And doing it when you're dead—I mean, that's a cop out. I don't think that's a good explanation. So where am I? Do I go clear to the end ... that there is no God? And this is the only life we have, and there is no afterlife? Well, I don't think I'm ready to accept that. I think we all have this hope that there's life after death, but I don't think it's the Celestial Kingdom. I don't know what it is. I can't see us all sitting on clouds playing harps either. So I'm not sure what's going to happen. It's real easy to say, No, this is it. Once you die, you're dead. But I think there's something in me that just said, Oh, there's got to be something after this life.

Could you conceive of a time when you might become active?

I don't know. I've thought about that. It would be real easy, I guess, if you were in a circumstance that you started going to church and doing everything again. I'm sure I could go through the motions. I don't think that would be a problem. I mean, I could sure give up drinking ... I'd hate to because I think that's an enjoyable part of life; I don't see anything wrong with it. I'm certainly not an alcoholic nor do I abuse it. But I could give it up, and I could go to church again, but I don't think my heart would be in it. I think I'd have the same doubts or questions.

On the other hand, could you see asking that your name be removed from the rolls?

I've never felt that I needed to do that. I guess if they came to me and said, "We're going to take you off. Do you have any objections?" I'd say, "No, that's fine." I think my wife would in a minute, but I just never felt the need to do that. For some reason, I don't want to go ask them. When we first moved to where we live now, the ward teachers used to come, and we went through several ward teachers. Pretty soon they stopped coming. They'd given up on us. Then all of a sudden a couple weeks ago, some people came and said, "We're your ward teachers." I said, "Fine."

Do you invite them in?

Oh, yes. We have good relationships with our neighbors, and I think they just all accept me as I'm not going to be coming to church.

Do you get any spiritual nurturing from anything else?

I don't think so. I think I enjoy life, and I'm very active in sports. In fact, many of my friends think I have the lifestyle they'd all like to have. I go skiing three times a week and play golf pretty near every day in the summer and take a lot of vacations, and enjoy intellectual pursuits. One of the real attractions for medicine for me was the great intellectual pursuit. There are new things coming out all the time. I enjoy reading the medical journals and keeping up with the new techniques and diagnoses in medicine. To me, that intellectual pursuit has sort of taken the place of religion. I enjoy everything—not just medicine. I like to read, and history's always been a fascination. My wife and I love to travel. When I was in the air force in England, we traveled all over Europe and England. Part of that was learning. I really enjoy that intellectual pursuit. In fact, it's gotten to the point that I can't read fiction anymore.

It's difficult to return to fiction after you've been deeply involved in something wonderful in biography or non-fiction.

In fact, my wife is discouraged because she says I don't read like I used to, because I used to read fiction all the time. It was mostly because I was going through all the famous literature. I just can't read the new stuff at all. I mean, I've read about airplanes, and it's boring. I'm back to the same thing with church—it's boring. So she's upset because I don't read much. But what I do is read magazines and newspapers. It's that kind of thing that I enjoy reading now. I joke and say, I'm a born-again hedonist. Now sports or activities and travel and food and wine, they are the good things in life. That's what gives me enjoyment or intellectual stimulation. I guess that's taken the place of this spiritualism. I don't notice a lack. I don't feel like there's something missing in my life. I'm afraid to say that maybe my original approach to religion was almost more of an intellectual approach. The gospel was quite appealing. I mean, it's a very logical explanation to why we're here. A mystical religion would never appeal to me.

Do you still think you have a basic belief in Joseph Smith's story and the gold plates?

I don't think so, but I don't know. I think one of the very best books I've read about this was the Emma Smith book, *Mormon Enigma*. I also read Fawn Brodie's *No Man Knows My History*, which I thought was an excellent book. How do you logically explain what happened to Joseph Smith? Was it fraudulent? Were these some kind of weird dreams he was having? I don't know. I don't really think the Book of Mormon happened.

You think it was a wonderful, creative mind that ...

Yes. And whether he plagiarized from other people, as has been speculated, or whether he made it all up? Boy, it's hard to believe anybody could make that up. So that's a little bit of a stumbling block. That's a pretty darn good story to make up. But it just doesn't ring true to me. It really doesn't. I mean, the natural explanation of population in North America—of course, if you even want to get into evolution and everything else, it makes so much more sense to me than the creative explanation. Even if you go back to the Mormon explanation of two creations in Genesis. You know, the spiritual and then the physical. That's just once again a cop-out explanation of trying to mesh creativity and evolution. I don't buy that. I think the natural explanation is so much more believable to me. But where do these things come in? Where does Joseph Smith come in, and how does he fabricate the Book of Mormon? That's tough. I don't know. I think there's something more than meets the eye. I can't believe that Joseph Smith set out to defraud people. How he justified this, we'll never know.

How do you think active Mormons view you and others like you? I mean, you're supposed to have seen the light and now you've turned your backs on it. Aren't there some heavy penalties for that?

I think so. I think my mom looks at me sort of as a lost soul. She thinks I'm going to come back. My wife and I were talking about it this morning. It seems like when we grew up Mormonism was a much gentler religion than it is now. People were just a little more liberal. I grew up in a neighborhood that—I hate to say this, but they were pretty wealthy. They were all good businessmen. I'm afraid six days a week they were sort of quasi-crooked. They knew they had their faults, so they came to church realizing they were sinners and trying to do the best they could. I'm afraid today that the people I know who live around us—they all think they're perfect. They don't make mistakes any more. They just go to religion to gloat with each other about how perfect they are. They're very intolerant of any other idea. Whereas, when I grew up it was a much gentler religion. People were extremely tolerant. They looked at each other as sinners, and everybody would try to do the best they could. We'd have a good time and people would swear and get mad at each other and accept mistakes. I think people are extremely fanatical about it today. I think they look at us with a real disdain and think that we've really fallen off—especially when we've had the knowledge and then given it up. I think they really think we're the worst of sinners. I think my neighbors think that.

Do you ever have any pangs of guilt?

No, I don't think so. I think I did at some time. I keep thinking, Gosh, have I thrown this all away? My chance at the Celestial Kingdom or whatever. Then I have one consoling thought that seems real strange. It's that, "Boy, if the people in the Celestial Kingdom are some of the same people I see in my neighborhood, I don't really want to be with them." I think my friends whom I play golf and ski with—I'd much rather spend eternity with them than these fanatical, hypocritical people who live around me and profess to be good Mormons.

If I were president of the Mormon church, would you have anything to say to me?

I'd ask you about this situation: How come so few people ever get exposed to the doctrine if it's so darned important? And you can't tell me that just doing the work for the dead in the Millennium's going to make up for these millions and millions of people who lived in China and Asia and Africa that have never heard of Jesus Christ or the Mormon religion or, you know, the doctrine. And the reason we're here. It seems to me that it just doesn't fit. I'd like to hear his explanation.

Would you ask him to change anything?

My dad always said if he was to become president of the church, the first thing he'd do is he'd kill the Word of Wisdom. So that would be a start.

I have only one other question: What have you done about religious training for your two children?

Very interesting. One of the jokes we had one time ... We were sitting around the table and my boy who was about seven or eight at the time said, "Now what's that church they've assigned us to?" We're always joking about that. Neither one has been baptized, which is much to my mom's chagrin. We've just let them be. My daughter, who's a very interesting person—she's twenty and now in college—is very much an atheist, very much so, and very anti- ... she thinks the Mormons are really silly and stupid. So she's a real interesting person. Extremely opinionated. We always joke that Katie has no gray in her life. Everything's black and white, and it's nice to live in a world like that where there's no gray—but it's certainly hard to live with her. All her friends have been Mormon, but she very much doesn't want anything to do with the Mormon church. My son—most all his friends go to church and they're all going to be going on missions. But he just has no interest. He's never gone to church; he doesn't want to. He thinks life's real good the way it is, and why burden yourself with having to go to church.

12.

Paul Rolly

Do not go gentle into that good night.
Rage, rage against the dying of the light.

—*Dylan Thomas*

Paul Rolly attended Uintah Elementary School, Wasatch Junior High School, and Skyline High School in Salt Lake City. "I was sort of a juvenile delinquent in high school, so I agreed to go to junior college military academy in Lexington, Missouri, called Wentworth, where I found out I liked learning." Graduating from Wentworth, Paul returned to Salt Lake City and graduated from the University of Utah with a bachelor's degree in political science. He started as a copy boy at The Salt Lake Tribune, *working on staff for ten years. Then for three years he worked at the Salt Lake Bureau of United Press International before returning to the* Tribune.

At the Tribune *he has been an obituary writer, night police reporter, general assignment reporter, assistant business editor, assistant city editor, legislative, state government, and political reporter, as well as having served a stint as business editor. Since the early 1990s he has been writing the "Rolly and Wells" column for the* Tribune *with JoAnn Jacobsen Wells. He also writes a behind-the-scenes Sunday column, "The Rolly Report."*

Paul is recipient of a Freedom of Information Award from the Soci-

ety of Professional Journalists (S.P.J.) for a series of articles he wrote on corruption in Daggett County. He is also winner of a first place S.P.J. Award for reporting on the LDS church's role in killing the "Fun Bus" bill in the state legislature. He has served as president of the board of the Utah Headliners Chapter, S.P.J.

Paul has a ruddy complexion and steady, dark eyes. We sit across from one another in a booth at Lamb's Grill, two doors south of the Tribune's *downtown Salt Lake City offices. The interview takes place over breakfast. Paul wears a bleached denim shirt with a black turtleneck, and his gray-streaked brown hair is parted almost down the middle, with waves flowing back from his forehead. I've forgotten a blank tape, and am wondering if I'll be able to find one at 7:30 in the morning. Then I remember the cassettes in my car, and I sacrifice a Prokofiev for Rolly.*

Paul begins, and as he talks, a piece of fried egg remains poised on his fork for fully five minutes before he finally consumes it.

~

I miss my writing.

You've got community demands on you now as a columnist?

Yes. Jo—JoAnn Jacobsen Wells—and I speak a lot. Rotary Clubs, Kiwanis Clubs, all of that stuff.

You were born in San Francisco.

I was born actually in Sausalito. Almost underneath the Golden Gate Bridge, there's a little army fort on a little peninsula on the Sausalito side called Fort Baker. It's closed now. My dad was a career army guy.

What year?

In 1948. My mother was a WAC [Women's Army Corps]. My parents met in New York. My dad retired from the army when I was nine months old. He'd been in the army for twenty-two years. So he was twelve years older than my mother when I was born. At the end of the war, he was stationed in the Philippines after we took them from the

Japanese. His career was basically in the military police service. And he was an associate or assistant commandant of a Japanese prisoner of war camp in the Philippines. Then he stayed there for some time after the war, because it took a while to process the Japanese and send them home. He came back to the States several months after the war ended. He and my mother got married about a year later. My mother grew up in Salt Lake. My dad was an orphan and kind of grew up all over the place. He joined the army when he was sixteen years old, and the army was basically his life and his family.

He wasn't from Utah?

No. He grew up in an orphanage in Pennsylvania. Anyway, they got married. His last assignment before he retired was in California. That's where I was born. Then as soon as he retired, he had to think about what he was going to do in civilian life. My mother was from Salt Lake City. She had two brothers and her father died within a three-year period, so she wanted to come home to be close to her mother. I was nine months old when they came back to Salt Lake. Then my dad embarked on a bunch of careers. He was very, very political in the Democratic party. My grandmother was a very staunch Mormon—she was a product of polygamy—from Spring City, Utah. She came from this very devout, pioneer-type Mormon background. For my mother, by the time she got to be an adult, the church wasn't important to her, although she'd been brought up in the church. She was basically Jack Mormon. When she married my dad, it completed that break, because my dad was totally non-religious ... never had any respect or anything to do with the Mormon church.

Did he denigrate it?

Yes, he made fun of it. He was pretty abrupt to ward teachers who would come over and try and convert him. So I grew up in a schizophrenic way because I spent a lot of time as a small child with my grandmother. Both my parents always worked. From the time I was in kindergarten, I can remember getting into Uinta Elementary School, getting out of class on Fifteenth East, taking a bus downtown, and then walking to my grandmother's place in the Belvedere Apartments. Everybody in the Belvedere Apartments was Mormon. They all belonged to the same ward; they were all old.

At the corner of State Street and Social Hall Avenue.

Exactly. I was the star of Belvedere Apartments, because I was five, six, seven years old. All these people were in their seventies and eighties. My grandmother knew everybody in the apartments. They went to church together. A lot of them had worked in the Church Office Building together. My grandmother worked in the Church Office Building—her career. They always really liked me, and they always had candy for me. So I was having a really good time there. I knew exactly what apartments to knock on in the Belvedere and who had the best stashes of candy. My grandmother also took me to dinner a lot at the Hotel Utah, at the coffee shop. She knew David O. McKay, the president of the church at the time; Hugh B. Brown who I was brought up to believe was some messiah because he was a Mormon general authority and a Democrat. My grandmother was a New Deal Democrat even though she was a very staunch Mormon. My parents ... their religion basically was really the Democrat party. But then my mother would make me go to church, pretty much to appease her mother. So I would go to church, and at the breakfast table and dinner table I would hear the opposite from what I heard when I would go to church, because most of the people at church were Republicans and conservatives. I would go to church and hear about how people like my parents were evil people and had the devil inside of them. When I got a little older and could start thinking for myself, I basically reached a crossroads where I had to decide whether my parents were bad people or whether the people in the church were full of shit. I chose the latter. Part of what helped me along with that decision was, from the time I was about ten or eleven years old, I noticed things when I'd go to church that I didn't like. I still believe that the Mormon young boy's clubs, and Primary, and then Mutual, and then Cub Scouts and Boy Scouts, can be the most vicious, mean groups of people around.

How's that?

When I was a kid, my parents didn't go to church. That was complicated by the fact that my Cub Scout leader was also the ward teacher assigned to my family. He would come over and try and get my dad to go to church, because my dad had no religious affiliation. Because I went to church, they felt that he could be a prime guy to convert. My dad basically told them to leave him alone. In fact, he very bluntly told them to leave him alone. So this guy decided to take it out on me, because I was this helpless kid. So I go to Cub Scouts, and then this guy would single me out for things. You know, my uniform wasn't right, I wasn't paying attention. You know, I'm not a good member of the church, I had my eyes open during the prayer. Then the other kids in Cub Scouts would pick up on this. Couple that with the fact that I was the only kid in that group whose parents didn't go to church, I got picked on a lot.

At that age peer groups can be so important.

Yes. We moved when I was eleven, and we moved into a brand new neighborhood where homes were just being built—out in Holladay, out by where Skyline High School is. At that time there were still mostly fields. New construction was just happening, so all the homes were new. I happened to be on a block where probably half the families were Catholic.

By then you were baptized?

Yes, I was baptized when I was eight.

Because your mother ...

Because my mother thought that was important, and basically she wanted to do it to appease her mother. Even though my mother didn't go to church, and she didn't like it for her—in fact, she couldn't stand it, going to church.

But she sent you?

Made me go. So some resentment developed that way. Plus, it was interesting, because when I was eleven and twelve years old, there were several Catholic families on my block. One of them, the Smiths, had a boy a year older than me and a girl a year younger than me—they had about four or five kids. They got to be very good friends of my parents. The mother was very, very beautiful. She died of a brain tumor. The dad mourned. He developed a fairly serious drinking problem right around that time because he had a hard time losing her.

The husband?

Right. He had a proclivity toward that kind of lifestyle anyway. So here's this sort of hard drinking guy who just lost his wife, has kids my age. He's very into sports. His kids went to Judge Memorial High School when they got older. They went to parochial school all their lives. He was a coach in a Catholic youth organization football league, and his kid was the quarterback. Here was a guy who had these problems. And, of course, if you're brought up as a Mormon and stuff, you look at a guy like him and think he's a piece of shit as a human being. He was the warmest, nicest guy to me you could ever imagine. He'd take me with him to the football games. They had father and son things at St. Ambrose that he would take me to as well. Everybody there was really nice to me. I mean, I could never be a Catholic. But by the time I was ten or eleven the whole notion of church was just something I didn't want to pursue. It was a negative force to me. I wasn't interested in any church. But it wasn't lost on me that the people who were the nicest to me when I was a young boy were Catholics who had drinking problems. The people who weren't nice to me and who I thought were cruel and vicious were Mormons who lived this so-called righteous lifestyle. So as I grew up and got older, I became very anti-Mormon. My dad was pretty anti-Mormon, so I got that influence a lot, even though on the other side I loved my grandmother very much, and I got a heavy dose of Mormonism from her. When I became real negative toward the Mormon church, it never affected my affection for her and my love for her and a lot of her friends who were so good to me when I was a little boy. I think that influence enabled me to soften my feelings as I got a little more mature toward the whole thing and have an understanding toward the Mormon mentality, even though it's something that I can never imagine myself embracing.

My first marriage lasted twenty-one years. I don't know how this happened because, at the time I got married, I was very anti-Mormon. I was twenty-three years old, and I was at the height of my anti-Mormon period. I had a habit of making fun of Mormons, making fun of BYU, told BYU co-ed jokes, and all that. But I met and married a woman who, even though she wasn't real active herself, came from a blue-blood Mormon family. To give an example: My wife's great-grandfathers were Joseph Fielding Smith and Heber J. Grant, both past presidents of the church. On her mother's side, her grandmother's brother was LeGrand Richards. That's what I married into. It was very strenuous the first few years. But even though I'm divorced from her, I still have affection for my in-laws. Her brother's kids still call me Uncle Paul. There's a good relationship there. As I've gotten older, I've developed a real affection for them, and I see the goodness in them. When we were first married, it was a strenuous relationship because they, like most staunch Mormons in Utah I've known, basically have very strong opinions about everything. Their opinions are such that if you don't share those opinions, you're not only wrong, you're evil. I never could handle that. A lot of times I'd become exactly what I hated, and that was an intolerant person who went out of my way to give shit to somebody who didn't believe the way I did—and that is to give shit to Mormons. This arrogance that they had ... I actually would be the same way, except in the opposite direction. My in-laws, for example, were staunch Republicans, so even when I knew better, I would taunt Republicans, taunt conservatives, taunt Mormons. I remember comments I used to make about Ezra Taft Benson. All my life growing up, Ezra Taft Benson was like the anti-Christ. Suddenly I'm married and I'm in my in-laws' house, and Ezra Taft Benson is like God. So there was a bit of a culture shock that I had to deal with, because I'm suddenly having Sunday dinner with my in-laws and the whole conversation is just the opposite of everything that I'd been brought up to believe. As I got older, I softened and then became more tolerant.

I think that's helped me as a reporter. You hear all the time that the news media is supposed to ignore the Mormon church as a social and political institution. I disagree with that. The Mormon church is the most important social and political institution in Utah, and if you're going to be a responsible reporter, you can't ignore the Mormon church.

Besides that, it's fascinating.

Yes. So I've got a strong feeling that way. The fact that I spent so much time with people whom I came to love, people who were very staunch Mormons and came from the point of view that the Mormon church can never do anything wrong, and nobody should ever criticize it or question it. I spent a lot of time with people with that mentality. These are people who for a good part of my adult life were very important people. On the other hand, I grew up with people who questioned everything about the Mormon church. One of those people was my mother who'd been brought up a Mormon herself. So I've had very close, long-term associations with those opposite points of view.

Did you ever feel conflicted?

From the time I was twelve years old, it was clear-cut to me. I kept going to church until I was sixteen, but I didn't like it and I had no respect for it and had no respect for the people who were there teaching it. So I never had internal conflict.

Did you ever rebel openly?

Very much.

How?

I started smoking when I was fifteen years old. As I look back on that, the reason I did that was to show people that I wasn't Mormon. The whole Mormon thing was the main reason I did that, because I remember it took me six months to inhale a cigarette without throwing up. I went through this hell in order to get this habit which was inflicting horrible things on my body, and it was basically to show that I wasn't a Mormon. I started drinking beer when I was sixteen. By the time I was sixteen, I used to go to church with a pack of Lucky Strikes in my shirt pocket. I wanted everybody to know. The final separation—and I initiated it—happened when I was sixteen and I had to go to the bishop for an interview to become a priest. They ask you all these personal questions in these interviews. Well, all the kids my age would go in there and they'd just lie. I mean, he'd ask them stuff, and whether they did it or not, they'd say, "No." They did that, and everybody knew it. I think the bishop knew it. It was just this phony game that everybody played. So when I went in there, I decided I wasn't going to lie. I was going to be absolutely truthful with this guy. I had no respect for him anyway. He eventually ended up getting excommunicated and his wife divorced him because he had an affair with the Relief Society president. These were the sorts of things that I would notice when I was growing up. It really gave me a negative attitude toward the LDS church.

So, anyway, I go into this interview. There's a lot of small talk involved and a lot of nothing-type questions. Then you get to the tough questions, and he kind of interspersed them. The first tough question was, "Have you ever smoked cigarettes or tobacco?" I said, "Yes." I think I was the first person to ever say that to him—you know, looking him squarely in the eye. All of a sudden, he's the one who became nervous. He went on this long thing about how I need to quit doing that, and the Lord loves me, and he, the bishop, loves me, and everybody loves me, and all this kind of stuff. And this was a habit that I needed to stop, and I should go home and pray about it. It's all going over my head, because by this time in my life I'm looking at this guy thinking he's a piece of shit. A few more small talk questions, and then we get to another tough question. "Have you ever taken alcohol?" "Yes, I drink beer when I can, and sometimes I sneak a little vodka out of my dad's liquor cabinet. Yes, I like it." Once again he's shuffling his feet, he's looking down like, "How do I deal with this kid?" And I'm not apologetic. I don't feel remorseful at all, so he's getting more and more nervous, and little beads of sweat are starting to pop up on him. It was clear to me that he didn't know how to deal with this kind of honesty. Then he gives me the same rigamorole again. Everybody loves me, the Lord loves me, and go home and pray and never do this again. He'll forgive me and I can still become a priest. So we're going on and we're getting to the big one. Because of my previous answers, I could tell this guy did not want to ask this question. He's shuffling his feet, and these little beads of sweat are popping up on his forehead. He finally gets to it. He has to ask it. He says, "Have you ever had sexual intercourse with a girl?" I'm being totally honest in this interview. I said, "No." He goes, "Phew," sighs, and all this stuff. Then I said, "But I'd really like to." That pretty much was the final straw that severed me from the LDS church.

Then I married this woman who was from this very blue-blooded Mormon family. She had a million cousins whom I liked, who were very nice, and they were very nice to me, and we had cousin parties. They were fun and I enjoyed them. I was the only guy there who hadn't gone on a mission. My wife and I were the only couple there who wasn't married in the temple. But they were pretty nice to me anyway, for the most part. There were a couple cousins who were jerks. I developed a softening in that marriage. Then I had kids. I had four kids, and, of course, they had heavy Mormon influence from all their cousins and grandparents and everything else. In some ways, they had the same upbringing as I did, because they had me there to kind of pummel their little brains with Democratic philosophy and liberal philosophy and principles and anti-Mormon talks. Then at the same time their Mormon influence was strong because they had so many relatives who were very, very Mormon, and they spent so much time with them. They all had cousins their own age and they were all their best friends growing up. It's interesting. My two boys aren't Mormon. My two girls are very Mormon. My daughter got married in the Mormon temple. I've got another daughter who went on a mission to Russia.

Did you help pay for it?

I paid for half of it.

You talked about your anti-Mormon days in your twenties. Clearly you've mellowed since then ...

I see a lot of sincere, wonderful, nice people in the LDS church today—who are as good a people as there are. My daughter married into a very Mormon family, and I couldn't be more pleased with the family she married into. I don't think she could've married into a better family, and they're really wonderful to her, and they're really nice people. When my daughter became engaged to this boy, his parents wanted to get to know me, and I wanted to get to know them, because we were going to share our children. So I had them over to dinner, and they had us over to dinner, and I really liked them. My former in-laws, even though I was kind of mean to them when I was younger—I have come to respect them and have warm feelings for them. In my adult life, I've gotten to know people who are staunch LDS who I really like. When I was young, it wasn't like that. Even the people who were good in the Mormon church—and I still feel this way—that I was treated very badly by a lot of Mormons when I was younger. At the time I saw it as an exclusively Mormon trait to be cruel. As I've gotten older, I see that more as a typical trait among particularly boys when they're in their puberty years, where there's a tight-knit club—when they're thrown together in any kind of a tight-knit club where they have this common club mentality. Now I don't think it's an exclusive Mormon trait. At the time, I did.

As a reporter, what do you see happening with the church and with Utah today?

I think the church has more of a positive influence than it does a negative influence. There are some aspects of a negative influence. But, you know, I don't see that from the top so much. I think when Ezra Taft Benson was the president of the church, even though he was incapacitated his last few years, it became very right wing. I see [church president Gordon B.] Hinckley as a calming, moderating influence, and I actually have a lot of respect for Gordon Hinckley. I think he's probably a great man.

Do you think there's a connection between being inactive in the church and being liberal?

I think there's a relationship there, and I think in Utah you're going to find a lot more Jack Mormons who are liberal than you are who are conservative. Conservatism, I don't think it's an institutionalized thing. I just think it's something that a great many individual Mormons have, and then it becomes kind of a club thing or a group thing in the ward environment where they talk about it. You know, you're growing up in a church that says you can't be a liberal and be a Mormon. I know a lot of Mormon Democrats. Kelly Atkinson, for example, who tried to run for Congress. Grant Protzman and Scott Howell [state legislators], who are active Mormons, get shit in church for being active Democrats. Now the other side of the coin is they get shit in the Democratic party for being Mormons.

With Gordon B. Hinckley as church president, do you think any inactives will return to the church?

Maybe some. It depends on where you are in your Jack Mormonism, you know.

Could you ever return to active Mormonism?

No, there's no way I could ever go back to Mormonism. On the other hand, I'm already in a position where I in many ways support Mormonism. My missionary daughter, for example. I'm sure that my grandkids born to my daughter who just got married are going to be brought up very Mormon. That's going to be important to my daughter, and it's going to be important to my son-in-law, and I'm going to make sure that I won't do anything to interfere with that. I'll even be careful not to share my personal beliefs about that with my grandkids, because I wouldn't want to interfere with my daughter and the way she wants to bring up her kids. But I personally could never do it. I've got my own beliefs.

Do you consider yourself a spiritual person?

Yes. I do consider myself a spiritual person.

Do you believe in a higher power?

Yes, and I believe in an afterlife, and I believe that things we do in this life can affect our afterlife. I've kind of got my own set of beliefs that aren't based in any religion, but they'd probably be closer to Buddhism than anything else.

I don't rule out the possibility of reincarnation. I believe there's a life force. Just like electricity, just like any physical force. I look at the natural beauty of the world. And I look around at the interdependency of life in the food chain, and how every creature on this earth has some kind of a purpose, and it's all interrelated with all the other creatures. I don't believe that could happen haphazardly. I believe that there's a natural law that has made it that way, and it's an intelligent natural law. Then I look at the difference between our species and all the other species, and I believe there's got to be, for lack of a better word, a soul or whatever—some kind of a force that creates that. I think that that force still lives after our bodies die. So that's my belief. I believe there's a higher power or a god, or whatever you want to call it ... you know, an intelligent force that makes sense of it all.

If I were Gordon B. Hinckley, what would you say to me?

I wouldn't have a lot to say to you. You know, I respect you, and to the very important people in my life you are a prophet. To people who are extremely important, whose opinions I will always be respectful of. I think you're a nice man. You don't have any spiritual power or control over me, but that's okay. I'm sure it'll be okay with you, too.

What about his ability to create political change?

I believe Mormon leaders have as much right to state their political opinions as anybody else. I've written about this where sometimes people of the Mormon church abuse that right or abuse that power because of the enormous power and influence of the Mormon church over the hearts and minds of a great deal of the population. It's when they try to affect political change secretly, because they have spiritual power, or whatever kind of power you want to call it, over decision-makers. An example, an illustration of what I'm talking about, is a story that I wrote in the 1980s that I won an award for in investigative reporting. It had to do with a bill that was before the legislature that was called the Fun Bus Bill. In Utah it's illegal to have an open container of alcohol in a moving vehicle. But this bill would've made an exception for the buses that go out to Wendover and the limousines and chauffeur-types of services where if you're not driving, and you've hired a chauffeur-type limousine or a bus or whatever, you can drink in that vehicle because you're being chauffeured by somebody else. It had the support of everybody. It had the support of Governor Bangerter; the economic development people liked it because it probably would help tourism. Law enforcement liked it because it probably would help get the drunk from behind the wheel and in the back of a chauffeured vehicle. So everybody liked it. The thing sails through the committee, sails through the house, goes over to the Senate, and all of a sudden it sits in the Senate Rules Committee for six weeks. The reason it sat in the Rules Committee for six weeks is because a couple people in the Mormon church told a couple of influential Republicans in the Senate that they didn't want that bill to pass. But they didn't say so publicly. Nobody said anything about it publicly. Finally, enough pressure was put on the Rules Committee that forced them to kick the bill out. It comes out on the board the last day of the session. It comes out about ten o'clock in the morning, so it's got all day sitting on the board. The Senate addresses bills in the order they appear on the board. So they're getting close to voting on this bill. Well, you know, nobody wants to vote against this bill publicly, because it's going to make them look stupid because everybody in the world supports this bill, including Governor Bangerter and law enforcement, and nobody's ever spoken out against it. So two key senators got a call from Dick Lindsey and Bill Evans of the Mormon church saying the church doesn't want this bill passed. Steven Reese, one of the guys who got the call—the other guy was Arnold Christensen, the president of the Senate—Steven Reese got up and said, "I move that we circle the bill because I've got a couple of questions. I want to see what the other state senators ..." They vote to circle the bill and move on to other bills. Well, it's getting later and later in the evening. Omar Bunnell—a Mormon, as well—goes over to Reese and says, "When are you going to uncircle this bill?" He says, "Well, I'm still checking on it." It was a ploy to kill this bill without ever voting on it. So Bunnell kept raising his hand to be recognized by the Senate president so he could make a motion to uncircle the bill and vote on it. Christensen ignored him. For two hours he ignored Bunnell, never recognized him. Bunnell was never able to make the motion, and the bill died. Then I found out about the telephone calls and did a series of stories on it. Now that's bad. When that happens, I think it's the press's responsibility to point it out and to make it public. On the other hand, I think that if Dick Lindsey and Bill Evans and Gordon B. Hinckley and anybody else, if they wanted to stand up and say, "I believe this way," I think they've got every right in the world to say that. I think that the hierarchy of the LDS church in recent years has been very responsible in the way that it has tried to remain neutral, and they send out a statement every year telling members to vote their conscience, and any way they vote is okay. They take no position or anything else. I think there's more pressure put on members at the ward level. I don't really fault the hierarchy of the LDS church for that. That's individual. Human beings are human beings. And Mormons are human beings like everybody else and suffer the same frailties.

Back when you were sixteen, you were smoking, drinking, not living the Word of Wisdom. Do you live it today?

I drink coffee, but that's it.

No beer, no tobacco?

No, no alcohol.

Was it hard to stop smoking?

No. I quit smoking when my first son was born. It was interesting, because I started smoking when I was fifteen. He was born when I was twenty-five, so I was a heavy smoker for ten years. When I made the decision to quit smoking, I quit smoking. I didn't do patches. I didn't cut down. I didn't do anything else. I just quit. That was it. Then I never smoked again, and that was twenty-six years ago. When I quit drinking, that was more complicated because I'd gotten a DUI. Then I realized that maybe I had a problem, because I was drinking a lot. So I quit drinking. But I had to make the decision that I needed to quit drinking. Once I made that decision, I quit. I didn't go through AA and all that other stuff. But I used to get drunk a lot. I've got memories of feeling out of control and some days wondering what I'd done the night before—if I did anything bad, did anything to offend anybody. One of the things I really love about not drinking is the feeling of always being in control. In fact, I've become addicted to that. I like to go to bars and watch the Utah Jazz on a big screen. I go to bars a lot because a great deal of my work is finding out things that are going on and talking to movers and shakers and talking with people behind scenes. The best place you can get that kind of information is in a bar. Usually the people I go in there with will be drinking alcohol, and I'll be drinking soft drinks. I have a distinct advantage. I love the feeling of going home and knowing that I did nothing to embarrass myself or embarrass my employer or embarrass anybody. Another great motivator for never drinking again is the knowledge that if I ever did anything like getting a DUI, it would make the front page of the *Deseret News*. I'd make the day of everybody over there. I'd never want to give them the satisfaction.

I'll tell you one more little anecdote. About three years ago, I did a story because several Democrats who were very strong Mormons were telling me about this. It was right after Clinton was elected. The Mormon church enjoyed a great deal of influence when Reagan and Bush were presidents, especially when Bush was president, his domestic affairs advisor and his foreign affairs advisor were both Mormons. So the church enjoyed a great deal of influence. Then all of a sudden Clinton was elected, and they had no influence with the president or his administration. Suddenly many people in the Mormon church became very concerned that they were perceived too much as a one-party church. They didn't want to be perceived that way. So some people—one of them was Gordon B. Hinckley, another was Jim Faust—met with people like Scott Howell, Bobby Coray, Wayne Owens—staunch Mormon Democrats—and told them they'd like to see more Democrats elected to public office. They didn't say, "We would support you," but certainly gave them the impression that they'd be very happy to see Mormon Democrats run for public office and win, because they wanted to get rid of that image that they were just a Republican church. I thought that was a great story, so I started pursuing it. I talked to several Mormon Democrats who'd been talked to. I called up Don LeFevre, whom I like a lot. He's a great guy, public relations guy for the church. I told him the story and told him I wanted an interview with one of the general authorities on this issue. They didn't really want to talk about it because they like to leave the impression that they never have anything to do at all with politics. You know, talking to Mormon Democrats, obviously, shows they do have something to do with it. It was an issue they didn't want made public. I don't see anything wrong with it. I don't see anything evil in it or anything else, but they were a little uncomfortable with the idea of a story. But I kept pushing and pushing. Finally, I told Don LeFevre that if I didn't get an interview I'd run the story without an interview. So he called me back, and he got me an interview with Jim Faust. I went over to the Church Office Building, met Don LeFevre at the elevator. We went up to the fifth floor, walked in. When I walked in there, he's got his hand out to shake my hand. The first thing he says to me is, "Do you go by Richard or do you go by Paul?" Well, I'd never in my life used my middle name, Richard. My closest friends don't know that my middle name is Richard. I've never used my middle name, and anybody who reads the paper knows that I go by Paul. But that was just his little way of saying, "I've looked you up, I've noticed that you're a member and you're on the books." But it was all with a smile on his face, and it was all pleasant, an interesting way to start a conversation, because the only way he could have known my name was Richard was to check to see if I was on the membership roles. I think he said that to let me know that he's checked and he knows I'm on the roles. I need to tell you that Faust is a great guy. I really liked him. I enjoyed my interview with him. I enjoyed my conversation with him, and we learned in that interview that he and my uncle—my mother's older brother who died of a bad heart when he was thirty years old—were mission companions together.

Have you ever considered asking for excommunication?

No. But if anybody ever wanted to, they could do that. I wouldn't go play their game. I mean, I wouldn't go to a bishop. I wouldn't do any of that stuff. Plus, I don't want to do anything to hurt my kids, either.

How do you think active Mormons view inactives?

It depends on the active members, because I've gotten to know both types very well. There are a lot of active members who view people like me as some kind of scum. I've got painful memories from my childhood of friends telling me they couldn't play with me anymore because my dad smoked. When my son was a little boy, he had friends tell him that they couldn't play with him because his parents didn't go to church. So there are those types. But there are also very active Mormons who don't look down on me. In fact, I think there are a lot of very active Mormons who've got a lot of respect for me, and they treat me that way.

13.

Shauna Adix

Failure is impossible.

—*Susan B. Anthony*
at her 86th birthday celebration, 1906

Shauna Adix has a bachelor of arts degree and a Ph.D from the University of Utah, as well as a master of arts degree from Ohio University. She has been program director of the Jewish Community Center; director of the Brighton MIA Girls' Camp; coordinator of the Project on Aging, Salt Lake Community Services Council; a staff member of the National Training Laboratory; acting chair, Department of Modern Dance, University of Utah; director, Women's Resource Center at the U. of U.; a director of Anytown Utah; a director of HERS/West, U. of U.; director and president, the Virginia Satir Network; dean and faculty member, Inner Light Institute; facilitator, Crone Connection; president, Crones Counsel, Inc. She was executive vice president of et al., inc., a Salt Lake City advertising agency, and was national president of Mortar Board, Inc. She has received awards from Women Helping Women, Soroptomist International, Rocky Mountain Region-Salt Lake Chapter. She was a 1980 recipient of the Susa Young Gates Award.

Shauna's a woman who thrives and grows by taking on new interests. Her dark blue eyes well with tears when we talk about death, and she speaks lovingly of her father, Frank McLatchy, who was sales manager at KSL almost until his death in 1954. Wearing a crew-neck sweater, and sporting white hair cropped short, she settles into a sofa in the living room of her home, built on Salt Lake City's east bench in 1912. We reminisce about her late husband, Vern Adix, also a professor at the University of Utah, who taught drama there. We explore some personal history before the interview begins; she self-consciously adjusts her posture to keep from folding her arms over the microphone. The ticking of a grandmother clock (her designation) punctuates the silences as she considers her answers.

~

One could pay a high price for sounding as though one is speaking against the church when you're speaking your own truth. That's one of the problems about church membership—that it calls you to ignore your own truth so much of the time to heed to what the brethren say.

Interesting. Do you think that's why I find that more women than men—especially women in the arts—decline my requests for interviews?

I think I can tell you exactly. Women in general, regardless of their religious backgrounds, have been subservient to the desires and the dictates of men—their husbands, their fathers, their religious advisors. I bet some of those in the arts are connected to men who've said they don't think it's a good idea for them to participate. They're not going to stand up against those men. I think there's both a real and sometimes an imagined penalty for speaking out. It's much harder for women to speak out than for men. Sonia Johnson is an example of that. I had dinner with her shortly before they called her excommunication trial. Several of us encouraged her not to go, expecting what was coming. She said, "Don't be silly; this isn't a religious matter." We all saw what happened to her. I have an idea that many of the women in the church don't call themselves feminists because somehow that sounds too liberal. Many women who do call themselves feminists saw what happened to her. I think it's not clear yet if there's too high a price to pay for women to speak publicly about what they feel and believe.

Let's go back to your growing up in Salt Lake City. You were born during the Great Depression. Your father wasn't Mormon.

Right. His story is interesting. Frank McLatchy met Charlotte Ulke in Yellowstone Park in the summer following her graduation from college. He ran the tour buses there and she had a summer job prior to beginning a teaching career in Utah. They were married by summer's end. She came back to begin her teaching job. Before a replacement had been found for her, she discovered she was pregnant. He agreed to come here long enough for her to have their child where she could be with family. They had to wait some months before my older sister was born. He needed a job. This was in the height of the Depression, 1929, after the stock market crash. When he arrived, he began walking the streets looking for work. He went into KSL—for what reasons I don't know or remember—and met Earl J. Glade who was then the manager. He asked for work and was told there were no jobs open, but if he wanted to try to sell some advertising time, he'd be given a commission. That day he sold time to Dinwoodey Furniture Company. That was the beginning of a career for him which lasted his entire worklife in Salt Lake. He never did go to the job awaiting him in South Dakota. I think for me growing up probably had a little different flavor than for people who grew up in homes in which the priesthood was held by the father.

But your mother was active?

My mother was very active. My maternal grandmother lived with us and she was also a staunch believer. My father didn't have a religious background. He didn't go to any church, but he agreed that we should have a religious upbringing, so neither did he balk at our being raised Mormon. The ward was just three houses down the street and we all went. He never joined us unless we were performing or receiving some award. I remember a time when he said if his children attended the ward, he thought he owed the system something. He sometimes served on the ward beautification committee or something that didn't require a testament of faith from him.

Did your mother encourage you to be active?

It was assumed we would be. We just did it. We would march every Sunday to church and Tuesday to Primary and/or Mutual. We lived at what was almost the edge of the city then. People farther out, mostly past 2700 South, were generally living on farms. They were building Highland Park Ward when we moved into the house I grew up in. My parents initially had a house on Highland Drive which they couldn't afford to keep. Next they rented on Alden Street. They bought the house on Stratford and Douglas when I was four or five. My growing up life was spent in that general neighborhood. I left Stratford Avenue to move into this house when I married Vern.

You've essentially lived in two houses your entire life.

Yes. I barely remember Alden Street, so there are just two houses of memory for me. Almost nobody I know has only two houses they've lived in for as long as I've been alive.

You said this wasn't a priesthood house.

My father liked to hunt on weekends. He had poker buddies in once in a while and usually played at someone's house monthly. The rest of us had different things going on, often associated with church. He never sought to undermine whatever we were being taught and always encouraged us in our activities, whether at church or at school. He was supportive without being particularly vocal about it. The irony is that at some point he was asked to join the church by J. Reuben Clark. It was during the time President Clark was in the First Presidency. By then Father was a major official at KSL. He didn't smoke and he didn't drink, at least not in front of any of us. However, he did like to drink coffee and he liked to hunt on Sundays. He said if he were ever to join the church, he felt he needed to do it totally and to practice it wholeheartedly. Since he wasn't interested in giving up coffee or hunting, he said no. Many years later, in the mid-1950s, he was diagnosed with lung cancer. He was never told he had cancer. He lived for two years after that. I had never thought KSL to be particularly magnanimous in their personnel policies, but they were for him at the end. Father thought he should resign because he wasn't able to perform his job the way he felt it should be done. My mother encouraged the manager to accept his resignation because he was in and out of the hospital frequently. The reply was: "No. If we had paid him everything he was worth to us all these years, we might feel that we couldn't afford him now." They gave him tasks which could wait for him to accomplish and kept him on full salary until he died. Every day he could manage it, he would go to work. In the last year of his life, he was sick more than he was well and he was at home most of the time. His longtime

Mormon buddies came regularly to visit him. During the final year he converted and became a member of the church.

This man who wouldn't join because he wouldn't do anything that wasn't totally integral to his personality and sense of complete honesty wouldn't have done that as a deathbed concession to my mother. I'm quite sure he didn't know he was going to die. The church had a policy then which I think is still operant today. There is a year waiting period after someone joins before that person is eligible to go to the temple. That policy was waived for my parents, I suppose, because many had deemed him worthy for a long time. He went through the temple in a wheelchair with my mother on one side and his doctor on the other. Thus it was that my mother realized her lifelong desire for a temple marriage.

You went to Mutual, you went to Sunday School, you did all the things an active little Mormon girl would do?

I paid my tithing, took my pennies to Primary. Absolutely.

At what point did you begin to question?

I could tell you the exact point. It was in a Mutual class. I was newly into Mutual, so I was twelve, thirteen at the most. The lesson was on dating. The teacher asked how many of us would date boys who weren't Mormon. Mine was the only hand that went up. As I think about it now, a kind of diatribe ensued about how foolish that was. If we dated boys who weren't Mormon, we might decide we wanted to marry them, and then we would crumble our eternal cookies, in essence. I remember sitting there that night having no idea what percent of the world's population was Mormon, but it seemed pretty stupid to limit yourself to possibly one-fourth of 1 percent, or whatever the figures might prove to be. That's the point at which I date my beginning to be what I came to call a malcontent Mormon. It seemed to me to be a system that didn't fully honor everything about all the members—like freedom to choose, freedom to date. That was the seed of why I couldn't stay active in the church. It became too limiting.

I progressed through all the stages. I did a lot of active things in and for the church. I spoke in church frequently; I narrated a pageant in the tabernacle for the 50th anniversary of Beehive. I taught and was on the stake Sunday School Board in Highland Stake. When I came here, I taught Mutual and served for many years on the Mutual Stake Board as the drama director. Vern, who wasn't Mormon, sometimes used to get aggravated when the stake secretary would call to find out what my attendance record at meetings had been for the month. He was soft-spoken and non-volatile about almost any issue, but when she called, he'd say in his loudest voice, "Shauna, the Gestapo is on the telephone for you." He helped me in many ways when I was stake drama director by building sets, doing makeup, etc. He even played a role in one production. His support for my activities in the church was very reminiscent of my father. When we adopted our children, Vern agreed to go to Sunday school and other meetings because he thought the children would benefit from that kind of parental modeling. He'd been a Baptist once, but hadn't practiced it or attended for years. Almost invariably when he'd go, if it was a testimony meeting, or even for the two-and-a-half minute talks, someone would say how sorry he/she felt for those who didn't have the truth of the gospel. He resented having people feel sorry for him or look down on him when he felt his life was full and lived well. He soon quit going.

During the early years of my marriage was the time of the Summer Festival—the time when the theater department mounted a musical and an opera on a stage built for that purpose in the north end of the football stadium at the University of Utah. For six of those years, I directed the MIA camp in Brighton and came home on weekends to see the shows. I paid my tithing for years even as my sense of malcontentedness increased. The day finally came when I wondered to myself why I would support with money a system I couldn't support as a belief system. It was the late 1960s by the time I ended any tangible support for the church.

You quit paying tithing about then?

Sometime around there. I still believe in the principle of tithing. I give away 10 percent of what I have even now, but I like to decide where it goes. I think that's not a bad thing to do, to share what you have with others who can use it.

There are many nice things about Mormonism. We'll get back to those in a minute. I have another question for you. Do you still consider yourself a spiritual person?

I do consider myself a spiritual person. I do not consider myself a religious person. I think religion often drives the spiritual sense right out the window by the call to adherence to form and structure that doesn't allow for one's own sense of connection or growth.

You haven't joined another religion though?

I did join the Inner Light Center from which the Inner Light Institute, which I helped create, grew. The institute is the teaching arm of the center. I was invited to join when the Inner Light Center began a few years ago. I said I'd be glad to join if they didn't expect me to be there all the time. They don't care what other affiliations people have. It wasn't a conversion experience. I liked what they stand for and the openness with which they operate. I liked the fact that they didn't have any dogma to espouse, didn't require you to believe in anything but values like goodness, harmony, truth.

Not exactly an organized religion?

No. They call themselves a spiritual community. They believe in love and peace and harmony and oneness of all with each other and Mother Earth. They affirm those values and want to assist people in helping find them as they can and will.

Were you nurtured by your Mormonism when you were growing up?

Oh, I'm sure I was. Whether I was nurtured socially or spiritually is a little hard to say now because the ward was the social center of my neighborhood. There were a few non-Mormons, but we didn't know them well. All the kids my age were Mormon as far as I can remember. The ward show was the big social event on Friday nights. We would've been very isolated in our neighborhood were it not for the social culture of the Mormon church, so I was certainly nurtured that way. I didn't think a lot about spiritual growth and attainment in those days. When I decided to marry Vern, a lot of neighbors and Mormon friends were worried about my future since he wasn't Mormon. They worried because of the notion of eternal progression which they thought I'd be foreclosing for myself. I was kind of relieved, actually, because I wanted to see how things would work out prior to signing on for all eternity, should the Mormon system prove to be right.

You had no conflicts?

Not about that, no. I don't know when I first thought about it, but my sense was that if this whole thing works, if what the Mormons believe about all the degrees of glory really happens, I'd rather be pruning the vineyards with people more like me than with people like some I know who think they're headed for the Celestial Kingdom. It seems to me that if that system were to be true, which I had serious doubts about, then there certainly ought to be a worthwhile place for someone who tried to live a life as thoughtfully and as spiritually and with as much sense of doing no harm as I could figure out. I used to hate to go to Mormon funerals where people would extol about the life of the deceased for having made a wonderful place in heaven. I disliked the notion that doing everything here was for some future glory. It seemed to me what we did here ought to make sense here and now. I didn't have any need to travel to the Celestial Kingdom. I thought I'd be more at home in one of the lower realms if degrees of glory actually were proven to exist.

Back then, did it ever strike you as unfair that you had to be married to a worthy male to make it to the Celestial Kingdom?

I don't know that it struck me then. It certainly struck me subsequently. I don't know that I would've embarked on a career, as one university professor saw it, as the University's "resident feminist" if I hadn't been aware of gender imbalances and discrimination. I didn't put it in a religious context then, but, yes, I suppose if there has been one thing that has really lighted and emblazoned my professional life and which made me more discontent with Mormonism than I already was, it was how restrictive Mormonism was to women. Vern and I didn't have a lot of conversations about religion. I didn't have any need for him to convert to something which didn't speak to the fullness of who I was. I remember the day, however, when he found out that in the temple ceremony a man could have more than one wife, but a woman couldn't have more than one husband. He suggested I ought to be willing to do battle against such patent injustice. I explained I didn't feel I had the tools or entree to take that one on.

I'll tell you about another time. A psychologist called me when I was at the Women's Center, someone I didn't know. He said he had a client he didn't know how to help and kept asking for referral names. Mine kept coming up. He asked me if I'd see her. The issue was that she and the man she was then married to had each been married to somebody else at the time they became intimately involved with each other. She became pregnant. Each of them left their first spouse and was married. At some point they felt guilty about their behavior and reported it to a bishop. The second husband was serving on the stake high council at the time. Separate bishop's courts were called for these two. He was disfellowshipped and she was excommunicated. She went wild. She didn't mind having justice meted out for their mutual transgression, but the fact that her punishment was different, to say nothing of being more severe, from his, just made her crazy. I saw her for several weeks. She finally worked through her frustration and anger. Last I heard, which was some years ago, she'd worked herself back into the church because that had become important to her again. Those kinds of stories make me a little crazy, too. I want to believe in a system that is love and not punishment, understanding and not censure, opportunity and not limitation. I just found too many limits for me and others—particularly women—to make it feel it was the place that fostered and nurtured my own growth.

What good qualities does Mormonism foster?

When the systems implicit within the ward structure really work for everyone in the ward, this is good. I think the bishop is the key to this. When caring is stronger than the letter of the law, especially when it's made available to the entire neighborhood comprising the ward boundaries, then it can be a very nurturing environment. Ward people often come to help others in times of trouble. It would be nice if it happened as a neighborly gesture on a regular basis. If the potential power of the two monthly home visits from the Relief Society and the priesthood was used not so much to teach a lesson, but really to find out what might be valuable assistance to neighbors, greater good might come forth. If we were as interested in living the lessons of the gospel as in preserving the ethnocentricity of the belief system, I believe everyone could benefit—including neighbors who aren't members of the faith, if they so desired.

I sat next to Apostle Mark E. Peterson on a plane once when I was working in the field of aging. I discussed with him how wonderful I thought it would be if the wards could be used as senior centers when not busy with regular ward activities. It seemed to me that a beneficial result of the power of the church would be to use its facilities for meetings which could help folks despite what their religious training might be. I didn't succeed, as you might've guessed. I understand there would be a number of problems attendant to opening the wards to non-church activities, including financial, custodial, and supervisory, but I'd love to see creative energy applied to exploring ways in which wards could be used to meet the issues faced by members in the community.

One of the recurring themes I heard at the Women's Center was voiced by newcomers to Salt Lake and the university. Many of them had heard horror stories about moving here, about how Mormon neighbors ostracized their non-Mormon neighbors. My sense from hearing these stories was that the Mormons in the neighborhood were often friendly initially in meeting the newcomers and often invited them to join their activities. If the invitation wasn't acted upon, it was often the last attempt at inclusion. Being a Mormon is a full-time job, not just something to do on Sunday. The Mormon neighbors remained busy in their own daily lives which, then, excluded those whose practices were different. The exclusion, it seemed, was usually as much a product of lack of time as of purposeful intent.

Do you find that your friends are more apt to be inactive Mormons or non-Mormons?

I have friends of all kinds.

You don't feel isolated from active Mormons?

No. I don't feel isolated. Some years ago the ward clerk called to tell me the bishop wanted to see me. I could think of a lot of reasons why a bishop might want to see me and none were particularly positive. When we met, he asked if someone in the ward had offended me because I hadn't been present for some time. I responded that the ward members hadn't offended me, but the church had. Some of the things I believe strongly in, the church had taken a public stand against. It seemed to me that to lend my support to a system which denounces things I stand for simply didn't make a good mix.

What were those things?

There were three. I'll tell you about them in a minute. To finish about the interview with the bishop, he said he was pleased I hadn't failed to come because of being offended by anything the ward members had done or said. He assured me that if I ever felt like coming back, I'd be welcome. He also assured me that I was valued as a neighbor. Another example of why I don't feel isolated has to do with a fence in my back yard which divides my property from the ward. A time came when the fence was listing badly and would've fallen on the ward property if it collapsed. I called to inquire whether the ward would be interested in sharing the cost of replacing the fence with me. The answer was no. They sent one of the ward members to shore it up as, I think, they knew Vern was in a nursing home and unable to do maintenance on our property. The next year they put a fence in and didn't ask me to share in the cost. No, I don't feel I've been isolated in my neighborhood.

And the three issues you've felt at variance with the church about?

Lack of support for the Equal Rights Amendment to the Constitution, abortion, and homosexuality.

Do you feel the church is threatened by the women's movement?

Well, it certainly worked hard to defeat the Equal Rights Amendment as far as I'm concerned. Yes, I think it's threatened. Maybe I can illustrate what I mean this way. The Women's Center brought Gloria Steinem here for her first speaking engagement in the state in 1975. That was also the year of the first Women's International meeting in Mexico City. The United Nations declared the decade 1975-85 the decade of women. Conferences were held in Mexico, Kenya, and Denmark as part of the observance. Our annual women's conference followed the Mexico City meeting. They used an open mike process which allowed for individuals to take the microphone and discuss whatever they wished. (Sounds a little like a Mormon testimony meeting, doesn't it?) We incorporated that into our conference as well. Gloria Steinem and I were sitting on the dais together. There were a number of women who identified themselves as students at BYU. Most shared a similar theme, which was that they wanted all gathered to know they were Mormons and they were also feminists. Gloria and I discussed whether we thought one could be a Mormon and a feminist, and we agreed that if feminism were defined as freedom to choose, then one could be a Mormon and anything you choose, so you could be a Mormon and a feminist. However, if you define feminism systemically, as we both did, then feminism requires openness in all systems for all people, regardless of gender, to move as thoroughly and as far as they can. Under those circumstances, you could not be a Mormon and a feminist. Since openness and equality are extremely important to me, you can understand why the church increasingly hasn't had a fit for me.

Another example of a manifest threat, I think, happened with some frequency at the Women's Center. I'd get a call from someone, not infrequently a bishop, who'd report that someone from his ward had decided to get a divorce after seeing one of our staff members. The caller would often lambast the Women's Center for encouraging divorce. All we ever did was try to listen to people and help them make decisions which they felt were right for them. I remember that happening several times. If a ward member's behavior was a violation of whatever the caller thought was proper, then we were viewed as the devil's advocates.

As far as abortion is concerned, I can understand that some men may not want their prospective children to be aborted, but it's the woman's body which is totally involved for nine months. Therefore, if any decision about what to do about a pregnancy is to be made, I believe the woman has the greater reason—and therefore right—to decide. I'm not persuaded that life is really life until it can be viable outside the uterus. As a result, I think the abortion laws as they have been laid down make sense.

Homosexuality deserves support and respect, I believe, because it's the place of belonging for many men and women. Attempts over generations to "cure" it or to stamp it out haven't succeeded. Rather than making the lives of those for whom it is the proper way to live more difficult, we would do well to ensure that those who practice it are afforded the same civil rights the rest of the world enjoys. The negative response by individuals and groups, including the banning of gay clubs in the high schools in Salt Lake, is a manifestation of the limits imposed by negative thinking. You know how strongly I feel about limitations imposed on persons from others, especially from established groups.

How do you think active members of the church view you as an inactive?

I don't know.

What's your guess?

I think if they know me, it doesn't matter to them. If they only know me by someone else's view or by hearsay, they might not know what to think. Maybe they'd just think that I've lost my way.

What do you think, in a general sense, actives think of inactives?

I think if they have any energy behind that question, they'd probably wish we'd get it right, because they don't like to see anybody fall by the wayside. They'd like us to help move the work along. If they think about it very much, and/or have some questions themselves, then they might envy us—or fear for us—that we had taken a stand. I think the power and the reinforcement capacities of the church are so strong that a lot of people don't even entertain the question about whether it's right or not.

I developed a metaphor about what happens to church-going believers. The container for holding one's faith is like a garden hose. Faith runs through the hose and comes out strong at the end. When something occurs with which one cannot agree or feels uncomfortable about, a kink occurs in the hose. The issue is lifted out and the general flow goes on only slightly diminished. You're fine unless you get so many kinks that only a trickle, or nothing, comes out the end. I think the process is something like that. I suspect there are a lot of people who are troubled by some things about the church, but they aren't sufficiently troubled, nor have so many kinks, that the flow is destroyed. When there is as much or more faith bottled up in the kinks as flowing through, then folks may be pushed to take a stand. It may range from remaining silent to deciding not to be involved any longer.

If you were president of the Mormon church, what would you do to change it?

If I were to be president of the church, I'd have to have a sex change operation. I might get so busy trying to figure out what it's like to be male that I might not do anything at first. [She laughs.] Seriously, if the mantle were to fall to me, I'd hope there would be compatible people with whom to work, people who feel and believe as I do. I don't know how many there'd be in the male councils of the Quorum of the Twelve and the Seventies as presently constituted who'd be supportive. I wouldn't have many female allies unless a lot of those bodies had changed a great deal along the way. I'd want to open up the system equally to all. See, I think that is where the threat is. I think we could give blacks the priesthood because it didn't require a marked change in the structure and systems of the church. To admit women to major leadership positions would be such a fundamental change in the basic structure of the church that I think it may be difficult for the present leadership to envision how it could happen and still keep the workaday things of the church on track. It would be a world-shaking change in the organization to change its leadership style and organizational structure from top to bottom.

It gets right to the heart of the Book of Mormon.

That's right. I was interested when the Equal Rights Amendment was an issue. In 1977, when each state had an International Women's Year meeting funded by the federal government, I was on the state planning committee. The chair of the committee went to the general president of the Relief Society seeking her approbation to tell Mormon women it was all right to attend. I don't know if you remember what happened, but Utah had the biggest meeting of any of the states. We had almost 14,000 attend our two-day meeting. It was bigger than New York, California, anywhere. About that time the Women's Center was contacted by women who said, essentially, they'd been called by someone from their ward to go out and collect signatures against the ERA and to attend the meeting and vote no on everything that was on the proposed national agenda. Our callers thought they might be well advised to know something about the amendment before setting out to collect signatures. They were surprised to learn it was made up of three short sentences, as the furor it had caused led them to believe it must be lengthy and extremely complicated. Several women I spoke to said they'd oppose it because they were busy enough already and didn't want to add the priesthood to their list of activities. It was at that time I came to believe there was an underlying, probably unconscious, concept operating in the lives of many Mormon women. The scenario read something like this: If I had been married in the temple and had done all the required work to earn a celestial reward, it would be enormously scary for me to question whether all the things I've done and the things I've supported might possibly be wrong—or not guaranteed to produce the results I'd been promised. If I began to question them and decided they weren't what I'd bargained for, I might become terribly angry. If I were that angry, I might be out of control. Who wants to risk being out of control because then people would very likely think you are crazy? I don't how accurate that is, or for how many, but I became convinced that something like that was operating for many women. It's safer to adhere than risk being pronounced sick, crazy, or angry, or not know where you belong. I think there's a great power in belonging, and especially if you belong to something that promises you glory from here to the end of everything. That's a powerful hold.

There's another process which happens that makes it difficult for many people, especially women, to question their church membership. The power of the promise of families together for eternity is so great that should one member of the family decide to leave the system, that person could destroy the whole family's capacity for future glory. It's the woman who generally is most concerned about the family and its functioning both here and in the hereafter, so the onus particularly falls on her. It's one thing to take risks and possibly ruin things for yourself, but to ruin something for everybody else is a huge burden to bear. A lot of people, even if they think about it, don't want the responsibility of possibly ruining things for anyone else.

Is there a chance you might return to active status?

The one moment I considered it was several years ago when my daughter died. She was almost twenty-four. Many of our friends suggested holding her memorial service at the ward even though she hadn't lived here for several years. I called the stake president, whom I knew from my days on the stake board, and asked if it would be possible to use the ward without having the bishop in charge. (One of the things I haven't liked about Mormon funerals is to have people conducting who don't know the person who's died.) I told him I only wanted people involved in the service who'd known her. After checking, he said it wasn't possible, but told me he thought I'd like the bishop. When the young bishop came to the house, I explained to him why I hadn't wanted to have him involved. It turned out he'd known

Alison as his wife had once been her Mutual teacher and he'd gone on outings with the class. He said the service was my show and he'd do whatever I wanted him to do. I asked if he'd have trouble dealing with cremation and he said he wouldn't. He was such a prince, I thought I could go back if there were more like him in leadership roles. Unfortunately, that didn't change the system and the stands I couldn't agree with which the church had taken. I can't imagine the system will open to women sufficiently in my lifetime for me to be comfortable there or feel my needs and values are acknowledged and/or met. I don't think there's much chance I'll go back. I'm not angry about it. I think it's terrific for those who find it to be true and right for them. I believe any system which helps people live their lives responsibly and with meaning has much more good in it than bad. If people think it works for them, fine. It just stopped working for me.

This is a good place to ask what happens to you when you die?

I believe that life force energy isn't lost. I don't really believe in three degrees of glory in the hereafter. I don't know where life force energy goes or precisely what happens to it, but I don't think it's lost. I happen to believe in past lives, so I guess that means I believe in reincarnation, although I don't have a system in mind about how it works. I can't answer the question, but I think it'll be a grand adventure. I've lived the best life I know how. If there are rewards to be given, then there has to be an adequate reward for that. I'm willing to take the reward at whatever level, however it comes. If what I'm comfortable with here is the measure at the final analysis, that's what I'll probably be comfortable with there. I look forward to it without fear or concern. I think it'll be most interesting. There are days when I think I've learned as much from this life as I need or want to know. Learning what's next will be exciting, I think. When my daughter died, there was as much relief as grief for me and a little bit of envy because she was able to move and learn something brand new while I'm still doing the same old stuff.

That's touching.

Well, that's the only thing that makes sense to me. She didn't necessarily want to be cremated, but we'd lost a younger cousin of hers three weeks before. At the funeral Alison had said to me, "Promise me something. If I die before you, don't bury me." I said, "If I don't bury you, I'll have to cremate you." Her response was, "I don't care. You know how I hate the dark. I don't want to be buried underground." I didn't promise, but when she died unexpectedly three weeks later, I felt I had to honor her request.

What was the cause of death?

Her death certificate reads suicide. She was an adopted child, and we didn't know her genetic history. She was subject to constant and severe anxiety attacks. Life was one continual anxiety for her. She was clinically depressed and on a prescribed anti-depressant. She'd started a new job on a Monday and felt completely overwhelmed by it. I think she lost track of her medication. As it turned out, she overdosed on it. Then she drove herself to an emergency room to say what she'd done. I think if she thought she wanted to die, she changed her mind. I think rather she was hoping for some time out to figure what to do as a next step as she'd decided to resign from the new job. Her boyfriend told me later she hadn't been taking her medication regularly during the week. I think she might've wanted to catch up and take some extra for good measure before telephoning her supervisor to resign. Interestingly, I was with her the day before she died. She told me then she wanted to have a major change in her life. She'd been drinking and smoking and exploring some things to try out to find out who she was, I guess. She didn't want to continue those patterns any longer. One of the last things she said to me was that she wanted to get religion back into her life, that she wanted a big change. I think she got what she wanted. I tend to think in terms of what the universe does more than God anymore. I think there's order in the universe. If people want to call that God, that's okay with me. I think the universe does interesting things in response to what it knows or is asked of it. She literally got what she'd asked for, I think, even though that may not have been the response she was consciously seeking. Her doctors told me she'd probably be in and out of hospitals all her life. She was no stranger to them as she had spent time in both psychiatric and medical wards. She was a young woman with a beautiful face and an obese body. She felt as though she was a prisoner in her body. All the diets and other attempts to change her body into one she felt good in hadn't worked. She felt she was a blight on the world because of her size. All the affirmations of love and caring from everyone she knew had never been enough to dispel her own sense of being unacceptable. I believe her death gave her an answer to her desire for a change. It gave her a new start without the prison she'd been locked up in all her life.

Our society puts such a premium on thinness. Did you ever drink or smoke? That seems to be one of the tests of active or inactive Mormonism.

There was a time when I was still living in my parents' house when I smoked. Not a lot, but I smoked some. My mother did a very wise thing about my smoking. She wasn't always so brilliant in responding to actions of mine which disturbed her, but this time she was right on. She came into my basement bedroom one day when it was reeking of cigarette smoke. Instead of giving me an exposition on the evils, she said, "Before you come upstairs and see your grandmother, I suggest you brush your teeth and change your shirt." I never smoked in that house again.

I was on a plane one time and happened to sit by a noted molecular biologist who told me of the discoveries coming out of his lab. What he said was that if he could make a major contribution to the world, it would be to keep people from inhaling any foreign substance. The lab tests were demonstrating that an enormous number of brain cells were destroyed through inhaling. I didn't know, of course, what lay ahead of me in life, but I figured I'd need all the brain cells I could manage to keep alive. I never smoked again.

And drinking? I drank, but only once in a while. I do it now very occasionally at social functions. That was one of the values of growing up Mormon. We didn't have the stuff in the house. By the time I was ready to expand my horizons, I found I didn't like the taste of liquor. I think my taste buds stultified and it was never important enough to try to acquire a taste. I suspect I didn't have a great need to rebel because my actions weren't tightly restricted. Except for my Mutual teacher, nobody ever tried to force me to do or think in ways which felt in opposition to my own desires. It occurs to me that it's no great sacrifice to avoid doing anything which isn't particularly inviting.

Why are you willing to talk about this publicly?

I'm wondering about that. I suppose because I think you can't make a decision unless you have something with which to compare. I guess that's why. If what I think or believe or have experienced can make a difference to somebody else's journey, I guess I'm willing to share that. I feel I'm comfortable with you. I've told you more stories about my life than I imagined I might. We don't know people's stories. That's a problem, that we don't know the stories. We see the façade, we see what we want to see or think is there, but we don't know what's underneath. It's what's underneath that troubles all of us. That's what sends people into therapy.

I'll tell you one of the most compelling stories of my life. It happened not too many months after I was hired as director of the Women's Center. Life became very complex for me. Besides trying to develop the idea of a center, there was a general telephone strike; we had little money budgeted for furnishing our space; my son was having difficulty learning to read in school; and my housekeeper was having problems with drugs. Additionally, I was president of a national organization for which I had many responsibilities and had to travel fairly often, and I was doing a lot of public speaking throughout the West. To top it off, I had the flu and was dragging about every day. I came home one night and found my children were at each other about some mutual grievance. At that moment it was as if something snapped in me. I just couldn't take any more cacophony. Some months before this, Vern had built what I called the blanket box. It was the base for a bed with a large storage compartment in which we stored extra blankets and pillows. We kept it in the basement. At that time it was mostly used for storage. When I could no longer stand the endless noise and confusion, I went downstairs and climbed into the blanket box, and lay there very still. I knew I needed respite and calm.

After a time I heard questions floating about from the family as to where I was. I hadn't announced my departure and that was very unusual behavior for me. They began searching everywhere for me. My daughter came to look for me in the basement. I could hear her opening doors and looking in every possible opening. I knew that she was going to find me. She opened the box and asked me what I was doing there. "Just resting," was my response. I didn't have any way to talk about my disappearance with my family. A little later I heard her on the telephone with a friend reporting my crazy behavior.

The next day a colleague came into the office and announced that I looked terrible. To look the way I felt was the first connected thing I'd experienced since the previous night. He invited me to tell him what was happening in my life. I reported what I termed my bizarre behavior of the night before. His response was that it made all kinds of sense, given the pace, the complexity of my life the previous months. He asked me if I'd give him two decisions about my life. I readily agreed. The first one, he said, was that I was leaving the center. I couldn't, said I, I had too many things on the docket for that day and several following. He responded—and told my staff, as well—that I was leaving and he couldn't tell them how soon I'd be back. The second decision was that I was not to return to work until he told me I could. I demurred, but he reminded me I'd given him two decisions and those were they. He called my boss and told her I had to get out of there, that I was in desperate need of time off. Her response was an acknowledgement that I'd been working too hard for too long and she'd wondered if or when I might break under the pressure. I was off for about two months.

I'd never been in therapy. The same colleague who furloughed me told me he thought I'd benefit from professional help. I called a psychiatrist and saw him five times. He kept waiting for me to talk. All I wanted to do was roll myself into a catatonic ball. I wasn't much help. Finally, he said he thought we ought to talk about my unresolved conflicts with my mother. I was willing to think I might have some, but even in my de-energized state, I didn't think that was what was at the core of my dilemma. Being burned out and over-programmed seemed a much more likely basis.

As part of his decision process for my life, my friend and colleague also arranged for people to take over the imminent pending commitments I had. They included out of town travel, lectures, and teaching. Freed thereby of all obligations, I spent many days at home trying to work on the puzzle my life had become. I was lying in bed one morning remembering a conversation with a friend and fellow staff member of a human relations training lab which had occurred several months before. He was an eminent psychologist whom I had known for some years. We happened to meet one afternoon and I had asked him what he felt he'd learned from his many years of practice. He said, "Funny you should ask. I've learned one thing. That is, if you know you need something, go out and get it."

During the first days of my mental health leave, there were many people coming and going in my house trying to figure out how to be helpful. Nobody knew what to do, least of all me. As I lay there remembering that conversation, I pondered deeply about what it was I needed. Pondering was a slow process as my mind was working at a snail's pace at the time. Finally the realization dawned that what I wanted, and therefore needed, was just to be nurtured in some tangible and affirming way. I thought of calling my friend who had set this whole process in motion. I thought I'd say I didn't know what a nurturing group was or how it would work, but could he put one together for me? About then my doorbell rang. Standing there was a woman I'd known only a short time. She'd been one of those called to fill in for me, so she knew something of my circumstances. She said, "I don't know why I'm here. I had to cancel an appointment to come, but I felt I should come now, today." In response to her query about how I was and what I'd been up to, I told her about my new-found recognition that I felt in need of nurturance and was considering requesting that a nurturing group be developed. She said simply, "Maybe I can help," whereupon she went to the telephone and made some calls. When Vern came home, she told him she was taking me out for a while and would deliver me home later. "Shauna will be with me all the time," she said, "and she'll be safe." She literally had to put my hands in my coat on that cold winter day as I had so little energy. [She cries softly.] It still moves me.

We drove to a downtown motel and she rented a room. She took my hands out of my coat, sat down on the bed, and opened her arms to me as though she were welcoming one of her own children. "Come," was all she said. I cried for five hours. We talked after for another long while. Finally as evening was coming on, she said she thought we needed to eat something and wondered if I wanted to stay all night. She was like a mother nurturing a hurt child. After dinner, this wonderful psychologist (that was her career as well as her intuition) called her husband and mine and told them we'd be a while yet, but that we'd be returning home. When all her arrangements for continuing child care were complete, I said to her that all my life I'd been somebody's counselor. I was number two sibling in my family of origin. Birth order expectations for number twos, according to some experts, include being a counselor within the family. People all my life had been coming to me to talk about their problems. I said how overwhelmed I felt that she'd do something so generous and helpful to me, especially since I had nothing to offer in return. I felt totally empty. "What could possibly be in it for you?" I wondered. She replied, "You've given me a great honor. You trusted me." What the psychiatrist had been unable to do, she did for me in that evening. She taught me more about acceptance, nurturing, trust of self and others, and connection in one day than I'd ever known before. I truly believe she not only saved my life, but gave it back to me to live with new understanding.

This story provides the underpinning for what spirituality has come to mean to me. This is a classic example of humanity at work: spontaneous, sensitive, and giving as it was in creating a way to meet a need. That's what spirituality comes down to, I believe—to try to meet needs where you find them and to live as fully and completely as you can while still being caring, kind, responsible, and forgiving. We talk all those virtues, but they're too rarely felt, called upon, or even enabled in many religious systems. At least, that's my sense of it.

The most important directive in my life these days is to know my truth and be willing to speak it. That's become really important for me ... trying to figure out what truth is for me and not be judgmental about anybody else's truth. I don't want to spend my time—my free choice time—with people whose truth is in opposition to mine, who'll try to change or alter my truth to fit theirs. I think there's enough space in the world for everybody's truth. A friend said to me long ago he believes everybody constructs a belief system in order to get through the world. If you don't construct your own, you agree with one you meet along the way. If Mormonism helps someone make sense of life, I think that's terrific. I'd rather be emperor of the world than president of the church. If I ruled the world, I'd want a place where everybody could find a place of meaning and purpose. Diversity would flourish. We'd live reasonably without hurting or harming each other. We'd value and honor our differences as well as our similarities. We'd allow things like gay and lesbian clubs in our schools. We'd encourage everyone to reach for the stars in his/her particular firmament.

Yes, if I ruled the world, it would be kind, gentle, invigorating, and diverse. Most religions would probably have to go, or change significantly, in order to fit in. Not just Mormonism, but most religions. They are, after all, corporations and businesses which want to keep people heeling (instead of healing) to what they think is the proper outcome. If you can agree with that outcome, then fine; but if you think you ought to be the architect of your own outcome, therein lies the rub.

14.

Civic Worker

We feel and know that we are eternal.

—Benedict Spinoza

She's an attractive woman, well-known, active in a variety of Utah projects.

~

You were born in a small town.

Technically, I wasn't born there, but I spent my whole growing up in central Utah.

Was your family active in the LDS church?

My mother more than my father.

Did you come from pioneer stock?

Oh, yes. My grandmother was particularly devout.

And you were active, I take it, as a young person.

Oh, yes. The whole town was, with rare exceptions. It's just part of growing up.

At what point in your life did you become less active?

It was a gradual process probably, but more after leaving college and after getting married.

Were you married in the temple?

Yes.

You became less active after that?

Yes.

Was that influenced by your marriage?

No, not necessarily. In fact, for a number of years in the early, early part of it, we still participated a lot, because our children were involved with the neighborhood children. It was more a cultural thing than a religious thing, though, as the years progressed.

Did you move to Salt Lake City shortly after your marriage?

Yes. We spent most of our married life here.

Do you have a bedrock belief, a faith, if you will, in the basics of Mormonism today?

No. If you want me to describe my beliefs at this point, they're pretty universal.

What do you believe?

I think there's a force or an order to the universe. I don't know what it is, but I think it's there, and that's good enough for me.

What were some of the factors involved in your withdrawal from active Mormonism?

I'd have to think about that. I think I was becoming less and less convinced that much of what was accepted as doctrine really lacked a lot of reality. I just couldn't quite accept that that's how everything happened.

The gold plates ...

Yes, and it was almost too man-made. It almost lacked the majesty of a God, and some of the things that were demanded seemed like they were very earthly rather than heavenly, if you will. Much of the ritual and the explanations seemed to be too pat and too cut and dried. I just couldn't see how anybody could be that absolutely positive that's how everything was. It makes life very simple for people who can accept it, of course.

But you can't?

Some of it's very difficult to deal with. Some of it's wonderful. I mean, there are the positives and the negatives.

The positives?

Wonderful, caring people. In my case, most of my association has been with people who are really very fine people, very willing to participate to support their community, particularly their friends and their neighborhoods who are part of their culture, as it were. I think the negatives though, you see in a broader sense—while I've never really experienced the insular part of the culture, the lack of acceptance of diversity. I live in a neighborhood where, even though I'm not active, the active Mormons are very ... That doesn't matter, we're still friends. In some areas I've heard that's really very difficult. But I've seen too much of it and I've heard too much about it from non-Mormon associates and friends, stories of their children having such a difficult time. That's a big negative to me. I think, too, if you want to go back in time, one of the things that bothered me, of course, was the exclusion of blacks. Way back. This was back when the whole civil rights thing was going on, and I never understood that. And the older I got, the less I understood it.

What about women?

You've opened a whole new door. Of course, it doesn't bother me that women don't have the priesthood because I don't care, personally. I do feel there's been a real patriarchal society that's made it very difficult for women. I never had to deal with that personally. But I've known people who did, again. So that wasn't my reason. It's just personal, developing my own philosophy, approach, whatever you want to call it.

How did you feel about the opposition of the church to ERA, for instance?

I never understood it. I objected to it because I supported the ERA.

Did you raise your children as active Mormons? Did you feel a need to send them to church?

They went. The older ones probably were exposed more than the younger ones. Their attitudes probably developed along with ours, parallel with ours because of what we were doing. So they're all inactive.

You were giving me a definition of your personal beliefs. Do you consider yourself a spiritual person?

I consider myself a very moral person, and if that's part of spirituality, then yes. It's your approach to life, and I think how you live your life is your religion. What's important to you becomes, to me at least, my religion. I don't have a great, great anger towards the church at all. It's just something I've gone beyond.

Can you see a time when you might return to active status?

No.

Can you see any circumstances under which you might ask to have your name removed from the rolls or be excommunicated?

Probably not. I mean, I'm perfectly comfortable with how things are.

Did you ever feel any conflicts internally—guilt, shame, anything like that—that you might've attributed to your upbringing in the church, conflicts that were later created because of your taking another direction?

If I did, it was so long ago I don't remember. I'm very comfortable with how I feel about things, and I'm very comfortable with how my children are dealing with it, too. It's sort of a live-and-let-live attitude, I guess.

Are many of your friends active members of the church?

Yes. It's about half and half, and I can move between both. They don't mesh a lot of the times, but I can be with a very religious group and be fine, although we don't often share the same topics of conversation like, "Where did my sons go on missions, and when are they getting back, and who's going to be a mission president." That's often their whole conversation, but it's interesting to me what they're doing. That's fine. Fortunately, they ask me about my children.

Some people say they believe that within a minute they can tell if a person is active or not. Do you believe that's true?

Not within a minute. Somebody would have to be really very overt in their discussion of the church. If they called me "Sister," then I'd know they were active in the church, yes. I guess that's your one-minute sign, but just in the course of a conversation ...

How do you think active Mormons view inactives?

I imagine some of them don't want to be around us. And that's their problem. I guess some of them would think we were really lost, but I don't worry about that. Again, if that's how they feel, there's nothing I can do about it.

What about a hereafter? What's going to happen?

I have no idea. Do you?

I have my theories. I think I'm going to continue existing in some form—whether it's in the sense of ashes to ashes, dust to dust, with the result being a tree that grows from soil that's replenished by my carcass, or whether it's something more literal as in the Buddhist or Hindu beliefs, where we come back as another human or another form of life. I don't feel like the energy of life is lost.

I don't either, and I still wonder if there isn't another dimension that we can't even see out there. It's possible.

Yes. If we were active, we'd have all that clearly defined for us.

It's much easier not to question, but too much of it begs the question.

Did your process of leaving happen suddenly?

I think it was gradual.

You felt comfortable as you passed through?

Withdrew. Yes. Withdrew is more the word.

My mother participated in the auxiliary units, but it was the social thing to do in that community. They really thought it was important that we went as children, and they certainly thought it was important that the grandchildren went.

I think our children got the picture, as well, that it's not the overt religious acts as much as how you're living your life—that basic core of integrity.

I agree.

And that's a very strong thing to hold on to.

If you don't have that integrity, there's a little bell inside that goes off as you begin to deviate, and it doesn't matter if you're active or inactive.

But you have to be exposed to knowing what integrity is. And I'm not discounting that some of the church experiences didn't add to that as I was growing up.

Some of the integrity, though, is universal. It's not just Mormon.

That's true. I wonder sometimes if some of it isn't genetic. I mean, there are certain things we do that we know are right, and other things that we know are not.

I'm sorry I don't have a more dramatic story to tell.

It's an honest story. It doesn't sound as though you've had much difficulty in dealing with it.

In fact, actually, it was easier to live with when we finally decided this really is how we're going to live our lives.

15.

Rod Decker

> Scrutamini scripturus. (Let us look at the scriptures). These two words have undone the world.
>
> —*John Selden*

We meet at Lamb's Grill on Main Street in downtown Salt Lake City, the so-called "Little Alta Club." It is summer, and Rod Decker has just returned from the Republican National Convention in San Diego. Dole will lose, except in Utah. Perot will not come close to recreating his big win in Utah in 1994. Rod predicts less than 10 percent of Utah's presidential vote will go to Perot. He's later proven right.

When the appointment for this interview was set up, Rod had one stipulation—that he could drink coffee. Wearing a dark sport coat and tie, he consumes several cups of black coffee as we talk. The shock of sandy hair that falls over his forehead is familiar to hundreds of thousands of Utahns who watch his news and commentaries on KUTV Television, Channel 2. As Rod related to the University of Utah's alumni periodical, Continuum, *recently, "I never had a journalism class." He wanted to teach political science.*

"Professors Francis Wormuth, J. D. Williams, and Jack Adamson had a great effect on me; they were influencing me to be an academic but I was a lousy graduate student. So when it became apparent I wasn't cut out to be an academic, I 'sank' to journalism." He subsequently

wrote for the University of Utah Chronicle, *then moved to the* Deseret News, *where he spent an illustrious career as a political reporter before joining KUTV. He has won numerous awards for his work.*

Rod Decker's most distinctive feature are his eyes—they seem to burn from beneath his brows, pouring direct heat on the subject of his vision. Rod is mostly business, alertly comfortable as he leans back against the red leather of our booth. Kitchen sounds bang intermittently. He seems to want to get right to work.

~

When were you born?

On July 18, 1941.

In Salt Lake City?

No, in New York.

Were your parents from Utah?

Yes. My father's family went through Hole-in-the-Rock and settled Bluff. My mother's family settled Lehi.

Old pioneer stock.

My father's great-grandfather was a Mormon Battalion member. My mother's great-great-grandfather was Joseph Smith's bodyguard.

Was he a Decker?

No, an Allred.

How long did you live in New York?

Until I was eight.

At that time were your parents active in the church?

Yes.

Both?

Yes.

You moved when you were eight?

To Utah. My parents had gone to New York thinking it would be temporary. My dad went to graduate school there and worked for a while.

They stayed about twelve years. Then they thought they wanted to raise their kids in Utah, so they came here.

Once you arrived back in Salt Lake, where did you live and go to school?

We lived at 1422 Perry Avenue, which is about 50 North and 14th East, in Federal Heights.

Close to the Pi Kappa Alpha house (just north of the University of Utah campus).

Yes. That's why I later became a Pi Kap. I went to Wasatch School for half of my third grade year, then to Stewart School for fourth to ninth grades, then East High School, and then the University of Utah.

Did your parents remain active after they moved back to Salt Lake?

Mom was always very religious. Dad became less religious, and finally not religious.

Was he ever openly critical of the church?

No.

He became non-religious?

My parents got divorced. My dad drank and caroused a bit. He was never a drunk, but he drank and caroused. He just was no longer Mormon.

Did you go to church as a child?

I went regularly. I was a faithful member until I was eighteen.

So you were almost an elder?

No. They said they'd make me an elder; I said I didn't want to be an elder.

Growing up, did you feel any conflict with the religion?

I felt conflict with the ward, with personalities. But not until I was out of high school did I really feel it.

Even as a child you felt worthy ...

I don't know that I felt worthy, but I believed it and practiced it. I felt it was what I ought to do my whole life.

How old were you when you quit going to church? Eighteen?

Yes, my freshman year in college.

What happened?

Two things. First, I went to the university and joined a fraternity, and it was an issue in the fraternity. My friends were anti-Mormon. Second, it then became an intellectual issue—is the church really true? I thought about it for a long time, a number of years, and finally decided that it wasn't.

Why did you choose anti-Mormon friends? Weren't there many active Mormons?

Yes, there were. But the kids whom I'd gone to high school with—most of them, not all—they'd been Mormon in high school but then had decided they weren't Mormon any longer. They decided this before I did. Then, in the fraternity, the older guys we hung around with were anti-Mormon. So it's true that I chose anti-Mormon friends, but ...

They were vocal about it.

Yes. They aren't anti-Mormon now. It was a phase one goes through in college. "Sophomoric" is the usual adjective. But the attacks were mostly: "Well, it's untrue. It's ridiculous, false belief." That was buttressed more or less by teachers at the university like O. C.Tanner, Waldemer Reed, Sterling McMurrin—those guys.

They wanted to make you an elder, but you declined. Tell me about that.

The bishop called me in and said he wanted to make me an elder. I said I don't want to be an elder. I guess the reason I didn't want to be one was because I was afraid they were going to pressure me into going on a mission, and I thought if I don't become an elder they can't send me on a mission. This was my first line of defense. Besides, I thought, I don't believe this stuff or, at least, I've got serious questions about it at this point. The best way to be was to say I don't want to be in the Melchizedek priesthood, given that I'm not a believer. So I said no. He said, Well, I'm not surprised, but you should keep coming to the priests quorum and things like that.

You said that you had some problems during those years with individuals in the ward.

I was younger than the rest of the kids. I was born in July, and was the youngest kid in my class, or one of the youngest. They kept dividing the Sunday schools and the older kids would go ahead but I would be left back with the younger. That distressed me when I was young. I couldn't get much sympathy out of the guys who were running things. My friends who went ahead made an issue out of the fact that they were older and I was the younger. I'd say, No, I'm in the same grade as you, but they'd say, No, our dividing line's different, you go back with the younger kids. It wasn't serious, but it bothered me when I was that age.

Your mother remained active. What did she say about your refusal to be an elder?

She didn't comment specifically on that but wanted me to be active. She's a serious Mormon, and it saddened her that I was not. We argued about it.

Is she still alive?

No, she died twelve years ago.

Do you have fond memories of those early days?

Yes, I was a Boy Scout and we had a good time. I had good times at Sunday school. I went with my mother to take classes at the institute of religion. I enjoyed those, as well. I took seminary classes when I was in junior high. I had a problem getting up early enough in the morning to go, but other than that I enjoyed them. A lot of my friends were ward kids. Yes, I was a happy Mormon when I was young.

Do you ever attend church today?

I occasionally go to a Mormon service if one of my friend's children is going on a mission. My wife and children are Catholic, so occasionally I go to the Catholic church, three or four times a year.

Do you consider yourself a spiritual person?

Not at all.

How do you reconcile the conflict between faith and reason?

I decided I didn't believe, not in Christianity or Mormonism or religion in general.

What happens when you die?

Probably you're just dead. I'm not dogmatic about it, but that seems to me the best bet.

Would you say you're agnostic?

Yes.

But you haven't left Mormonism.

No, I haven't.

Did that ever occur to you?

Never very seriously. Sometimes I think, What will I do if the bishop says to me, Okay, either come to church or get out. I'll say, Okay, I'll get out. But as long as they leave me alone, I'll just let things go.

Has your inactive status ever caused problems for you in a social or business sense?

When I worked for the *Deseret News,* they didn't have any problem with my belief, whatever it was. Surely, had I been interested in becoming "the boss," it would have been a problem at some point. I suppose there's a spiritual ceiling at the *Deseret News.* But that wasn't what I wanted to do anyway. So as long as I was a reporter, they didn't care about my beliefs. However, I wanted to "poke" journalistically at the church and at some of its beliefs, and that led to problems.

Such as?

They suggested that I not write about Planned Parenthood or about pornography. I'd stick up for the First Amendment. I'd chafe under the strictures such as that.

Was that one of the reasons you accepted the offer to work for KUTV?

Yes, that was one of the reasons.

Do you think KUTV is viewed as the station for inactive Mormons?

I don't know. It isn't an especially inactive LDS station. Mostly it's non-LDS. Most of the people there are non-LDS. The boss, nowadays, is active LDS, however. And Michelle King's active LDS. But most of the people there are from out of town and are non-LDS.

I've wondered about the composition of the viewing audiences of the television stations ...

I don't know what it is. I'm sure somebody's got those numbers. I guess we get some Mormons, but probably not as many as KSL does.

Have you ever called yourself a Jack Mormon?

I don't know that I've ever said Jack Mormon. I call myself an inactive Mormon.

Do you think there's a stigma to the term Jack Mormon?

It doesn't bother me.

Why do you think some people leave the church?

I think for most of them Mormonism is an onerous religion. One of the things Mormonism does is to pattern your life for you. It's one of the reasons it's successful. But a lot of people don't want their lives patterned that way. They don't want to put up money, they don't want to put up time, they don't want to live at slight odds with the rest of society. So they become inactive. I would think some people become inactive because they think hard or read hard and decide it isn't true. In my own case, it became a social issue from friends, and then an intellectual issue. I thought about it and decided that I didn't believe it. To some extent—I suppose it's true for many religions but more so of Mormonism—Mormonism intrudes on your life more than most other religions. To some extent, you have to want that kind of intrusion, that kind of direction, if you're going to stay an active Mormon. Some people want that kind of patterning, and feel good in the ward. Mormonism is like a dance step; it helps you to move gracefully to the music and time. You go to church and they tell you what to do when you get married. I don't mean this in any derogatory way. You get married and they have plans for your kids and uses for your time, and they offer you a community and the chance to be an important person in your community—or as important as you choose. It's a way of living. People who are good Mormons and people who aren't. It seems to me to be the major factor.

We often hear the term "good Mormon" contrasted with "inactive Mormon." We never hear "bad Mormon," but it's certainly implied when they say an active Mormon is a good Mormon. Is there any shame or guilt around what Mormonism may do to some people?

I guess in some instances there is. I felt guilty when I left the church. I still feel guilty, though in a very abstract way. I really believe the church isn't true.

Why do you feel guilty?

I was raised a Mormon but no longer am, that's all. Though far from perfect, I still try to be a good person, to obey the law, pay taxes, raise a family.

Do you think the Word of Wisdom has anything to do with it?

I guess it did when I was younger. I was raised to be a Mormon, to go to church, to be in the community, and to be active. Giving up coffee and booze wouldn't be especially difficult, if I decided that I wanted to be a Mormon.

There seems to be more of a stigma attached to smoking than to drinking. Perhaps that's because smoking is more visible.

That may be so, I don't know. Drinking is more episodic. You drink occasionally. Yes, I still feel guilt, I think. I don't feel guilty about anything in particular now, just guilty that I should be a religious person.

Could any of it be connected to your having descended from a long line of active ancestors?

No, that's not the big thing. The big thing is that, while I'm sure in some respects that most of Mormonism's specific claims aren't so, whether they are or not seems to be less important. I guess I could be a Mormon now and still say that Jesus didn't appear to Joseph Smith or that the Book of Mormon isn't historical, that those teachings don't matter much. Even if the Book of Mormon isn't historical, one can choose Mormonism as a way to worship. Most of Christianity is like that. My wife's a good Catholic, and literally believes that Jesus rose from the dead, but a lot of Catholics don't. A lot of Christians don't worry about it either. They think it's a good way to live and that's the way they live. They think and have a desire to worship, so they worship in a traditional forum. I could do that with Mormonism, if I chose. But I don't want to go to church a lot and sit through all those meetings. I don't want to be a ward member. I don't want to feel limited, to feel in any way afraid of what I say or write for fear they'll excommunicate me. I don't think they'll excommunicate me as long as I don't care if they do or not. I don't want to live the discipline.

Can you foresee any circumstances under which you might return to active status?

I guess it's possible, but I think it's unlikely.

Can you think of a scenario where it might be possible?

It would be primarily an internal process. It wouldn't be a change in my outward life or in my circumstances. I left the church largely because I thought hard and became convinced it wasn't true. I'd go back, perhaps, if I thought first that the truth doesn't matter. I suppose it might happen if I were to become persuaded it was true. I think that's unlikely, though. I'm also persuaded now that its untruth doesn't matter very much. I might go back if I thought this would be somehow good for me.

How do you think active Mormons view inactive ones?

By and large, actives see themselves in the business of saving souls. They believe souls are saved through the Mormon church, and they'd like to get inactive people active again. They don't like people who oppose them or ridicule them or set themselves up as enemies to the church. Other than that, for the most part, what they'd like is for an inactive person to have some kind of conversion experience and become active again.

How do you think the church could reactivate the inactives?

In my case, the church would have to be true. But it isn't. I guess they could change the universe, so that it conformed to what they say it is. But I don't think it's like they say it is. Or they could change my beliefs. But I don't know how they're going to change my beliefs. Otherwise, Mormonism's extraordinarily successful. It's astonishingly successful as measured by its growth. The reason it seems to me to be successful is that it provides, as I said before, a strict patterning of life. It seems to me that they have to work. They don't do it consciously, or not entirely consciously. But they have to work to get the right amount of discipline, the right amount of friction, of dissonance, between themselves and the rest of the world. Polygamy was too much. The kingdom of God on earth was too much. They had to get the right amount so that Mormons who join the church, or who are active in the church, feel that this is something real, a commitment, and that it's a religion, that they feel God is a presence in their lives. But not so much so that it marks them as too different from other people or too weird or provocative. They seem to have it about right. Now I'm not going to tell them to change. Would it be easier on me if they said, Okay, you can drink coffee? Yes. But would I then believe that Jesus rose from the dead? No. So surely there are things they could do to appeal to some inactives. They could adjust the mix. Maybe a few inactives would like even more discipline, though most would like less. But it seems to me that they have the mix about right. Some people aren't going to like it, but enough do. I'm not going to tell the Mormon church how to tweak their belief system.

Are there any negatives with being inactive?

If you're an active Mormon, then you believe the biggest negative is that you're deprived of the benefits of the church. You don't get the help of the church in raising your children. You don't get the fellowship of the priesthood members. You don't get feelings of worthwhileness that come from paying tithing. And you don't feel that you're living in tune with the universe and with the commandments of God. Active Mormons tend to have strong feelings about Mormonism, but inactives are so scattered and few that nobody else in the world shares their strong feelings. There's a whole culture regarding to what extent one should believe or disbelieve in Judaism or Catholicism or Christianity. In Mormonism there are people writing books, but few of them read each other's books. There's no real culture. Active Mormons don't pay much attention and non-Mormons can't figure out what all the fuss is about. So Mormonism by itself is small and marginalized, although it's becoming larger. Moreover, it chooses marginalization. It chooses to be different. Inactives are at the margin of the margin, so the things that seem important to an inactive Mormon are doubly marginalized. There are those, I guess, who just go away and aren't Mormons at all anymore. I obviously chose not to do that. It was never a conscious decision. But it's clearly what I've chosen. So I live in the rock pool at very edge of the Great Salt Lake. It isn't the ocean; it's just a little puddle somewhere.

Is there an overall Mormon character that you can describe?

Yes, and its strengths and weaknesses seem to me to be exactly the same. Mormons are provincial. There are Mormons who think seriously and deeply about their faith, but by and large Mormons don't. They aren't any different from everybody else. But they are different in this respect: the church is very skeptical of independent scholars. In most religions, a person can obtain status and respect by studying very hard about that religion. There are Catholic theologians who are theologians simply because they have read all the Fathers and know the scriptures and have read the Greek and the Hebrew. Their words are listened to by everybody in the church and are respected. That's eminently true in Judaism. It's not very true in Mormonism. In Mormonism people respect you as a scholar as long as you provide apologetics for the views of the brethren, who themselves are not scholars. The fact that all Mormon men are clergy means that the clergy is not learned in the sense that they go to school to become clergy. So while Mormons think of themselves as an intellectually respectable religion, in the church as a whole intellect plays a very subordinate role. Anyone who thinks things through and comes to a conclusion different from that espoused by the brethren, no matter his or her evidence, is simply wrong. If he insists on his position, they may kick him out. No matter how respectable scholastically his or her view may be, to be a Mormon is to live somewhat at odds with the rest of the world—to be different, visibly different, in some respect. The brethren seem almost to need to be at odds with enlightened opinions. First they were polygamists, then they wouldn't admit black men to the priesthood, now they're anti-feminists. That may not be quite accurate, but they're seen as being a target of feminists. They're like a man who has walked so hard into a cold north wind that he's afraid if it stopped he'd lose his sense of direction. In part, they need that idea of being provincial and being at odds with avant-garde thinking.

That helps bind the flock, too.

Yes.

ROD DECKER

It's us versus them?

A little bit, although this may be too strong. They have no animus, I think, toward enlightened liberals. They simply don't believe that. That makes them different and provincial. Now you could emphasize that side of things too much. Mormons want to succeed in the world, to be respected and praised by non-Mormons. But they want to be a little different, too. They want to live on Mormon terms.

Do you think the political influence of Mormonism has a bearing on whether one is inactive? I ask that because my father, who was raised by devout Mormon parents, was politically angry with the church.

Nowadays the church tries to steer clear of politics for the most part. They don't succeed entirely, and I don't know if they ever can. They are conservatives—moral conservatives and economic conservatives. I suppose there are some people who aren't Mormons because of politics. I'd guess in most instances if somebody has a problem with the church's politics, the real problem is something else. You don't have to fight with them. You can be a liberal Democrat and a Mormon. They say you can be that, but they may never pick you for bishop. But, heck, you don't want to be bishop anyway. Liberals tend to think that liberalism is Christ-like, that welfare is like alms, that the church ought to be in the forefront of social activism, and that's following the teachings of Jesus. They can't understand why the church can't see that those are the teachings of Jesus. Well, they may be the teachings of Jesus and they may not. Some liberals accuse Mormons of being self-righteous, but liberal Mormons seem to me to be self-righteous in their own way. They say we need to vote Democratic and increase welfare payments, that Christ would have us do that. That bothers people who don't believe that's what Christ wants. So, yes, the church is conservative. Yes, the church participates in politics some. Yes, in the past the church has participated in politics a lot. The church is a bit hypocritical about its participation in politics in that it's been kind of secretive in the past. They tend to sneak around, and even when they're participating in politics, they tend to say, Oh, no, this isn't political. They do that out of habit. There's no good reason for it; they just do it. I guess you can fault them on that. But politics isn't a terrible problem for me.

How many inactive Mormons do you think are in Utah's legislature?

Some, but not many; maybe 10 percent; maybe not even that. There are non-Mormons in the legislature, but most Mormons are active. A lot of them are big-time Mormons: stake presidents, mission presidents, bishops, former bishops, people like that.

Is inactivity a hindrance to a political career in Utah?

No. Look at Cal Rampton or Scott Matheson. No, I don't think it's a hindrance. Being an active Mormon is probably a help, though. Being a devout something else is probably a help, too. Being an inactive Mormon probably makes it more difficult, but it doesn't make it significantly difficult.

Did you ever pay tithing?

Haven't since I was eighteen.

Have you ever been confronted by an active Mormon about your degree of faith?

Yes, maybe a dozen times.

How did it make you feel?

There was a time when I used to relish arguments with them. But for the most part now, I don't want to argue with them. I just tell them what I believe. Usually what they'll say is, What do you mean, you don't believe? And I'll say, I don't believe Jesus was born of a virgin. I don't believe he rose from the dead. I don't believe he appeared to Joseph Smith. I don't believe he'll return in glory. I could go on, but you get the idea. They usually leave me alone after that.

Do you ever feel lonely or isolated because of your inactivity?

No.

16.

Ardean Walton Watts

> **I shall be telling this with a sigh**
> **Somewhere ages and ages hence:**
> **Two roads diverged in a wood, and I—**
> **I took the one less traveled by,**
> **And that has made all the difference.**
>
> —*Robert Frost*

Ardean Watts's career has been steeped in music. He took his bachelor's degree in music theory at Brigham Young University, and his master's in performance at the University of Utah. He was for a time a student at the Academy of Music in Vienna. At the University of Utah his career brought him many honors, including a Distinguished Teaching Award. He served as chair of the ballet department, and as a Dee Fellow, to name a few of his achievements. He retired from the U. in 1993 and is now professor emeritus.

His activities with the Utah Symphony will recall him to many readers; he was associate conductor for eleven years, and was musical director and principal conductor for Ballet West, as well. He was also piano soloist with the symphony under Maurice Abravanel and Paul Whiteman, and was the official pianist of the Utah Symphony Orchestra for twenty-two years.

Not all of his performing has been classical. He was leader and conductor of dance and show bands at Lagoon, Saltair, and the Rainbow

Randevu in Salt Lake City in the 1950s. He was a Grammy Award nominee for best classical performance-choral in 1962, when he prepared the University of Utah Chorus to record Honegger's King David *with the Utah Symphony. He has also been a vocal coach and was founder of the University of Utah Opera Company. Recent creative projects include incidental music for Shakespeare's* The Tempest *at Pioneer Memorial Theater, electronic realization of the orchestration of* Carmina Burana *by Carl Orff, and the composition of* Mark V Marimba Toccata.

Ardean is active in Rotary Club, was a member and chair of the Music Committee of the YMMIA General Board of the LDS church (1958-74), and was appointed to the Utah Arts Council in 1987, serving as its chair in 1993-95. He has been president or a member of the board of the B. H. Roberts Society since 1987. He was also the founder of the Mushroom Society of Utah, and is a member of the board of HawkWatch International.

Ardean ushers me into a room in his home whose walls seem composed entirely of books. A grand piano sits near a window, through which winter sunlight filters across a green-blue carpet. The piano is draped with a throw woven with a piano key pattern in black and white. A madonna hangs on a wall, a framed Egyptian papyrus rests on a shelf. The place is dotted with pictures of family. This man is imposing, with white hair and jet-black eyebrows setting off a white Brigham Young beard. He wears suspenders and black glasses. His hands tremble slightly, but his voice is steady and mellow, and he frequently enjoys a laugh at his own observations.

~

Were you born in Utah?

I was born in Kanosh, Millard County, Utah, but my father left the farm and became a grocer in Idaho. I was raised mostly in Idaho Falls. I left home at age seventeen when I graduated from high school to attend Brigham Young University; fulfilled a mission in the New England states 1947-49; and then completed a degree in music at BYU in

1952. Married, settled here, and I've been in the music profession ever since.

Let's go back for a moment to your childhood. Were both of your parents active church members?

Yes.

And dedicated?

We've already talked about how many kinds of Mormons there are. My father at one time decided that Sunday was his only free day of the week and that justified hunting and fishing on Sundays. But that represented an aberration of some sort. Generally my parents were very dedicated. But I've come to accept that there are thousands of variations on being Mormon, and I'm one of them.

I know you're concerned about the term "Jack Mormon." The church calls them "less active."

I don't consider any description that I've heard yet adequate to describe my situation accurately. Jack Mormon, in spite of the fact that it is very ambiguous and could probably mean anything to anybody, is most often associated with people who don't adhere to the Mormon lifestyle. But I still do, as I did for the first forty-five years of my life. It would be more accurate to describe me as a "heretic." The church likes to refer to us as "intellectuals," but that doesn't apply to me either. One time I was asked to give a lesson to the high priests on "What Is a Mormon?" The recommended chapters in the book we were using as a quorum manual contained a definition by J. Reuben Clark that maintained a Mormon believed this, this, this, and this—a half dozen or so essential beliefs. I started my lesson by saying, "I'm not a Mormon by his definition." I think he was dead wrong. You're a Mormon if you say you are, and I say I am. The first forty-five years of my life were very orthodox Mormon. I spent about fifteen years as a member of the general board of the Mutual Improvement Association (MIA) working very closely with general authorities. Some of my colleagues became apostles. I prefer to reserve the right to call myself whatever I wish. And I'm neither a Jack Mormon nor an inactive, although right now my bishop is still looking for a place where I fit in, where I won't cause too much trouble.

Describe what kind of a Mormon you are.

First of all, I'm an historical Mormon. I was raised in the church, and I'd say that most of my habits of living, the way I think, and my values have been inherited from the Mormon tradition. I don't repudiate them in any way. I consider the church essentially a human institution. As a human institution, it stacks up very well against other human institutions, like the Democratic party, the Elks Club, etc. I think that the big problem that many people have is that their expectations are too high because the church claims to be a divine institution. I have lowered my expectations to the extent that I can still smile a little bit once in a while when it comes to the church. I think they do a great deal of good for individuals of all ages. In my ward they nourish old people in ways that are very often rare out in the world. And they do the same for the very young. We used to be very good in the field of youth programs, but I think we've slipped somewhat where that's concerned. There are many programs sponsored by religious and secular societies that probably do as good a job as we're doing in that area. But I'm still amazed at how many good things happen, and they've happened in my family, and I personally feel they're worth investing in. It's just that I don't believe that the officers are called of God, and I'm under no obligation to believe what they say.

That's unconventional.

It sure is.

You have eight children?

I do.

You're married to a woman who is a ...

A strong believer.

You were at one time a strong believer?

Definitely, until about age forty-five.

What happened?

A moment of grace came into my life, which I can describe more specifically, but it's not worth the time. It was simply a moment when I realized that change was possible, and I wanted to make it. I wasn't dissatisfied. I've never been persecuted by the church. Nobody hurt me as a Mormon. I did dislike Boy Scouts, and I wasn't a good one as a result, but I have an Eagle Scout in my family, so obviously I'm not against Boy Scouts. It just didn't work for me. That event (the moment of grace) happened at 3:20 in the afternoon.

Please describe it?

I was reading a book, and the name of the book I know, but it doesn't matter. The idea occurred to me that in order to be a better person, I would have to be more receptive to what I thought were God's messages for me. And so I said, "I'll do whatever You want if I know it's You speaking, and hang the consequences." And that was it. Everything caved in within a few minutes, and I had to start from scratch to build a new faith.

A genuine epiphany.

I think it was. I consider that the most important, single moment of my life.

Was it a freeing moment?

There was no lead up to it at all. It was just, Wham! And I did respond in the way that I said I would.

What were the first things you did?

I was on my way to Denver with the Utah Symphony. The first thing that I did was to decide to buy a pair of roller skates—pretty irrational. The second thing was I felt compelled to read a book which in my mind at that time was forbidden. That book was one I had run across when I was a missionary in New England and had more or less put into a file to be dealt with some other time. The next morning in Denver I was waiting on the library steps when it opened, and I spent two days nonstop reading that book.

What book was that?

It's a book called *Oahspe*, and it's doubtful that you've ever heard of it. It's a mystical book, and dates from the middle of the nineteenth century. Its content was startling to me, although I can say it has little impact on me today. It was a catalyst, and it did accelerate the process of flushing out the old and making room for the new. It happened very, very fast. Most of my library, which you see, I gathered during the period immediately following that event when I felt I had to fill in the blanks. Generally Mormons are not encouraged to study all faith systems seriously, but I had to. So I became a voracious consumer of literature about religion. I'm at least four things. I'm a father and husband, a musician, a naturalist, and a religious nut. But I don't own a church. I make up my own theology to fit the need.

You're very spiritual, aren't you?

I don't know what that means. I've succeeded in erasing the line between what is spiritual and what is not. I think every human activity has the potential to be a spiritual act—an act of worship, an act of thanksgiving, of rejoicing—or the opposite, damning and hellish. I choose to make life experiences, as much as possible, fun and glorious. That may be spiritual to some, but it's not a conventional way of looking at spirituality. They wouldn't buy that in my ward, but they wouldn't buy it in a lot of other places, either. My modes of prayer and worship are so many that they're indescribable and constantly changing.

When I was tracting in New England as a missionary, people would often say, "I'm very open-minded but I'm not interested." Bam! We'd walk away and I'd remember saying to myself, "Yes, they're so open minded their brains are falling out." One could say that about me perhaps, but I have my own solid convictions. I have a very strong belief system, but it is unconventional by Mormon standards. I care little if there's a hereafter. I find most descriptions of God uninteresting. I believe in doing compassionate things and having fun. That's about it.

How does that impact your wife and children?

My children are close to each other and to my wife and me, very close. It's inconceivable that we do important things without sharing them. We have four families who live here in the valley, and we have four families from sea to shining sea. And I'm good friends with all of them. We do much better than tolerate each other. I respect their religion and they reciprocate. I encourage them to be good Mormons if they believe that way. But my heresies are a source of great pain to my wife whose upbringing was also conventional Mormon. She's opened herself considerably over the period of twenty-plus years that I've been floating free out there. That's made our lives together tolerable, better than tolerable—we have a wonderful life together. We've been married almost fifty years. But it hasn't been especially easy for her. Once in a while things get tense and it's hard for her. But we'll survive that.

Is it conceivable that another epiphany could return you to a conventional kind of Mormonism.

Any moment.

That could happen?

I consider myself open to that possibility, but most of my problems with Mormon beliefs are that I really don't like them. It's not that I don't believe them so much. I don't want to believe. They don't fit into a cosmic scheme my brain can deal with.

Does your brain create a cosmic scheme of its own?

I have dozens of them that I like. I don't pretend that any of them is the right one. I think that they're constructs that may be useful to us humans when thinking about that which is beyond our ability to comprehend. I probably feel more comfortable with aspects of Hindu philosophy or Buddhist than the Judeo-Christian tradition, which I feel is burdened with an overall notion of a chosen people. When God selects from all of us offspring, so to speak, a few to give them either favor or a special mission, I get very uncomfortable. I say, "No way, I'm sorry." Whatever god set that up is alien to me. I think that situation is at the root of many of the world's ills—the religious conflicts including Ireland, Israel, and Bosnia. Much of the conflict in our world history has been fanned by the idea of some people being God's chosen—or having his favor or his authority or some other thing—and others not. Being dominated by those who think they are is an idea that is abhorrent and sickening to me, almost inconceivable.

Alma in the Book of Mormon begins his lecture on faith by saying that first you have to have a desire to believe—that's the beginning of it. I agree wholeheartedly with that, but I have little desire to believe the Mormon myths. So I don't. But Mormons are still my friends, my best friends. What a person believes is such a private thing. It's inconceivable that we can think that the things that we hold dear or have defined for ourselves are somehow so lofty and wonderful that other people can't be happy without them.

If somebody wants to know my story, I'm glad to tell it, but it's more in the spirit that there are lots of kinds of faith. One of our close friends is Hindu. In her little shrine in her home is a ceramic elephant head. That representation is one of the Hindu pantheon of gods. I don't care at all what symbol a person uses to focus their attention on that which they may call God. It could just as well be an ant as far as I'm concerned, and would be just as close. However, I don't believe that all beliefs are the same. That is, if somebody's belief system teaches them it's okay to take advantage of somebody else, then their belief system is inferior, by my standards. Period. So I do have strong values. I'm grateful to various religious traditions who've articulated those. People have done that, and they continue to do that today. I wept when Nelson Mandela became the president of South Africa, and he brought together a cabinet of his enemies. I think he's a prophet to our world. In my sense of a prophet, he's showing us a very lofty way to live. Prophets are wherever you find them, and I think there are a whole lot of them to learn from.

I reject the traditional idea that there's such a thing as scripture. All the books in this room, to me, are scripture. That is, every one of them has ideas of worth, of inspiration; I'd be willing to cross-out the titles and all of the authors' names and judge every book by its content. If it's profitable for instruction and virtue and so on, then it becomes scripture to me. So I don't have four scriptures. I have more like 4,000. Some of them I value more than the traditional four Mormon scriptures because they're more in line with where I am at the present. But I'm prepared, as you said, that tomorrow morning the world may look different to me.

Not everybody should do what I do. You have to have a certain disposition or personality to make your way alone where the religious enterprise is concerned. I certainly wouldn't advocate that anybody follow me. I enjoy people who grow their own because we get so many new ways of looking at the world, whereas when we get institutionalized, we are encouraged to all think similarly or to not think at all. Maybe I wouldn't have done it at another time in my life. I think that what happened to me was appropriate when it happened, and probably shouldn't have happened earlier—for reasons I don't know.

Given the philosophy you've just articulated, I'm not sure you'd want to say anything to the president of the church, if you could. You might simply accept the way things are. You seem to be a very accepting person. But if you were to say something to the president of the Mormon church, what would it be?

Only to lighten up with regard to intellectuals, gays, the woman's movement, etc. I like President Hinckley very much. He's a gifted public spokesperson for the church. I wouldn't for anything want to be in his shoes, but there are zillions of things I'd do differently. For instance, the recent controversy over [BYU basketball coach] Roger Reed and the recruit he was trying to sign up. [Reed had attempted to use church influence to have the young recruit sign with BYU.]

I think that BYU's course is tragic. It's not because they're trying to teach values in addition to science and other disciplines—that's wonderful. But the fact is they're not practicing good values. They're putting athletics ahead of scholarship, for one thing. That was very clear, not only in what Coach Reed said, but when I heard [BYU] President [Merrill] Bateman address the Rotary Club a few months ago, he said virtually the same thing. I wanted to stand up and say, "I don't want to have anything to do with an institution of higher learning that has such skewed values." At the time that I went to BYU I thought it was, of all places, the place I wanted to be. After I graduated, I even dreamed of coming back there to teach. But things change. I taught for thirty-two years at the U. of U. instead, and I love that institution very much. So where the church's attitude toward education is concerned, I see serious problems. I think that our kids are encouraged to obey rather than think. I consider that a terrible thing, a human tragedy—at the very time when they have the most energy to devour things, to learn, to contribute. The students are at the age of Joseph Smith when the church was founded, and the attitude seems to be "don't trust them as far as you can throw them." This isn't my big message, it's just one that occurred to me because it's been in the news recently.

What do church authorities make of Ardean Watts?

I don't know, but I can imagine. One of my friends who became an apostle told me that he thought that my epiphany was from the devil. My response was that if I pray to God and God allows the devil to answer, then he's not my God. On the other hand, I had a number of other interviews with the brethren at the time that were very positive; some were quite understanding and said things like, "Well, you'll probably be back some day when you wake up out of your funny dream," which is better than saying that it was the devil. One former general authority friend responded, "I understand where you're coming from." I'm sure there's a large file maintained by the committee organized for the purpose of keeping track of folks like me dealing with the times that I have appeared in public and spoken critically of church policies or programs. But I've always tried to do that politely and respectfully.

Respectfully?

I do respect them. I do respect the gentleman and ladies who contribute much to many lives through their service in the church. But I get to choose my own prophets. So I guess that's fair.

Do you have anything you want to add?

Is my story different from your other interviews?

Altogether different from any of the others. A little more mystical than almost all, except maybe Ed Firmage. He didn't have a lightning-strike epiphany like you.

I value Ed as a friend, and I've been quite close to him and several others. The people I gravitate toward the most are liberal Mormons, then liberal non-Mormons, and then straight Mormons. I should retract that. It sounds condescending to say some of my best friends are straight Mormons. Nobody could have had a better church life than I did. I graduated from BYU and settled in Salt Lake Valley. After a few years I was invited to become a member of the MIA general board. I worked on a daily basis on that board with people whom I respected as much as any who existed in our town. My church service was doing something in harmony with my professional ability. That's as good as it gets. My life has been so rewarding that there's nothing I can complain about. I have a good family, I've been healthy. I don't have any sense that I earned that at all. I'm not comfortable with the notion that

God singled one out for such lavish gifts, but I'm perfectly happy to enjoy them while I can. I can understand that somebody who's been beaten up repeatedly would have a totally different attitude, depending on who beat them up. That's not something that I understand existentially. I understand only that I can't imagine that life then or now could be any better. I'm retired and can do anything I please within reason. I hope that I contribute to other people's happiness in the process.

May I make a request? Would you play something for me?

No.

You won't?

No, I've never played the piano well enough to match my standards. Now, for the first time, I'm playing for my own pleasure at home. I don't do it excellently, so playing in front of anybody makes me ill. The only exceptions are a few family occasions when the family understands, and occasionally I support others as soloists.

Fair enough.

I do find ways of contributing musically. For instance, I'm on the search committee to find a new conductor for the Utah Symphony. I dig into that with my heart and soul. I do things my way. I do everything with passion. My life is full and varied. Tonight I'm taking my first scuba diving lesson. I'm going to the Yucatan Peninsula next winter to have that experience for the first time. I've snorkeled a little bit in the Caribbean and in the Gulf of California. Never done the deep stuff, and I wanted to do that before my body and mind deteriorate to the point I can't.

So you plan to be certified?

I'm going to be certified by Christmas.

When were you born?

In 1928. I'm sixty-eight.

17.

Edwin Brown Firmage

I believe that in the end the truth will conquer.

—*John Wycliffe*

Edwin B. Firmage teaches constitutional and international law at the University of Utah's College of Law in Salt Lake City. A Hinckley Fellow at Brigham Young University, he graduated with high honors in political science and history; received a master's degree in history from BYU; was a National Honors Scholar at the University of Chicago Law School; and served on the editorial board of the Chicago Law Review. *He received Doctor of Law, Master of Laws, and Doctor of Jurisprudence degrees from Chicago.*

Ed was a White House Fellow on the staff of Vice President Hubert H. Humphrey, with responsibility for civil rights. He also served as United Nations Visiting Scholar and attended sessions of the U.N. General Assembly in New York and the arms control negotiations in Geneva, Switzerland, in 1970-71. He was a Fellow in Law and Humanities at the Harvard Law School, and received the U. of U.'s Distinguished Teaching Award and BYU's Alumni Distinguished Achievement Award. He was named Samuel D. Thurman Professor of Law by the U. in January 1990.

In 1987 the U. of U. invited him to deliver the annual Reynolds Lecture, "Ends and Means in Conflict." He was awarded the Charles Redd

Prize by the Utah Academy of Science, Arts and Letters for outstanding contributions in the humanities and social sciences. Recipient of the 1989 Governor's Award in the Humanities, given by the Utah Endowment for the Humanities, he delivered the McDougall lecture at the Cathedral of the Madeleine in Salt Lake City in March 1989.

Ed is author or co-author of numerous books and publications. His book with Collin Mangrum, Zion in the Courts: A Legal History of the Church of Jesus Christ of Latter-day Saints, *was the first legal history of the Mormon experience in the nineteenth century and was named best book of 1989 by Alpha Sigma Nu, the Honors Society of the National Association of Jesuit Colleges & Universities in the United States. With the late Francis Wormuth, he wrote* To Chain the Dog of War: The War Power of Congress in History & Law; *and with J. Welch and B. Weiss, he edited* Religion & Law: Biblical, Jewish and Islamic Perspectives.

Ed was a participant in a Fulbright Seminar in the Soviet Union during the summer of 1990, and worked with Vietnamese refugees in Vietnam, Thailand, and Hong Kong in 1990 and 1991. He was the 1991 recipient of the Rosenblatt Prize for Excellence, the highest academic award given by the University of Utah. In 1991 he was also awarded the Turner-Fairbourn Award for significant contributions to peace and justice. He has been an invited speaker at many institutions here and abroad, including lectures to Justice and Peace Representatives of the International Congregation of Men and Women Religious in Rome in 1993. That same year he delivered the Kellogg Lectures at the Episcopal Divinity School in Cambridge, Massachusetts.

It is autumn, and the University of Utah campus is particularly lovely. As you approach the law school, the trees of Cottam's Gulch are resplendent in golds and tans. Ed's office is on an upper floor with a view of Pioneer Memorial Theater and, beyond, Salt Lake City's Avenues. Ed greets you, and immediately you're at ease. He wears tan slacks and a plaid shirt which make his eyes seem very blue. A small scar marks his chin. He asks to change chairs, and leans back in a lounger. He's just had an inner-ear operation ("caused by sediments from the Balboa beaches") and is still affected by it. He moves to a nearly prone position, and you feel like a psychiatrist looking down on a patient.

His office is small. On one wall is a striking poster of Desmond Tutu. Shelves are filled with books—books on war, international law, Constitutional law. A candle glows on a poster for Amnesty International. There are numerous photographs—of his mother, of himself with Vice President Hubert Humphrey and President Lyndon Johnson. Also hanging are a BYU Alumni Association Distinguished Service Award, and a U. of U. Distinguished Teaching Award. His Doctor of Jurisprudence degree from the University of Chicago is framed and sealed in wood.

~

I was born in Provo, Utah, in 1935. I had an active Mormon mother and a humorously semi-active father. Dad took organized religion with a substantial dose of humor. He was a spiritual man. I came to realize that in my adult years. He had to be coaxed or coerced into church. He found God in the mountains.

On horseback, we took a frying pan and coffee pot any Sunday he could because he worked twelve-hour days, six days a week, at Penney's and then later the Firmage store. So there was conflict between Mom and Dad in that regard. I always felt deeply close to God. I never doubted. Not a Mormon god particularly, just simply God. But I didn't have any particular interest in theology in my young days, and didn't read scripture, including Mormon scripture, until my honeymoon. I was called on a mission when I was on a honeymoon. It wasn't as astounding as it sounds in that it had been sort of planned. I became engaged to my former mate after one year at Brigham Young University. I always planned on a mission. I'd grown up in such a totally Mormon environment that one didn't even think of a choice. It was not *would* you go, but *when* would you go. On my honeymoon I got a mission call to England. And in that two-week honeymoon I read all the standard works. It's an interesting way to spend a honeymoon, but I did actually read all of the Old Testament, the New Testament, the Doctrine and Covenants, the Pearl of Great Price, the Book of Mormon—all essentially for the first time with any seriousness.

And you'd attended all your services regularly?

I'd been a pretty active attender except when I was off with Dad.

Was there ever any open discord between your mother and father about your going off with your dad?

Oh, yes, frequently. I remember being recruited by Mother to try to help convince Dad to stop smoking; he smoked a pipe—thoroughly enjoyed it. I approached him when I was just a little kid, three or four. Mother was a very artful, manipulative woman who, for all good purposes, didn't want him smoking. So he stopped. He still enjoyed a cold beer every now and then. But due in part to my letters, mainly from the mission field, Dad became a Mormon bishop of two student wards at BYU and was a superb bishop because he was a very humane, kind man and didn't care too much for the rule book. He simply spent his time counseling, giving good sage counsel to young people about life. Dad excelled at the sunny side of the haystack "reasoning together" on religion, and did extremely well. He was a very loved bishop. But I think he viewed God as a great mystery—he didn't doubt God—but felt that many of the strictures that organized religion placed upon human beings (not the Mormons particularly more or less than others, but it was the Mormons he experienced) were rather severe and sometimes unfeeling. The trouble he got into as bishop was always with a superior, who wanted a harsh verdict of some sort. Dad also leaped over them occasionally and appealed to N. Eldon Tanner or Grandfather Hugh B. Brown on behalf of a young kid. For example: A youth going on a mission whom the stake president wanted to keep from going for doing something that 99 percent of young men have done (and the other 1 percent are liars). Dad wouldn't go along with them and got Eldon Tanner to agree and that irked his stake president. Dad was released. But he was always very friendly toward the Mormon church and modestly active in it.

You mentioned Grandfather Brown. He was your mother's father?

Yes, Mom's father. When I came back from the White House after service with Vice President Hubert Humphrey, I lived almost next door to Grandfather, and so for the last decade more or less of his life we were very close. We'd been all of our lives; he was a loving father and mentor in my childhood and youth. I'd worked with him when he was in Canada. I was in my mid-teens. I worked as a young man roughnecking the long end of a shovel on an oil rig. We had long talks in the evening, and there was never a censure or a harsh kind of ecclesiastical, authoritarian "this is the way it is and so you better believe" sort of thing, but rather he took seriously relatively childish questions. "Who's God's father" type questions—if that's childish, it's pretty profound really—and give them serious attention. I always saw reflected in his vast library and in the way he conducted his own life, a very humane, broad-gauged man, who didn't fit comfortably within the conservative, authoritarian structure in which he worked. He was the odd man out. I grew up Republican because my parents—being mercantile types—were. And in Utah County and Provo, what else could I be? I always wondered why Grandfather was a Democrat among so many Republicans. I once asked Grandfather, "Why are you a Democrat?" His answer at the time seemed simple-minded. Since then I've found it rather profound. He said, "Eddie, I think the Democratic party is more sensitive to the poor." He didn't say anything else, no big theological or political thing ... just "they're more sensitive to the poor." I now think that's a pretty good way of judging politics and religion.

What comes first, the liberalism or the inactivity? I've talked to many people in the course of this project who are liberal and inactive, more so than of conservatives who are inactive. Any thoughts on why this may be the case?

I think it can be both. For me it was both simultaneously and before I knew either was happening. You could date a liberalizing influence when I was a young boy with Grandfather Brown having religious talks, and borrowing books from his library, most of which I never returned. As I consciously look back, it began for me probably in the mission field because I smuggled into my digs in England and Scotland the writings of the early Fathers, Greek and Latin Fathers—Origen, Tertullian, Clement of Rome, Clement of Alexandria. (And quickly thereafter, the writings of others—living people whom I would view as Christian disciples, like C. S. Lewis and Tolkien.) And the writings of Fredrick W. Farrar on Jesus and Paul. As I read these writers of the second, third, fourth, fifth, sixth, and seventh centuries, I felt that they had been touched by God. I was too unconscious of what was happening to understand the awkwardness of what I was teaching as opposed to what I was reading. As far as I was concerned, I was strengthening my Mormon testimony. But I was laying the groundwork, laying some mines that would be detonated later, because the idea of preaching an apostasy and a restoration were antithetical to concluding that there was an unbroken line of writings from the gospel writings on; that there wasn't any huge chasm between the end of the first century and the nineteenth. The idea that God was sort of snoozing until 1820 now seems to me absurd. Many deeply spiritual people were living, and I came increasingly to feel a deep affinity with them—like I knew them. That continuity increasingly came to be terribly important to me. The Mormon explanation for it seemed to trivialize God, and them.

I read a speech of Grandfather's as I did a biography of him. Grandfather bought into this too, seeing all this as prologue, a great big drum roll for 1820. Years ago I finally said, "My hell, that's a long drum roll." Seventeen centuries of apostasy or at best prologue trivializes enormous actors on the stage: From Origen, Tertullian, Clement of Rome, Clement of Alexandria to St. Augustine to Thomas Aquinas; Wesley, Luther, and the entire Protestant Reformation. These people were not a Greek chorus, prologue to Hamlet walking out on the stage. All of them had more impact than Joseph Smith in reality, in my mind now, in Christian history. But the more I read and the more I pondered and the more other life events began to hit me, my fundamental Mormon paradigm began to show fissures and then finally it cracked wide open. That is where political liberalism and theological and spiritual inquiry joined.

By 1960 Ezra Taft Benson had returned from Eisenhower's cabinet and had begun preaching a powerful John Birch line, often disguised as if it weren't, but it was—it was straight out of Robert Welch and his *American Opinion* magazine. Grandfather was the checkmate to this as best he could be. And I worked with him. I was a young law student just beginning my first year at Chicago when Benson had first raised the John Birch thing. Grandfather asked me to do a report for him on that subject. "Eddie what is this John Birch Society?" So I did a research paper for grandfather in 1960-61. Benson had returned and his son would become a coordinator for New England or some area for the Birch Society, and a lot of this stuff was being infused by Benson into Mormon speeches and teaching. Grandfather was busy trying to checkmate this. About the same time I had just moved from the BYU environment to Chicago's South Side. I'm asking myself theological and sociological and political questions exactly at the same time.

Why did you go to Chicago?

I was going to the University of Chicago Law School. Rex Lee and myself and a fellow named Larry Wimmer, who was a missionary companion of mine in Manchester, England, had all decided to go to the same school. We applied to Yale, Harvard, Stanford, Berkeley, Utah, and Chicago. We were accepted by each of them and had money offered by most of them. Chicago offered us the most dough, and as young marrieds, we followed the scholarship funds. We also felt that Chicago was perhaps the premiere law school in the country. Larry Wimmer wanted to join the economics department at Chicago to study under Milton Friedman.

I took the Goldwateresque political views that I had acquired in a Provo environment to Chicago's South Side, and that paradigm collapsed. I couldn't see reasonable social and political answers coming through a sort of, "If you had any gumption, you'd inherit your own department store" sort of mentality. Though the university had an impact, Chicago's South Side had a lot more.

After graduation and the acquisition of a few graduate degrees, I taught for a year at the University of Missouri Law School and then went to work on the staff of Hubert Humphrey in civil rights. The president had given Humphrey two big mandates: one over civil rights and the other was over relationships with the mayors and the governors. I ended up working with Roy Wilkins of the N.A.A.C.P., Whitney Young of the Urban league, and Martin Luther King, Jr., of the Southern Christian Leadership Conference. And, particularly with Roy Wilkins of the N.A.A.C.P., I formed an intimate friendship. We often talked and he talked about the blacks and the Mormon priesthood and his sadness at that policy. He believed that both groups had much to give the other. He even offered to fly secretly into Salt Lake and meet with Grandfather and church leaders about this topic and not make any public to-do about it, make it absolutely secret.

So those things were festering in me: what about the blacks? What about the priesthood? What about the constant, reactionary drumbeat of Mormon ecclesiastical teaching as it interfaced with politics that I was by then deeply involved in at the White House. For example, I spent a good part of my time planning the White House Conference on Civil Rights. Tickets to it were like gold. University presidents were turned away, governors were turned away; there was very limited seating capacity for it, although hundreds and hundreds would be there—everybody wanted to come. There had been no invitations to Mormons sent. Now the president and the vice president have what you call "night reading." That is, they will read overnight some portions of the thousands of letters and memoranda that they didn't write but bear their signature. Humphrey would take this correspondence home each night and glance through it. He saw a memo that I'd written to Clifford Alexander, who was the president's man on civil rights (I played a similar role for Humphrey), saying, "Look, there isn't a Mormon in this whole group. I admit that this group will not contribute to the cutting edge of debate on this topic—they're way behind. But part of governance is not simply getting the best and the brightest to create new law, but also to bring the country with you through dialogue with many groups as you move into a radically different time—so won't you invite two or three Mormons?" Humphrey happened to see this memo sent over his imprimatur—my name but on his stationery. He wrote back on it, "Eddie, I will support you. Tell me who you want invitations to go to." So I chose four youngish Mormon general authorities whom I thought were up-and-comers at the time. Tom Monson was one and two or three others. [Marion D.] Duff Hanks received an invitation. But the word came down from the top: no Mormon general authority would be allowed to go. I know that Hanks would've come. They sent Milan Smith who was, as I recall, stake president in the area of the Capitol. The other major religious traditions had national and international church functionaries attending. You could multiply that incident a hundred times and those were the things I was bumping into.

Up to this time, did you have a basic bedrock testimony of the Joseph Smith story?

Absolutely. The whole thing. I was deeply disturbed by the black and the priesthood issue, but I don't choose my religion by a particularly disturbing single issue. Whether it's the ordination of women or blacks or a more authoritarian structure than I feel comfortable with, I don't leave, even de facto, an organization on the basis of some level of discomfort on one issue. There'd be no home that one could institutionally find if one did that. It was more fundamental things like Christian continuity. Increasingly I felt the need of continuity. I just felt uncomfortable with an 1820 beginning. I felt enormously deprived, spiritually hungry. When I got into the literature of other churches at a later time, I saw how thirsty I truly was. When I discovered in 1980 the writings of Thomas Merton and Francis of Assisi, it connected back with my meeting (through their writings) Lewis, Tolkien, Bonhoeffer, in the 1960s, and Farrar and the Fathers of the early church in the 1950s. But they came to have a deep impact on me. I felt the need institutionally to connect those centuries, and this feeling was utterly at odds with the Mormon response of apostasy and restoration; all those people in all those centuries were but a prologue to the Restoration. That idea for me disintegrated.

What happened at that time was a critical point in my exodus. The MX missile debate. Paradoxically so, because while I was chasing air force generals around the desert (debating MX), I was meeting wonderful religious figures, many of them Franciscans. I had long dialogues with Mormon leaders which lead to three Mormon messages by the First Presidency: a Christmas message, an Easter message, and finally an MX message, all dealing with nuclear weapons. The first two statements essentially condemned the nuclear arms race and expressed horror at such weapons ever being used. In addition, whenever KSL would editorialize in favor of MX, I'd be allowed KSL air time to rebut. Gordon Hinckley at the time was the head of the Public Affairs Committee, a euphemism for the "church-state committee."

The "church-state committee"?

I'd call it that, if you scraped away the euphemism. Its jurisdiction concerned the relation between church and state. I'd been meeting with and writing Gordon Hinckley long memoranda based on the teachings of the Old Testament, New Testament, Book of Mormon, and the Doctrine and Covenants, and the teachings of Joseph Smith, Brigham Young, et al., on force and violence and the Christian gospel of love. There was great disharmony between those teachings and having a base in Utah and Nevada of the greatest collection of genocidal power that had ever been known. There was almost dark humor in basing such weapons in an area seen by the original settlers as "Zion." Finally, I was asked to brief the First Presidency on this, which I did. I spent two hours with Spencer Kimball and Presidents [Marion G.] Romney and Eldon Tanner. I'd gone in with long memoranda. I knew but didn't emotionally remember or realize that they were functionally nearly blind in old age. I had to tell them the story of MX and why I thought it was such a threat. I was due to fly off to make one last effort to dissuade Jimmy Carter from supporting MX. It was the one time in my life when I single-issued a candidate. I was on his reelection committee, and I said to members of his staff that if they went ahead with the MX, I couldn't support his candidacy. Eldon Tanner called and said, "Delay your White House trip. We've found a later flight for you. We want you to come in and brief the Quorum of the Twelve and tell them what you told us." So I did. This was the culmination of a year of private meetings with Gordon Hinckley. I briefed the quorum and the First Presidency (the First Presidency joined the Twelve in their meeting room). I wrote a draft statement that I hoped would be of some use. A week later the church's statement on MX was released. I was then ready to start a nationwide speaking tour with a navy vice admiral, John Marshall Lee, and one of the heads of the Western Shoshone and the head of the Nevada Cattlemen's Association—a four-person truth squad, in our view of truth, at least, going across the country preaching against MX. I was just at that time going to brief the *L.A. Times* religion editor, John Dart, when the church called and read the statement to me. I said, "That's great." My interview with John Dart came out banner, front-page headlines: "Mormon Church Comes Out Against MX." I think formal Mormon opposition is without a doubt what killed it, given the proposed MX location. Had it been located in New York's Central Park, the Mormon First Presidency statement wouldn't have found the obituary page. But given the location in the heart of the Mormon Great Basin, the idea of force-feeding a missile down the throat of a group now utterly opposed was politically not possible.

The whole culture, basically.

It's simply not acceptable in a democratic state. I believe the First Presidency statement killed MX.

Long before that, I put together what was called "Utahns United Against MX." It included our then new Roman Catholic bishop, William Weigand, and our Episcopal bishop Otis Charles, the Jewish rabbi, AFL-CIO leader Eddie Mayne, Maestro Maurice Abravanel, Chase Peterson of the University of Utah, and about seventy other luminaries. In this process I also had met people who'd change my life dramatically. They were more simple folk, mainly the Women Religious of Roman Catholicism. I met some spectacular nuns who were at the forefront of MX opposition in their communities; Franciscans in the main, but not always. A Franciscan sister in Las Vegas, Rosemary Lynch; Mary Luke Tobin of the Sisters of Loretto, who'd worked closely with Thomas Merton earlier in an abbey near his at Gethsemane, Kentucky. One of the few women invited to Vatican II. She introduced me to the writings of Thomas Merton. Rose introduced me to the writings of Francis of Assisi. By that time I was also into more secular writing—but writing directly relevant for me and my own pilgrimage—and that was the writing of Carl Jung—depth psychology. I was into a form of depth spirituality and depth psychology simultaneously from 1980 on. This was new to me, utterly new, without a Mormon counterpart. The "inner journey" rather than seeing simply a transcendent God out there sitting on some star near Kolob. There was another aspect of spirituality, I learned—God wasn't only the transcendental "ultimate Other." He was also a subjective God, in my heart, the *Imago Dei*. I'd been speaking without a means of spiritual, emotional, and physical renewal, almost alone, for over a year. The governor was still in favor of MX. He later became a valued opponent of the MX, but in 1979 he'd send a letter inviting MX to Utah.

That would've been Scott Matheson.

Scott Matheson, friend and colleague. He did a wonderful turnaround and became a powerful opponent of MX, but at an earlier time he was in favor of it. As were all of our Congressional delegation, my own party's president, and the Congress which was Democratic. So it was a very lonely war. For a long time I was meeting privately with Gordon Hinckley, but other than that I was speaking around the state, doing everything I could to help people see not only the genocidal nature of this weapon, but also to see the deep spiritual and moral issues central to this question. I came to a point where I was really burned out. I needed a source of renewal. And I don't think my Mormon tradition gave me the teaching or the tools to renew. Maybe this is my fault, not any institutional fault, but as I saw my institution it didn't provide an obvious way of renewal. Subjective spirituality wasn't emphasized in Mormon teaching. We could make a desert blossom as a rose, but our own heart could be an arid desert. And the idea of meditation, of contemplation, of an inner journey, of Christian mysticism—or for that matter Buddhist spirituality or Hindu spirituality or Sufi spirituality—were utterly beyond my horizon.

Were you conflicted by this?

I was intrigued, fascinated, drawn by the rich mixture of history and spirituality. Of course, a lot of this was overcoming fearful stereotypes. Brick by brick a paradigmatic structure that had worked well for me for a long time was being dismantled. I couldn't see Catholics through the lens of older stereotypes after Sister Rosemary. I couldn't preach apostasy from the readings I'd done even as a young Mormon missionary. Lutherans, Jews ... I mean, it all seemed like there was one huge central truth—and that was our common humanity. Then there was a secondary truth and that was the wonder of our individuality. This secondary truth could sometimes be controlling. For example, if I were single, which I am, I'd want to marry a woman, so the fact that I'm a man means that I'd be looking for a woman, and our common humanity, though a larger truth, wouldn't control my decision to date women rather than men. But in human rights you could never have the secondary truth as being controlling. Whether I was black, or Catholic, or Mormon, or male, or Hispanic, an alien, or legitimate, or illegitimate—these ways we categorize ourselves in law and sociology—shouldn't overpower for human rights' purposes the primary truth of a common humanity. I saw this universality preached better by different organizations than my own.

I have to go back now because I've missed one terribly important man in my life. Other than Jesus—and that's unfair competition, to compete with God—it would be St. Paul. I wrote a little book on Paul; it was meant as a little morality play for my brothers and sisters of the Mormon church. I first read Paul as a young missionary in England in a version of the Bible that wasn't King James (and I think that was important because I needed to see it afresh without a sing-song familiarity). When I read the second chapter of Ephesians and Paul talked of a universal humanity, it blew my mind. Here's this provincial young man from Provo, Utah, never seen a black guy, and Paul is talking in Ephesians about an absolutely universal humanity. He's fighting the problem of whether a gentile must first become a Jew before becoming a Christian. In the earliest period of Christianity, all Christians had also been Jews. But then the Christian church had to confront the seemingly paradoxical phenomenon of gentile Christianity. By then you're having this phenomenon of gentile Christianity and it would foment the first Christian Council of Jerusalem in Acts 15. Paul wins. The gentile Christian need not be circumcised or obey any other of the Jewish law to become a Christian. Jesus becomes the door for the gentile Christian convert.

Paul's vision of universal humanity makes him one of the four or five great people in history. Though for Paul, it didn't extend to women. (Even here, however, Paul's personal practice must have transcended his traditional notion of the role of women in religion. We owe to Paul and his traveling companion Luke almost all of the names of women we have in the New Testament.) This Pauline vision of universality made it possible to evangelize the whole world.

This universal statement to this Provo boy simply blew my mind. Later my experience in Chicago, then falling into the arms of Hubert Humphrey and Roy Wilkins and Whitney Young and Martin Luther King would explain my growing sense of human universality. Later I'd begin to meet, through literature, Francis of Assisi, Thomas Merton, Mahatma Gandhi, and Carl Jung. These would be my guides to the center of my own soul.

Now I have to qualify all this. As I've aged, I see the reality of the objective God, the ultimate Other. I don't think the inner journey is the whole story; it's simply a yin and yang. I believe in an objective God who's different from me, utterly different than me, and who's somewhere. I believe that Jesus is Christ, God's son, and somehow God incarnate himself. I believe that historical fact and that objective reality. I also believe, as Jesus said, that "the kingdom of God is within you." There's the need of an inner journey, of creating one's own myth, the story of subjective spirituality. And there I had no Mormon help, no theology, and no institutionalization for me to go out on a dream quest, to go inside. Yet in the MX controversy I desperately needed it because I was burning out. A sister in Cheyenne, Wyoming, Francis Russell, who was a Franciscan and who headed opposition to MX right there under the noses of the air force, introduced me to the retreat process, as did Sister Mary Luke Tobin. I met Mary Luke when I was the house-Mormon in an ecumenical service opposing MX in North Dakota, sponsored by the Methodist and Catholic bishops of the state. Mary Luke and I were the keynote speakers at the ecumenical service. She introduced me to Merton. (She runs the Thomas Merton Center for Creative Exchange in Denver.)

The Episcopalian and Catholic view of history, of continuity, deeply appealed to me. I feel the need for connection of centuries. Episcopal practice, for me, performs the necessary though awkward precarious job of accepting the Christian teaching through every century before the Reformation, and equally accepting the central teachings of the Reformation.

Mormonism didn't give this to you?

Mormonism didn't do that. I read one of Grandfather's speeches again. At one point he'd talked of the importance of the Reformers and the importance of what had gone before. But again, to him, it was a big drum roll. A big drum roll for the restoration in 1820. And I thought, My hell! Augustine isn't a drum roll! You know, the great Protestant reformers, the Church Fathers; this isn't a prologue to something else. Christian teaching and spirituality have continued from the beginning through the centuries. God is speaking in every century in a magnificent fulfillment in and of itself—not as a prologue to something else. I thought, How tiny we make God. And how tiny we make these figures. Could I really worship a God that snoozes around from the end of the first century until 1820? What the hell was he doing?

At the same time, going back to your original question—it was happening simultaneously, these things were interacting, like an antiphonal chorus. For example, after my work with Martin Luther King, Ezra Benson sent a statement directly after Martin Luther King's death, attacking that great religious leader, to the general authorities. He referred to King as an agent of the Communist conspiracy and all this horseshit. I'd worked with the man. So at the time I'm having deep theological questions, deep center-pieces of Mormon theology are coming unglued for me. Simultaneously the radically reactionary, almost paranoid conservatism, of Mormon politics and sociology was also alienating me.

You can't get a more secular issue than MX. And yet in God's wonderful paradox, it's the process of fighting a war against the MX and the decision by the air force and the president to base the MX in the Great Basin that would become the springboard for an enormous spiritual awakening for me: meeting Francis of Assisi, Thomas Merton, Carl Jung, and another big name for me, Gandhi. In preparing for the Reynolds lecture in 1987 in Canterbury, I took mainly Gandhi, Jung, Francis, and Thomas Merton; those were the big four.

You were the University of Utah's Reynolds lecturer in ...

In 1987. I wrote it in part in the Canterbury Cathedral, with an appointment at Kent University. The Reynolds lecture was a deeply personal lecture; it was my story. Then in 1989 came the supposed sequel. I viewed the McDougall lecture—which was to be a great defining point for me, in both my marriage and in my church—as simply a sequel to the Reynolds lecture—part two of my story. The Reynolds lecture was in three parts. The first part dealt with the nuclear issue in international law. The second part dealt with the constitutional issue of how we go to war (based on my book *To Chain the Dog of War* written with Francis Wormuth). The third part was beyond law. Law can help, but it leaves you hopelessly short of where we must be. Even if by law you could eliminate all nuclear weapons from the earth by fiat, you don't lobotomize a generation of physicists. You could begin the whole process of arms racing again. How do you change the souls of human beings? How do you change your mind? I went into the depth psychology of Jung, and Christian and Buddhist and Islamic spirituality. Then in the McDougall lecture, I began where the Reynolds lecture ended: beyond law. Going where law can't get you. Spirituality and psychology. The inner journey and the outer consequence. I gave the McDougall lecture at the invitation of the Catholic bishop. I didn't view it as an assault on the Mormon church. It was perceived as that because as a very small part of a thirty-page tome on Jesus, Gandhi, and Jung on reconciliation and spirituality, I said I longed for the time in my own church when several black people, some of them women, would sit on the stand as general authorities in our holy house, meaning the tabernacle. The Cathedral was packed—about a thousand people in attendance. They, hearing the whole thing in context, reacted extremely warmly to the message. But the media, quite correctly I suppose, highlighted the statement on the ordination of women. That was the newsworthy portion, in their opinion. Well, all hell broke loose. I had hundreds of letters, three death threats. Overwhelmingly most were positive, including all the communication from Catholic priests and sisters: they favored the ordination of women. But the reaction from the Mormon church was different. I think they misunderstood. I'm an old political pro and had I wanted to tack my thesis on the Mormon temple door I'd know how to do it. I hadn't put out press releases. I viewed the lecture as my personal story, more of a *mea culpa* regarding my own patriarchal past: "Here's how I should be viewing women, and I haven't in my life." Well, the speech—this is an overstatement but not too much—ended my marriage and changed fundamentally my relationship with the Mormon church.

The McDougall lecture in 1989 was a defining point. But it was more than the straw that broke the camel's back—it was more like a two by four. The response at church headquarters was immediate. There was formal rebuttal in the *Salt Lake Tribune* and all through the media. It was talked about in thousands of congregations. I received letters almost instantly, from all over the country and around the world. The issue was the role of women in religion—the feminine face of God.

Was it serious enough that you thought you might be called before a church court?

My stake president called me, and many have been excommunicated for far less. I was the first active Mormon male to make this call for women in the priesthood. Many have done so in frankly a more tepid fashion later and most of them have been excommunicated, men and women. I don't know why I haven't. I've done what I've done with great respect. I've never spoken disrespectfully of a general authority.

You obviously have very warm feelings for ...

I have warm and intimate friendships with many general authorities. All this time during the MX struggle, some of those friendships had significantly deepened. But truly I didn't see my actions, as naive as it may sound, as leading any crusade. I saw the McDougall lecture as my most intimate statement of my own spiritual journey, which included not a little acknowledgment of my own blindness and insensitivity in my attitude towards women. I bore witness. I didn't intend to lead a movement.

My Christianity is far more central to my being than my partisan political beliefs. I'm an active Democrat, I'm a liberal Democrat. I love the old social gospel, as unfashionable as it is right now. So I find my Christianity and my liberal Democratic inclinations very compatible. I've often been a sort of Lone Ranger leading off on some crusade on the First Amendment and the Utah Supreme Court, or civil rights in Utah for blacks or Hispanics or women, arms control, peaceful resolution of disputes, the MX missile, etc. But like any other human being, I need group worship and group association. In a Mormon context, I was finding that it would take me Wednesday to recover from Sunday service. I was no longer renewed by a Mormon service. I felt assaulted and degraded, or at least beat up on, not personally, but ideologically and spiritually.

In the early MX meetings in 1979 and 1980, I'd begun to go to St. Mark's, the Episcopal cathedral, in Salt Lake City. First came a retreat with Otis Charles, then Episcopal Bishop of Utah ... a silent retreat. I had no idea what I was getting into, three days of silence.

Was that difficult?

It wasn't; it turned out to be rather nice, but I was utterly astounded. I thought we were going to have three days of discussions on religious topics, and I said, "My hell, Otis, you mean we're going to sit here and not say anything for three days?" He said, "Essentially, yes, Ed. We'll have conversations in the evening, but basically we'll be silent." That was a big first for me. Since then, silent meditation and contemplation have come to be the center of my spirituality. Prayer is at the heart of my spiritual life. A deep love of the New Testament would be a second moral and spiritual worshipful element. As a young Mormon missionary, I read the New Testament nineteen times. I just loved it. I kept a copy in an open jockey box in an English Ford that I drove around. I was second counselor in the mission presidency, traveling all over the United Kingdom. When I'd stop at red lights, I'd read one paragraph and put it back. I had a love affair with the New Testament that has never ended.

You're very spiritual.

I won't put tags on myself, but my spiritual journey is the center of my life. Without it my life would have no meaning. My center isn't law professoring, it isn't fighting for constitutional issues. They're important to me, but the centerpiece would be Jesus as Christ, and St. Paul as a spectacular disciple of God with a universal vision. It has huge implications for civil rights and civil liberties, for the fight in California now regarding aliens and scapegoating, to issues of race and gender. I draw huge political implications from my theology, but it's that direction and not the reverse. In finding a religious home, I had two powerful attractions: Roman Catholicism and the Episcopal church, and I still do.

Could you embrace either of these today?

Yes. The reason I have in the last couple of years gravitated toward the Episcopal church is that on several core issues I find the Episcopal tradition more compatible with my own views. Everywhere sexuality touches the church I find myself uncomfortable in Catholicism. These include issues of the requirement of a celibate clergy; divorce and remarriage; the role of women in the church government, including ordination; abortion and choice; and birth control. I think Protestants have a blind spot when it comes to celibacy. Through my dear Roman Catholic sisters, I've come to understand the need for many who feel called to celibacy, but I oppose celibacy as a requirement for ordination. I find a comfortable theological ambiguity in the Episcopalian faith, while offering me the same episcopal and apostolic continuity through the centuries.

The Episcopal faith wonderfully acknowledges a paradox in the Reformation. They are partially a Reformation church, accepting the Reformation, but they don't denounce the Catholic tradition which came before. Where I will eventually be, I don't know, but I'm in contented communion at St. Mark's. I'm a member of the Mormon church. My tribe or ethnic group is Mormon. My religious practice is Episcopal, my theology is catholic—small "c"—and my spirituality is a blend of Catholic, Episcopal, Buddhist, and Hindu spirituality, with one huge center—Jesus as Christ.

You sound very confident.

I know who I am and where I am. I can be damned wrong on many things, but this is where I am. And I've been public enough about it that I'm not in the closet on any issue.

Can you see a time where you might ask to be excommunicated from the LDS church?

Yes, if I felt tension between my Mormon membership and my Episcopalian communion and practice. The Episcopal church looks upon my baptism as valid. I'm a baptized Christian. I'm invited to take the Eucharist. My dear Dominican friends never denied me, and I often took the Eucharist at St. Catherine of Siena Parish, at the Newman Center here, but they were violating their rules and I was forcing them to violate their rules. I came to be uncomfortable in this. If I were to marry after being divorced, unless I went through the annulment procedure, which I find deeply offensive, I couldn't take the Eucharist even if I became a Catholic. So the invitation to receive an ecumenical Eucharist "for all who are searching after God" at the Episcopal church again is an invitation, an ecumenical invitation, to me. I don't renounce my Mormonism. I'm proud of our nineteenth-century heritage of suffering for the right to practice a peculiar religious tradition. I also acknowledge the power of Mormonism as an ethnic and tribal phenomenon. I personally think you can understand Mormonism far more clearly by seeing it as dominantly an ethnic group and secondarily as a church.

Interesting.

I think it's deeply tribal with all of the empowerment that allows, and that's great. I mean, when you talk about social organization, and taking care of your own, and organizations for young people, the Mormon church is formidable in its power. But tribal power has its shadow side. The shadow of a tribe is that you can excommunicate God. God is no longer at the center, the tribe is, and you're involved in a strange group self-worship. That's a form of corporate ego-centrism, where the center of the group becomes itself, that is the tribe. Tribalism has great power. You belong. There's no anomie, there's no "lonely crowd." You know who you are. But God isn't at the center. The tribe is at the center. That's what makes it a tribe. The cost, however, is the excommunication of God. The First Commandment is obliterated.

I'm of the Mormon tribe. My biological great-great-grandfather is Brigham Young, and, by temple sealing, Joseph Smith. My great-great-grandmother, Zina, was married to Joseph Smith, sealed before his murder. After Joseph's death, she was married to Brigham. I've never felt embarrassed by, or in need of, renouncing my Mormon roots. It's just that the paradigm of life that they offer me now at this time in my life, in my spiritual journey, won't work for me.

On the other hand, how does your paradigm accommodate Mormonism's teachings regarding the after-life, especially regarding your former mate and eight children?

I don't think Joseph Smith interpreted Jesus correctly on marriage in the New Testament any more than I think the Catholics interpret Jesus' statements on divorce correctly. I simply appeal to C. S. Lewis and to my sense of a loving God. I believe that we'll be with those whom we love; what the relationship is I haven't the foggiest idea. In one of Lewis's great books, he says, All we really know about the hereafter is that if we try to picture the most beautiful picture that can possibly be, the reality will be incomparably greater. I fully believe that. I have no fear of death in that sense. I've had to bury one child, three months of age. And my father. And loved friends. I miss people as they die. I hope to be missed when I die. But I've had plenty of dreams and plenty of contact that tell me that life is forever, that if we love each other here we'll love each other there. The Mormon paradigm on life after death isn't without its problems. I can't imagine anything more hellish than to be with someone for time and all eternity if, even though not divorced, you didn't get along very well. I don't think entrance into heaven will be determined by a handshake or a sign or signal, nor do I believe associational rights will be determined by a temple ceremony. I think the temple ceremony is beautiful in that it presents an opportunity for someone to go in, shed earthly clothing, to put on white, and for a time try to determine spiritual true North. But when one makes it terribly literalistic, you're dealing with what Jesus was talking about in straining at gnats and swallowing camels—why Jesus seemed to hyphenate lawyers and hypocrites, why "the hearse horse snickered as it drew the lawyer away." I don't think that literalism is what it's about. It's about love. I think we'll be with whom we love. I have no doubt of a resurrection; I have no doubt of an afterlife. The McDougall lecture came as a dream. I reentered a dream. I've been studying Jungian psychology with a fine Trappist monk who's also a certified Jungian analyst, who studied in Zurich for many years. I tried dream reentry. It worked. I talked to the woman in my dream. I won't tell you the whole dream—it's intimate. But basically the McDougall lecture was merely my recitation of what I received in the dream. Is that the "other side"? I don't know; it's probably the other side of my psyche; but within that dream, I was in touch with some aspect of divinity.

Have you ever been in analysis or therapy?

I've studied with professionals in study groups. I was in therapy before divorce and after, but it has nothing to do with what we're talking about. The friend I'm talking about was a Trappist who came out here from Gethsemane [Kentucky] where he'd known Merton and was for twenty-odd years in Huntsville but also spent years in Zurich training as a Jungian analyst. I worked with him for a long time. I worked with him personally in a study group, not as a patient.

I think I got derailed on one little point, probably a minor one, but you were asking about friendly relations with general authorities. I mentioned the Rosenblatt prize. Gordon Hinckley was at the university convocation. This was two years after the McDougall lecture and all the public debate about ordaining women. We had a very friendly talk. There never was a word of censure, never a word of criticism, or even raising the issue. He said how much he appreciated the award being given me and that he appreciated this renewal of an old friendship.

I was called in by my stake president directly after the McDougall lecture. The issue, of course, was my statement about the ordination of women. I said to him that I supposed that Elder Dallin Oaks or some other of the general authorities had directed him to do this, and the president's facial expression confirmed this. My stake president wasn't an intimidating kind of man; he's a very kindly guy. By this time a media fire storm had erupted over my comments about the ordination of women and the general role of women in religion. Hundreds of letters and calls had come in, including several death threats. I was separated from my wife and was soon to be divorced. Personally I was in a shambles. So I was agitated, apprehensive. I arrived at the stake president's office before he arrived. After some time his secretary came in and said he'd been delayed in traffic. With this unexpected delay, and amid the stress and agitation of that time, I sat back and meditated. The same woman I had had contact with in the dream was there as I was meditating. She put her hand on me, and we seemed to dance through the cosmos. She gave me a blessing. When he came in, I was utterly relaxed. He was flustered and very upset that he'd kept me waiting. Spontaneously, trying to put him at his ease and without any premeditation, I said, "President, I know why you've called me in. I've had a lot of time waiting for you to arrive ... I've really had a chance to rethink my own positions on things. I don't think I can accept a call to the stake high council at this time." I said it dead-panning you know, absolutely serious in my expression. His jaw dropped down and he couldn't get his mouth to close. He looked at me in shock. Then I couldn't resist laughing. I started to laugh, and he laughed, and then we both embraced and our entire time together was very friendly. All he basically said was, "What is this thing?" referring to the McDougall lecture. I took him through it page by page, and he said, "Well, you've had death threats, can we do anything for you?" I said, "No, I don't take them seriously. I had serious death threats in the MX controversy. This time, I think, I simply pushed some good old boys beyond where their vocabulary for invective could allow them to respond. Had they grown up in Provo when I did, they'd have the profanity sufficient to say what they really meant." I said that a Mormon sister across the street from my home had come over to me and said, "Ed, we don't know what you're talking about half the time, but we know you and we know you're something of a pacifist, but if anybody comes around here with death threats we'll beat the tar out of them." I said I felt quite secure and don't worry about threats. We hugged and that was that.

For some prolonged time I did have some attempt at institutional intimidation directed from the general authority level, not from my ward or stake. Everywhere I spoke for several years after that lecture I had someone taping my talks.

Is it possible that your positions have in the past helped become catalysts for change within the church?

It surely did in the MX controversy and perhaps on some other issues related to civil rights.

Perhaps some day we'll see changes in the status of women?

I know it'll come. Whether it comes because of anything I say or do, it'll definitely come.

But you're adding to the many voices, and your voice carries a lot of authority.

There isn't a down side to the ordination of women. That's the impelling point, I think; that is why I think it's inevitable. If you talk Roe v. Wade, abortion, I can give you as powerful an argument on one side as the other. Either side you take, and I have a definite side, it's the opposite side than I had for a good part of my life. But I see a powerful down side to it. An ethical, legal, moral down side that is awesome either way you go. In other words, you pay a huge cost by accepting any position on the question of abortion. But the day after the Mormon church ordains women, they're going to say, "What in the hell was the fight about? That didn't hurt a bit." Mormons have yet to have their Vatican II. They need it badly. Within Catholicism, at Vatican III, I expect bishops to bring their wives. And at Vatican IV bishops will bring their husbands.

Several months after the McDougall lecture, I finally sat down and cogently wrote an op ed piece for the *Salt Lake Tribune* as I had written the first op ed piece opposing MX, the first voice against MX in 1979. The next day the Mormon church came out with a statement against my position. They quoted Boyd Packer. The statement was basically an appeal to tradition. There wasn't a substantive reason given. I'm not diminishing the importance of tradition in church practice, but there has to be something undergirding the tradition. The article basically said, "We do it, because we do it, because we do it." He said, "Motherhood is the equivalent of priesthood. Men have priesthood, women have motherhood." I responded that "men have fatherhood as women have motherhood. Fatherhood and motherhood are each other's equivalent. Priesthood is entirely apart." The vacuousness of the church's position seemed to me apparent. The reality is that there's no reason that I can perceive why men must mediate God for women.

Can you foresee any circumstances under which you might re-embrace Mormonism and become active again?

I can't. It would take a huge, almost impossible, institutional change to accommodate where I am spiritually. I don't think Mormonism could transmute itself in a time span that my life would demand. If there is no apostasy, then there is no Restoration. That doesn't mean there isn't a first vision. Joseph Smith's first account of the first vision sounded almost the same as John Wesley's. Hundreds and hundreds of Christian mystics have had a similar experience—a sort of personal witness that their sins are forgiven, that God loves them, and that God is. There was nothing about all the churches having been in error and utter apostasy. There was nothing in it about forming a church. It seemed to be a personal vision. Now, having had dreams of importance, I understand that one can ponder a particular meaning, and perceive a meaning and a richness that one didn't understand at first. How much more I understand about my 1989 dream now than I did in 1989. So I can understand Joseph Smith in spiritual dialogue internally trying to figure out what happened in 1820. It's possible that his various versions of what happened can all be legitimate in a sense. But the integrity of his original statement, not condemning other churches nor denying their authority, would allow us to adopt and use the riches of all the authors of Christianity through two millennia. If the Mormon church came to adopt that kind of an idea, it would allow all sorts of ecumenical outreach. Great incomprehensible riches in theology, in spirituality, and in social and political ethics could be ours. We could use the richness of all Christian tradition. We could also honor and use the best of Hindu, Buddhist, and Islamic spirituality. Mormonism stripped of hubris, slimmed down to be *a* true church rather than *the* true church, could have God at its center, not its ethnic tribal self. The first commandment would be honored by eliminating the corporate or tribal ethnic self-worship that presently relegates God to the periphery.

What about your children? How have they dealt with your becoming inactive, with this new awakening? Are they active? Are some inactive?

All of the above. As divorces go—and they're savage things—ours was a love fest. We see each other almost daily. I have open access to the home. We regularly enjoy meals and family parties celebrating birthdays, or simply all getting together. We have constant association with the kids. And the kids are often at my house. We live only two minutes from each other. Davey, my youngest, slept at my house last night. We go on family vacations together. Gloria gets one home and I get another, on Balboa Island. We're much better friends than we were mates for the last decade, let me put it that way. Her final letter to me was very tender; it basically said, "You're like a huge boulder and every where you go people and things kind of get in your orbit and I'm there too." But then, mixing her metaphors, she said, "I have a song to sing too and it's not your song." It wasn't on civil rights, it wasn't on the First Amendment. She's a very conservative person. So when I'm out doing stuff with Hubert Humphrey, that's not what she'd have me do. When I'm working with Martin Luther King, it wouldn't be where she'd be. Surely on the ordination of women—she was simply appalled. And on this last article supporting gay rights at East High School and analogizing same-sex marriage to polygamy in terms of some of the invective that was heaped on both—it just blew her mind. She needs to be where she is ... the marriage ran out of gas. We were wonderful partners during the time we could be together, but for the last decade that was increasingly impossible. I was moving too far—and she rightly said, "You're the one who changed." We started in the same position in the Provo of the 1950s. I changed radically during that time. This doesn't mean friendship can't remain. The kids range from one active son who just returned from a mission to several children in some modest level of activity to several who are completely alienated. But each child had reached her or his own position as part of their own journey. On Thursday we're all gathering as a family to fast for my oldest son for a particular purpose—a venture he's engaged in. We'll all do that with various degrees of belief in the efficacy of a fast or prayer. I have one daughter who had her name removed from the church, having to do with the role of women. She and her sister faced particularly harsh realities in their own personal life based upon what I think is, very accurately, a subordinate view of women in the Mormon tradition. They don't want to take it any longer. One's out formally and one's out informally. So it ranges from an active returned missionary from South America right down the line to some kids who'd think I was an old fuddy-duddy for my very orthodox belief in Jesus as Christ and my belief in a personal God. But we're very close, enormously close as a family. They like to be together; they choose each other as social partners over other people.

We haven't talked about one important issue, but I can hand you a document that explains my thinking and experience. I'll give you the article that I wrote for the *Event* magazine on the gay-lesbian support group at East High School. I'd spoken at the Capitol Hill rally protesting the state legislature's hate speech and hateful action taken against the appeal of young high school students to form a gay/straight support group at East High School. Several days after the speech, I was asked to write an article for the *Event*, a local alternative newspaper. It was a deeply personal thing for me. Serendipitously, the night that I was asked to write the article, I was due to fly off the next morning to spend some time with my wonderfully Mormon mother who was in Nauvoo serving as a guide and host. Two days later, coming home, I found all these letters on my desk from the Capitol Hill speech, hundreds of them, from Family Fellowship, which is a Mormon support group of Mormon parents of gay and lesbian children. These letters and articles included horrendous stories of suicide of children, of what I'd term ecclesiastical abuse—not from vindictive bishops as much as ignorant bishops—and stories of wonderful love from some of them. As I continued to write or rewrite this article, the scapegoating of other human beings by legislative and religious leadership was apparent. My mind returned to Nauvoo where my mother and I stood on the banks of the Mississippi, reliving the history of our own people who were savagely persecuted for, among other reasons, practicing a form of sexual relationship—plural marriage—which the country found shocking and unacceptable. The painful paradox of a people formally persecuted for polygamous marriage now persecuting their own people who are homosexual struck me like a punch in the belly or a knife in my heart. As I wrote this article, it seemed apparent that every contact and event for this short intense period of time had a direct bearing on the article. It came to the point where I knew that if a person entered my office or my life in any way it had to do with the article. I had people pull me off the road to tell me their story. I'd be approached as I was eating in a restaurant repeatedly by people who said, "My son, my brother, etc., is gay," or "I'm gay and I want to talk with you." It became painfully clear that hundreds of thousands of Mormons were living in some degree of fear, pain, and rejection by their church—gay and lesbian men and women, their parents, other relatives, and friends. Many have formed virtual "churches in the catacombs" of houses of worship of other religious traditions. Others are excommunicated or have left voluntarily, disillusioned or disgusted with the treatment they received from the church. It came to my visibility in a way that had not been before; but I've told this story so I'll just hand it to you.

18.

Government Administrator

Nothing in the world lasts save eternal change.

—Honorate de Bueil, Marquis de Racan

This formerly active Mormon holds a position of power and responsibility in government. As you read this interview, it becomes clear why he wishes to remain anonymous.

He's a scientist. We meet in his office. The morning light pours in as the red October sun filters through the pines outside. He wears an open shirt. His mustache and dark hair are streaked with gray. He lowers his glasses as we talk.

~

You've been on a lot of television and in a lot of magazines recently.

The place where I work attracts a lot of attention, and I guess I'm still dumbfounded by the fact that the smallest possible decision we make here can make it in the *L.A. Times*, the *Washington Post*, or the *New York Times*. People just look at this place as sort of an American icon.

It is.

And those of us who are workers here just have to get used to that kind of attention. Anyway, being thrust into that, I've been on shows and in magazines and met with people who amaze me. I have to say this: It's a very boastful story, but it's also humorous. Our director called me a couple months ago and said, "A good friend of mine, the

Israeli ambassador to the U.S., is coming your way, would like to see your operation, and I'd consider it a personal favor if you'd show him around." Great. We do a lot of that. So I took the ambassador and his wife around, and we had a very pleasant day, and I think that they enjoyed the hell out of it. Well, a couple nights later the ambassador was at a cocktail party with Barbara Walters, and he said, "Barbara, you've got to get this guy to take you on a tour; it's just wonderful." So Barbara Walters called me and asked if she could spend a pleasant day with me touring. I said, "What day is that, Barbara?" She said, "Friday, this week; is that possible?" I said, "Barbara, this kills me to say this, but no. I'm going to be with the president that day." And I don't say that as some ego trip or anything. It's just that kind of a place. You don't ever get used to it. You're just thrust into it by being here.

Let's go back to your childhood. Did you attend church regularly as a child?

Yes, I attended every Sunday. Went to all the meetings. I went right on up through the hierarchy. It was the dominating force in the life of myself and my family.

You went to Mutual, as it was called then?

Yes.

Was that fun for you? Boy Scouts, for instance?

Boy Scouts was a lot of fun. It was a very positive experience in my life. And, of course, all the Boy Scout troops were sponsored by the church, so you got sort of a double dose. You not only learned how to use a pocket knife, there was a strong dose of religion associated with it, but that was a pleasant ... I have fond memories of the Boy Scouts; I have fond memories of Mutual. As a very young man, the church was a good influence on me and I enjoyed it.

Were your parents active, too?

Very active. Devout.

Did you at any time rebel against their activity in the church?

Yes. And that grew with time. I think the first memory I have of wanting to be some place else other than in that pew, I must have been about eight years old. It was a beautiful day, much like today, and I was in there in a wool suit, and it was just scratching the hell out of my skin. You know how uncomfortable that can feel at certain times? I remember thinking, Why am I here? This is torture. That was the first recollection I have of not wanting to be there. Then I had another experience with a group of people, young boys. I don't even remember who these pals were, but we vandalized the ward house. It wasn't serious vandalism. We sprayed aerosol shaving cream on the walls—didn't even break a window. But I remember feeling so guilty about it that I contemplated suicide. I mean, overpowering guilt. I'd just done the most heinous thing to vandalize this house of the Lord. I was probably ten or eleven at that time. I recall lying in bed that night just knowing that I should go over and get that .22 and do myself in. It was that bad.

So an enormous sense of shame came with that act?

Yes, overwhelming guilt and shame.

Do you think that's part of growing up Mormon?

Yes. I think the whole concept of the Holy Ghost looking after your every move is something very powerful to grow up with, because that means any time you're in any kind of mischief, no matter how harmless, then somebody's looking over your shoulder. Someone's always watching. I certainly felt *that* growing up.

Did anyone ever tell you you'd get black marks in heaven if you behaved improperly?

Oh, yes. Doesn't everybody believe that? You know, I mean there's a dossier being assembled up there in heaven, and you get good chips and bad chips, and the sum total is going to affect you when you arrive there.

At what point did you begin not attending church regularly? Were you still living at home?

Yes. I was fifteen or sixteen and then I started to seriously rebel. My father'd come and get me up early Sunday morning to go to priesthood meeting. From time to time, I'd feel strong enough to rebel against him and say, "I don't want to do this." But it wasn't very often, and so I'd go as a prisoner, in essence, because I didn't have the nerve to go against my dad. So I'd go at sort of a gun point—not literally, but figuratively. Then I'd just hate it. I'd just sit there in church and seethe. That's a complex feeling. Not only was I being forced to do something I didn't want to do ... How would I put this? I mean, you're put into the situation where you're angry at your parents, and you're also angry about the thing that they feel most strongly about—that being religion and the church. I think a lot of guilt and shame came up in me for having that feeling. Knowing all along as an underlying force that also the Holy Ghost was looking at these feelings.

So you still believed, but you were beginning to rebel against the outward trappings of it?

Yes.

It must've been very conflicting.

Oh, yes. Ripped me apart for many years.

You were in high school when this started. What other events were in your life at the time that seemed to feed this rebellion? Girls, peer group, ...

Yes, all of that. I met in priesthood meeting a guy—I don't even remember his name—who was in the exact same boat as I was. His dad was, you know, taking him to priesthood meeting at gun point. So we became soul mates. We'd show up there in our coat and tie with our dads, and then we'd meet, and then we'd leave and go have coffee. Then show back up at the end of the meeting and connect up with our dads and go home. I don't know if our dads ever knew we were doing that, but they probably did.

He was your first reinforcement toward your mutiny?

Yes, the next stage in the rebellion. You've acceded to your dad's wishes by going to priesthood meeting, and you show up to the chapel and then you duck out, you play hookey. There were stages to all of this.

What was the next stage?

The next stage was to leave home. I couldn't break that cycle without leaving home, so I did that, again, in stages, starting at about eighteen. I started spending summers away from home, and that was just great. The freedom of that feeling, not having that constant pressure to be the good, solid Mormon child. That just grew with time, so that eventually I abandoned Utah. Part of that was getting out from under that constant Mormonism oppression.

Describe that.

It's the constant pressure on inactives by active members of the ward. The ward teachers always trying to bring you back into the fold. I just couldn't deal with it. I wanted to erase it from my mind and suppress it. In Utah that's hard, because they all know. Everybody in your community knows you're an inactive, and so all of your interactions with your neighbors and your community, and even friends, are oriented towards pulling you back into the fold. And ultimately I said, I can't deal with this. So I looked for things that would remove me from the culture altogether. That's how I ended up far away from Utah.

But while it removed you from external pressures, you still carried an ingrained cultural Mormonism with you wherever you went.

Absolutely.

How did you deal with that?

In a variety of ways. I certainly brought with me the traditional Mormon role of the male and had expectations of my young bride that were very Mormon-oriented, and over the years caused a lot of strife because she wasn't that kind of woman. I mean, she was and is a great mother and a great homemaker and all of that, but she wasn't going to take the traditional Mormon woman role—the mother and subservient role. We've resolved that over the years, but I had those kinds of expectations about women, mothers, and family. Despite the problems that it caused in my marriage, it still produced some good kids who are very squared-away and happy with life. I went through a period in my thirties when I was anti-Mormon, still trying to extract myself from this guilt and the shame. During this phase I bought everything anti-Mormon that I could, read it, studied it, all of that. That's part of that incremental separation that's taken me my whole life fundamentally to deal with that guilt and that shame from abandoning the church.

There was a seminal experience. When I turned nineteen, they called me on a mission, and the bishop took me into his office, and I just dreaded that. I knew it was coming and spent a lot of time worrying about what I was going to do. I mean, that was the thing I think my parents wanted from me more than anything else—to have a missionary son. So we sat in there and I didn't have my mind sufficiently made up. I told the bishop that I wanted to think about it. I said, "I don't want to give you an answer today." In retrospect, I think I just didn't have the guts to say no, because I certainly didn't want to go on a mission. But I made one request of him. I said, "I don't want you to tell my parents that I've received this call while I'm thinking about it." He said, "Okay." I went home from the meetings that Sunday and walked into the door of my house, and my parents were as joyous as ... I mean, they knew. They'd told them. They were so excited, and I was just angry as hell. I felt like I'd been had. They'd set me up. Not only did they ignore my request, but they turned my parents into people who were as happy as I'd ever seen them in my entire life. I was just furious, because I guess I knew deep down that I was going to have to give them the biggest disappointment of their life, which I hated. Nobody likes to do that to their parents. So I let everybody down, in essence, when I said no to the mission. It's a very, very vivid and unpleasant memory of mine in the whole scheme of things.

Were tobacco and alcohol ever outward signs of your rebellion?

Yes, they were. My rebellion interested me in both tobacco and alcohol. I thought for a long time that they were the primary reason, but I don't believe that anymore. I think they were just peripheral. When you're going through that kind of separation, you have to identify with some peer group. That's probably natural for people who are trying to step outside of their religion. Rather than being the reason, they're a by-product because of the peer groups that you want and need to associate with. You want people who understand how you feel.

Did you ever feel that, in spite of those outward symbols of your pulling away, you weren't accepted by non-Mormons either? That they still considered you Mormon, no matter what?

Yes. I've always thought and still feel that it's almost a racial thing, that being born and brought up a Mormon puts you into a kind of race. I had a lot of Jewish friends. In the Utah society they felt that they were sort of racial and I felt I was sort of racial. Yes, there were always some barriers there, especially because teenagers and young people can be so cruel about other people's beliefs. When you'd get angry at somebody or wanted to get under their skin, then that was always a good place to start, you know, with your politics or your religion. Though it was kind of mean-spirited in a way, it got to the truth of that fact. Does that make sense?

Yes, it does. Does your Mormonism tag along with you sometimes?

All the time.

Can you give me any examples?

I can give you 10,000 examples. I live right next to a chapel, and when they have services there every Sunday morning, I'm reading the Sunday paper and drinking a cup of coffee or something like that, and I hear the choir. It's an immediate transport back.

"Come, Come Ye Saints."

Yes. And organ music. I still like organ music. Actually, choirs and organ music and so forth are a very positive memory. I still like it. I still like the Mormon Tabernacle Choir. Got most of their CDs and tapes and play them.

You've talked about the relentlessness of ward teachers and of actives in your ward and your community. What about after you left? Did they find you?

I was forty years old before I told the ward teachers to quit coming to my house. I said, You know, I'm not interested in this. It took me that long to be able to openly express my true feelings.

Ever think about requesting excommunication?

No, I couldn't do it.

You couldn't do that today?

No.

Do you ever think you could become active again?

No.

You can't foresee any circumstances? A deathbed need or anything like that?

No. Why can't I? Well, I'd like to think it just isn't worth the time to go through, but I think it's deeper than that. And regarding your question about asking to be excommunicated: I think that in the small chance that I'm wrong, that I want that insurance policy—I think that that's the real answer. Yet I don't know why I'd want that insurance policy, because by the theological rules I've already done everything wrong that I could possibly do. So I'm not going to be saved in the afterlife, if there is an afterlife. It's something I haven't sorted out, that I haven't resolved in myself. I couldn't become active. I'm adamant about that. I have a knee-jerk, negative response not only to my own religion but to every other religion. I just don't like organized religion, whether it's Catholicism or any of them. Yet I'd not take my name off the roll. Isn't that curious?

It's honest. Do you consider yourself in any way a spiritual person in spite of your feelings about organized religion?

I think I'm a very spiritual person.

How so?

I think that my spirituality is what brought me into the profession that I'm in, the love of nature and all things in it, and I have spiritual experiences in nature almost on a daily basis. But I can see a god or a higher power in nature, and that's an important part of who I am. I just don't think you need to sit in or on a pew in order to appreciate. You know, I see a lot of value in the teachings of Jesus and especially of love and how you treat your fellow man and so forth. I haven't walked away from that stuff. The way I view my separation from the church is having walked away from organized religion.

How many children do you have?

I have three boys.

Are they in any way religious?

No. But they're spiritual and they abide by what we could loosely call the Ten Commandments. They're very moral and ethical young men. There's another Jack Mormon in this town—a woman. Every once in a while, generally after the third glass of wine, she and I will talk about our Mormon culture and so forth. One evening she said, "I don't understand this. Your sons ..." This is a small community. We all know each other's kids. She says, "Your sons are the most moral, the nicest, the most polite, the best students." She says, "How can you do that without religion? How can you do that without Sunday school imbuing the Golden Rule and the Ten Commandments and stuff like that without religion?" I said, "I don't know, it must be their mother's fault." I just dodged it. I don't know how you do that other than being a good parent.

You teach morality.

I guess so.

As you now look with some degree of detachment on active Mormonism, what are the positive things about it? What sorts of things do you look back on with fond memories, both for yourself and for the community?

My quick answer is their music. They bring good music into your daily life. I mean maybe it's as simple as learning how to play a trumpet. They foster that. There is substance to that answer even though it's a quick answer. I think that their views about family and community are stellar. Probably the best in the land. My substantive answer is that this whole notion of community-motivated spirit and the family and the essence of the family, it's the best. I think that's why they're so damned successful in growing their numbers. It certainly can't be the theology.

You're not a believer in the gold plates?

No, can't deal with it.

What do you think happens when you die? Can you go to the Celestial Kingdom or ...

No, I don't think I'm going to be there. In fact, I don't believe in an afterlife. You have to have faith in order to buy into that one, and I don't. I've seen nothing outside of faith, nothing in my entire experience, that would suggest that I'm wrong on that. Ashes to ashes, dust to dust—that's it. Recycle me back into nature.

It's kind of nice, though, isn't it? Returning to be part of nature?

Yes. The way I've put it together in my own mind is not unlike reincarnation.

The Buddhist or Hindu view of reincarnation.

Perhaps. You're being recycled into trees or bugs or birds or whatever. I can see something that's very much like what they call the soul as going on after you die. Certainly your elements. The elements—the calcium, magnesium, and the potassium, and all of it—they go on. Nothing's wasted in nature.

I don't know if I have any more questions for you.

You haven't asked me the fundamental one.

Which is?

Why did I rebel and leave the church? It's taken me fifty some years to figure that out. Why? I've got two brothers, and they did the exact same thing I did. Now how does that happen in a devout, loving family? Here's my answer. I think that my siblings and I all rebelled and left the church because we felt like our parents loved their church more than us. Now I've sorted that out with assorted therapists over the years. After my anti-Mormon period, I sought psychiatric therapy to help me straighten these things out, because I could see how debilitating it was to what I wanted out of life, which was joy, love, and happiness. That's what everybody wants, right? The peace and so forth. Both of my parents were from—as a result of deaths—broken homes. Neither one of them had good mom and dad role models, because they both grew up in a house where one of the parents was absent as a result of these deaths. I truly believe my parents did the best that they could, but they just didn't have the skills. So when they put their primary interest and love into their religion and made their children feel that they were second best, that there was nothing more important than the church, then I think we quit playing with the church. I mean, we started to separate ourselves from the thing that we couldn't compete with.

That's quite an observation.

It took me a lot of years to figure that out. Which is why I want to be anonymous, because my mother and my stepfather are still alive, and I can't hurt them at this stage. They're eighty-six years old, you know. I can't hurt them that way.

I simply don't talk to them about religion anymore. When I was about thirty—my father had died by that point—my mother was still after me. "Come back into the church." I'd married a non-Mormon. "These little boys have to have an anchor in their life; you've got to get them involved in the church"—and stuff like that.

I was the first in our whole lineage to ever get a master's degree, and that was I thought at the time a real achievement. Nobody in either my father's or my mother's family had ever got a master's degree, very few of them even a bachelor's degree. So I was rather pleased with my achievements. She told me during this angry exchange that I'd always be a failure in her eyes as a man, as a father, as a human being, because of my rejection of the church. We've never spoken about the church since then. It's been twenty-five years.

You still carry that thought with you, don't you?

Oh, I sure do. That was the most hurtful thing that anybody has ever said to me.

She's never spoken of it since?

No.

She's never retracted that statement?

No. Now we have a very loving relationship. I mean, I make sure her children and her grandchildren are around her and that we have happy times together and that we visit each other and all of that. But it's just we don't talk about it.

Are you able to accept her without condition today?

Yes.

It comes to that finally, doesn't it? You get a divorce and then you finally reconcile and just understand.

Yes. It's a perfect metaphor.

That's what I had to do.

Divorce your mom ... and dad, if he were still alive. Anyway, to the extent that I've sorted any of this out, that's my story.

GOVERNMENT ADMINISTRATOR